1985

Media Ethics

ANNENBERG/LONGMAN COMMUNICATION BOOKS
George Gerbner and Marsha Siefert, Editors
The Annenberg School of Communications
University of Pennsylvania, Philadelphia

Clifford G. Christians
University of Illinois

Kim B. Rotzoll
University of Illinois

Mark Fackler
University of Minnesota

MEDIA ETHICS
Cases and Moral Reasoning

Longman
New York & London

Media Ethics
Cases and Moral Reasoning

Longman Inc., 1560 Broadway, New York, N.Y. 10036
Associated companies, branches, and representatives
throughout the world.

Developmental Editor: Gordon T.R. Anderson
Editorial and Design Supervisor: Diane Perlmuth
Manufacturing Supervisor: Marion Hess
Production Supervisor: Ferne Y. Kawahara

Library of Congress Cataloging in Publication Data

Christians, Clifford G.
  Media ethics.

  (Annenberg/Longman communication books)
  Bibliography: p.
  Includes index.
  1. Mass media—Moral and ethical aspects.
I. Rotzoll, Kim B. II. Fackler, Mark. III. Title.
IV. Series.
P94.C45   174   82-7761
ISBN 0-582-28447-3   AACR2
ISBN 0-582-28371-X (pbk.)

Manufactured in the United States of America

Contents

Cases

Foreword

To be a journalist today is to know that there are people out there who do not like what you do, how you do it, or the explanations you offer for both. We all grew up with that old refrain, "People who live in glass houses should not throw stones." It is one that the public applies with growing fervor to the nation's media, whose all-pervasive reach touches and brings under scrutiny virtually every aspect of life.

If you have ever been victimized by a poorly done news story, or know someone who has, it is not hard to sympathize with the sentiment, but it comes at a very real problem from the wrong direction. To suggest that the media should shut up, turn off the spotlight, and go away is to offer a prescription for the sure death of important freedoms in this country. What the situation requires is that the media rethink the way they—we—approach our work. It is time that the ethical vacuum that lies at the heart of most media institutions be filled with something better than situation ethics or a value-free approach that substitutes a hazy concept of the general welfare for a more rigorous moral accountability.

To put the matter in plain language, the domain of the mass media today is an ethical jungle in which pragmatism is king, agreed principles as to daily practice are few, and many of the inhabitants pride themselves on the anarchy of their surroundings.

This reality stands in stark relief against a background of profound media change over the past several decades. The archetypical newspaperman of *The Front Page* is no more, if in fact the hard-drinking moral illiterates who populated that prize-winning play were ever more than caricatures. Education, including the upper reaches of higher education, is more prized today than the school of hard knocks. The apprentice reporter or producer must bring a great deal more than enthusiasm to the job if he or she hopes to succeed. The level of technical competence has been raised significantly. The machines are extraordinary, as must be the imaginative creativity of those who use them.

By contrast, when it comes to ethical values, the media would rather punt than play. Of course there are the hour-long handwringing sessions at the professional organizations' annual meetings, preferably in the early morning ghettos of convention scheduling. There are the anguished editorial-page responses to a Janet Cooke scandal or a *New York Times* interview that wasn't. Behind that thin line lies nothing— no systematic study of media ethics, no media-wide set of standards, no serious attempt to include such study or standards in the basic training for entry-level hopefuls.

In a profession that specializes in bringing judgment to bear on everyone else, this amounts either to hypocrisy or to something worse, a blatant protectionism that tries to silence outsiders' criticism by claiming there are no agreed grounds for judgment. What the public sees is the vast corporate enterprise of communication, presenting daily critiques of the rectitude and performance of others while refusing to concede that it should be subjected to an identical evaluation based on the same kind of standards.

At work here is less the arrogant abuse of power than the blind response of institutions practically untutored in ethical considerations. In the realm I know best, daily journalism, many of us are acutely uncomfortable with any discussion of the subject. What excites our interest is the surface quality of the product. The highest accolades are reserved for a display of skill. "It may not have been much of a story, but it was great television." When the conversation turns to whether a particular approach or account did harm to those depicted or failed to meet certain ethical tests, there is considerable throat-clearing, followed by a quick change of topic.

We are uncomfortable because the terrain is unfamiliar, but it is terrain for which *Media Ethics: Cases and Moral Reasoning* is a first-rate guide. It speaks in the language of the case study and asks the hard questions about situations that are as familar as this morning's headlines and tonight's evening news. But it does something more valuable than simply ask questions, which, after all, journalism does regularly. It also provides the framework for thinking and reacting ethically in the workaday world in which most of us find ourselves.

This book is, in short, an invaluable addition to the literature on and about the media. It offers a wealth of insight to student, teacher, professional, and layperson alike. By bringing ethics down from the theoretical to the practical dimension of known dilemmas, it all but eliminates any excuse for ignoring the challenges they pose.

Some people in my business claim to believe that the public's antagonism and mistrust of what we do is primarily the result of the human instinct to blame the messenger for the news. "We don't make it, we just report it" is one of our favorite clichés. The attitude is contemptuous of the people and plain wrong to boot. While, as I suggested earlier, there are those who wish the media would concentrate on "good news," most Americans know better. They do not want pap. They know it is a tough world out there.

What they do want is to be able to understand the principles that guide the media and to have some assurance that there is as much media practice as media preaching when it comes to those principles. What the public senses is the reality that there are no articulated guidelines, no ethical philosophy worthy of the name that undergirds the way the media work. We in journalism in particular presume to speak in the name of the people and to offer ourselves as their surrogates in the battle with those who would diminish liberty, despoil the world, or assault the common good. The people have the right to demand in return that we worship at some higher altar than that of professional expertise. *Media Ethics: Cases and Moral Reasoning* provides a blueprint for building one.

Hodding Carter III
Chief Correspondent—"Inside Story"

Preface

Media ethics has been traveling a rough road at the junction of theory and practice. Occasionally textbooks will include an ethics chapter at the beginning, but will not integrate it with the workaday problems that follow. Principle and practice do not merge well in such endeavors, nor in our daily actions. The rush of events forces us to make ethical decisions by reflex more than by reflection, like a driver wheeling around potholes, mindful that a blowout sends him into a courtroom at one ditch and into public scorn at the other.

Two different mindsets are involved, making fusion difficult. The study of ethics requires deliberation, careful distinctions, and extended discussion. The newsroom tends to emphasize other virtues: toughness and the ability to make rapid decisions in the face of daily crises. Advertising and public relations professionals are expected to be competitive and enterprising. Entertainment writers and producers value skepticism, confident independence, and hot blood. For the teaching of ethics to be worthwhile, the critical capacity must emerge; reasoning processes need to remain paramount. Yet executives of media firms tend to value people of action, those who produce in a high-pressure environment. If media ethics are to gain significance, the gap between daily media practices and serious study must be bridged creatively.

This book attempts to integrate ethics and media situations by using cases and commentaries. Communication is a practice-oriented field. Reporters for daily newspapers tend to work with episodes, typically pursuing one story after another as they happen. Advertisers ordinarily deal with accounts and design campaigns for specific products. Actors and writers move from program to program. Communication is case oriented and media ethics are uninteresting and abstract unless practical experiences are addressed. However, media ethics ought to be more than a description of practitioners' ethics. Therefore, in this book, cases are analyzed and connected with the ethical guidelines set forth in the Introduction. Those who work through these pages will be prodded and stimulated to think ethically. Considering situations from a systematic framework advances our problem-solving capacity; it prevents us from treating each case independently and thereby reinventing the wheel too often. The commentaries do not insist on one correct answer, but pinpoint some crucial issues and introduce enough salient material to aid in resolving the case responsibly. Much of the book's inspiration has come from Robert Veatch's award-winning *Case Studies in Medical Ethics*, published in 1977 by the Harvard University Press. Mr. Veatch mixed his commentaries, and we have followed suit—raising questions for further reflection in some, introducing relevant ethical theories in others, and pushing toward closure where that seems appropriate.

All the cases are taken from actual experience. In order to ensure anonymity and increase clarity, names and places are changed in many of them. Though our adjustments do not make these cases timeless, they help prevent their becoming prematurely dated and shopworn. We attempted to find ongoing issues that occur often in ordinary media practice and did not only select exotic, once-in-a-lifetime encounters. In situations based on court records or in a few instances of historic significance where real names aid the analysis, the cases have not been modified.

As the integration of theory and practice in ethics is important, so is the integration of news with other aspects of the information system. The three sections of this book reflect the three major media functions: reporting news, promoting products, and entertaining. Since we want readers to do ethics rather than puzzle over their immediate experience, we have chosen a broad range of media situations. Many times by encountering similar issues in several phases of the communication process, new insights can be gained and sharper perspectives result. As the Cases by Issues list in the Appendix indicates, deception, economic temptation, and sensationalism, for example, are common in reporting, advertising, and entertainment. The issue of how violence is handled can be explored in reporting as well as in entertainment. Stereotyping is deep seated and pervasive in every form of public communication; cases dealing with this issue occur in all three sections. Moreover, the wider spectrum of this book allows specialists in one medium— television, newspapers, or magazines, for example, to investigate that medium across all its uses. The Cases by Medium list in the Appendix organizes all the cases according to the major media involved. Often practitioners of journalism, advertising, and entertainment are part of the same corporation and encounter other media areas indirectly in their work. As a matter of fact, the Supreme Court has specifically included journalism, advertising, and entertainment under First Amendment protection.

The Potter Box is included in the Introduction as a technique for uncovering the important steps in moral reasoning. It is a model of social ethics, in harmony with our overall concern in this volume for social responsibility. It can be used for analyzing each case and reaching responsible conclusions about it. This book is intended for use as a classroom text or in workshops for professionals. We are especially eager that communication educators and practitioners read and think their way through the book on their own. Whether using this volume as a text or for personal reading, the Introduction can be employed flexibly. Under normal circumstances we recommend that the Potter Box be studied first and the theoretical perspective at the beginning be learned thoroughly before proceeding to the cases. However, readers can fruitfully start elsewhere in the book with a chapter of their choosing and then return to the Introduction later for greater depth.

Whether used in an instructional setting or not, the book has two primary goals. First, it seeks to develop analytical skills. Ethical appraisals are often disputed; further training and study can improve the debate and help lay aside rationalizations. Advancement in media ethics requires more attention to evidence, more skill in valid argument, and more patience with complexity. Second, this book aims to improve ethical awareness. Often the ethical dimension goes unrecognized. The authors are not merely content to exercise the intellect; they believe that the moral imagination must be stimulated, until real human beings and their welfare become central.

Improving analytical skills and raising moral sensitivity are lifelong endeavors that involve many facets of human behavior. Studied conscientiously, the terms, arguments, and principles introduced in these chapters may also improve the quality of discourse in the larger area of applied ethics. We trust that using the Potter Box motif for the 76 cases in this volume will aid in building a conceptual apparatus that facilitates the growth of media ethics over the long range.

We are fully aware of the criticism from various kinds of radical social science that ethics is a euphemism for playing mental games, while the status quo remains intact. That objection warrants more discussion than this preface permits. However, it should be noted briefly that we find this charge too indiscriminate. Much of the current work in professional ethics *is* largely a matter of semantics and isolated incidents, but this volume does not belong to that class. The social ethics we advocate wrestles forthrightly with organizational structures. Many of the commentaries, and even entire chapters, probe directly into significant institutional issues. Certainly that is the cumulative effect also. Reading the volume through in its entirety brings into focus substantive questions about economics, management and bureaucracy, allocation of resources, the press' raison d'être, and distributive justice. While raising and addressing these fundamental questions, we also have felt constrained to communicate effectively. The case and commentary combination, we believe, has instructional benefits—allowing us to dissect issues into their understandable dimensions without slipping into tiny problems of no consequence on the one hand, or attempting a complete dissolution of the democratic order on the other.

We incurred many debts while preparing this volume. The McCormick Foundation generously supported our research into ethical dilemmas among media professionals; many of the cases and the questions surrounding them emerged from this research. Ralph Potter encouraged our adaptation of his social ethics model. Louis Hodges wrote the initial drafts for the commentaries in 2, 4–5, 9, 12, 14–15, 20, 23, 25–26, and read earlier editions of the Introduction and Part I. Richard Streckfuss prepared the first draft of cases 4–6, 9, 12–15, 19–20, 23, 25–26. Robert Reid provided a detailed response to a previous version of the manuscript and spared us several inadequacies. Dick Christian and Jim Fish appraised many of the advertising cases from the wealth of their practical experience. Jay Van Hook and John Ferré edited the Introduction along with other chapters. Diane Weddington recommended the Potter Box as the organizing idea and wrote the original draft applying it to the Cinema theatre. We absolve these friends of all responsibility for the weaknesses that remain.

Clifford G. Christians
Kim B. Rotzoll
Mark Fackler

Introduction

Ethical Foundations and Perspectives

The Cinema, a metropolitan movie theatre, was gutted by fire. Advertised as "the best spot in town for gay film buffs," the Cinema fire killed 16 men, including a minister, a politician, and a banker. The police did not release the names of the casualties until three days later. One victim's next of kin could not be located before then. Another carried false identification and was finally recognized through a dental examination.

Both city newspapers, the *News-Print* and the *Sentry-Citizen*, normally reported the names and addresses of disaster victims after the official investigation and release of information. On the day of the fire, each newspaper printed a brief account of the disaster and an explanation for withholding the names. On the third day, the *News-Print* published the names and addresses of the deceased; the *Sentry-Citizen* dropped the story completely. This event aroused the curiosity of media ethicists across the country. Both editorial staffs were called to defend their decisions.

The *News-Print* editor claimed "legitimate reader interest." The fire was obviously a significant local event, and the newspaper had always carried complete accounts of public disasters. The editor reasoned that this fire was no exception. The *Citizen* claimed to be protecting the interests of survivors. "We are not sure the victims were homosexuals, and we do not wish to plant that suggestion in the public mind."

Both editorial staffs gave a specific reason for justifying opposite decisions. Why? Who was right?

When this case was presented to a journalism ethics seminar for discussion, the students argued passionately without making much headway. Analysis degenerated into inchoate pleas that suffering survivors deserve mercy or into grandiose appeals to the privilege of the press. Judgments were made on what Henry Aiken calls the evocative-expressive level, that is, with no justifying reasons.[1]

Too often media ethics follows such a pattern. Students and practitioners argue about individual sensational incidents, make case-by-case decisions, and do not stop to examine their method of moral reasoning. Instead, a pattern of moral deliberation should be explicitly outlined where the relevant considerations are isolated and given appropriate weight. Those who care about ethics in the media can learn to analyze the stages of decision making, focus on the real levels of conflict, and make defensible ethical decisions. This test case can illustrate how competent moral justification takes place.

The Potter Box

Moral thinking should be a systematic process. A judgment is made and action taken. One paper concludes survivors ought to be protected and withholds the names. What steps are used to reach this decision? How does a paper decide that an action should be done because it is right or should not be done because it is wrong? The second paper considered it immoral to hurt innocent people, so the names were not printed.

Any single decision involves a host of values and they must be sorted out. These values reflect our presuppositions about social life and human nature. We often find both positive and negative values underlying our choices. Newspeople hold several values regarding professional reporting. Readers, the family members involved, and reporters all value homosexuality in varying ways. These values taken in combination with ethical principles yield a guideline for the newspaper such as "protect the innocent." The good end, in this instance, is deemed to be guarding an innocent person's right to privacy. The means for accomplishing this end is withholding information about their family members.

Likewise the *News-Print* came to a decision and based an action on it. The public has a right to know public news, the newspaper concluded; we will print the names. What values and ethical principles determined this decision? This paper judges it wrong to withhold information from people who rightfully deserve it. The staff argues that everyone ought to be told the truth. Guidelines may be stated in positive or negative terms. Finally we establish a policy: "Tell the truth under all conditions."

If we do this kind of analysis, we can begin to see how moral reasoning works. We understand better why we really disagree about this case. Is it more important to tell the truth, we ask ourselves, or to preserve privacy? Is there some universal end of actions that we can all respect, such as truth telling, or do we choose to protect some persons, tempering the truth in the process? Thus we do ethical analysis by looking for guidelines and we quickly learn to create an interconnected model: we size up the circumstances, we ask what values motivated the decision, we appeal to a principle, and we choose loyalty to one social group instead of another. Soon we can engage in conflicts over the crucial junctures of the moral reasoning process, rather than bogging down in personal differences over the merits of actual decisions. One disagreement that appears to be at stake here is a conflict between the norm of truth telling and the norm of protecting the innocent. But differing values and loyalties can be identified too.

Creative ethical analysis involves several explicit steps. Dr. Ralph Potter of the Harvard Divinity School formulated the model of moral reasoning introduced above. By using a diagram adapted from Professor Potter and therefore conveniently labeled the "Potter Box" we can dissect this case further (see Figure 1.1). The Potter Box introduces four dimensons of moral analysis and aids us in locating those places where most misunderstandings occur.[2] Along these lines we construct action guides.

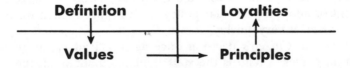

Figure 1.1 The Potter Box.

Note how this box has already been used in our analysis of the Cinema fire. (1) We gave a definition of the situation, citing newspaper policy, police activity, and possible options. One newspaper printed the names when the police completed their investigation; the other did not. Both always followed the policy of printing the names of disaster victims, but in this case they chose differently. (2) Why? We have examined some of the values, both positive and negative, that might have been operative. But we clearly see that we have not exhausted all the values. We could have stressed that public persons—in this case, the banker, politician, and minister—must be reported consistently in news dissemination or readers will not trust the paper's integrity in other situations. Nor may we suppose that a person is a homosexual simply because he dies in a gay theater. Nor can we simple-mindedly assume that being caught in a theater catering to gays is embarrassing to everyone. Each value influences our discourse and reasoning on moral questions. (3) We named at least two principles and could have listed more. One paper invoked the ethical principle of truth telling and the other a person's right to privacy. But other principles could have been summoned: Do the greatest good for the greatest number; do the just action; love your neighbor. The one newspaper feels obligated to print the truth, even if some innocent people get hurt or are misunderstood. The other newspaper will not print the names, even at the risk of losing some credibility. (4) From the outset a conflict of loyalties is evident. The *News-Print* claims it is acting out of sympathy to its readership in general. The *Citizen* claims to act out of sympathy for the victims of the fire.

Moving from one quadrant to the next, we have constructed our action guides. But the problems can be examined in more depth. Conceive of the box as a circle and go one step further. This time around, concentrate on the ethical principles. Next time in the cycle, focus on the definition or loyalties. In the process of clarification and redefinition, each element can be addressed in greater detail and then the deeper insight connected to the other elements.

The matter of choosing loyalties usually needs the closest scrutiny. The Potter Box is a model for social ethics and consequently forces us to articulate very precisely where our loyalties lie as we make a final judgment or adopt a particular policy. And in this domain we tend to beguile ourselves very quickly.

Examine the *Citizen's* decision once again: "Protect the innocent; publish no names." Who is the staff thinking about when they make that decision? Perhaps they consider only themselves. They say they do not wish to increase the suffering of survivors and the grief of the victims' families. They claim they do not want to inflict pain. They contend they do not want to lead people to label the victims as homosexuals when the victims might not have been gay. They seem to be saying that they could not live with their conscience if they were to print the news. But on additional reflection, their loyalties may actually be different. Are they really protecting the innocent, or protecting themselves? Certainly, not reporting names is a means to an end, but the end could be their private comfort. The staff members appear to be interested in a gain for society. They appear to protect the innocent, maximizing their privacy and minimizing scandalous gossip. But the crucial question must be faced once more: For whom did they do all this? If they do not return to the top right-hand quadrant of the diagram and inquire more deeply where their allegiances lie—for whom they did it—they have not used the Potter Box adequately.

Probe the *News-Print's* decision in the same manner. Tell the truth, print the names, it was decided. If the paper had always printed the names of victims, why should it make an exception this time? If it excludes them now, will it make an exception again and again until its credibility is ended?

The paper's readers have certain expectations; must these not be met? If decisions are made that undermine credibility, has the company's long-range ability to contribute to society been damaged? What is more important, the welfare of the community's citizens at large or the welfare of those in the fire accident? Even if the rumors are untrue, will some of the stigma of homosexuality be removed by implying that certain prominent people might have been homosexuals?

In the initial analysis, the *News-Print* did not seem to be concerned for the survivors. Its imperative was to tell the truth or lose the trust of advertisers, readers, and employees. But maybe this newspaper's loyalties to its readers can actually benefit the Cinema victims also. It could be reasonably argued that if the truth is told often enough, the public will be less shocked about homosexuality and less curious about private affairs. In time the survivors of the tragedy could become more than objects of curiosity. The truth of the tragedy may finally outweigh idle speculation.

Choosing loyalties is an extremely significant step in the process of making moral decisions. As the preceding paragraphs indicate, taking this phase seriously does not in itself eliminate disagreements. In this arena, honest disputes may occur over those who should benefit from our decision. For media personnel who are sincere about serving society, choices must be made among various segments of that society: readers and viewers, the sources of information, politicians, ethnic minorities, children, and so forth. In any case, the Potter Box is an exercise in social ethics that does not permit the luxury of merely playing mental games. Conclusions must be worked out in the rough and tumble of social realities. Often professional ethics makes a final appeal to moral principles and rests content if a decision can be justified according to some reasonable guideline arising from that body of scholarship called ethics. As developed in the next section, ethical principles are crucial in the overall process of reaching a justified conclusion. However, in the pursuit of socially responsible media, clarity over ultimate loyalties is of paramount importance.

In addition to considering each step carefully, the box must become a circle (see Figure 1.2).

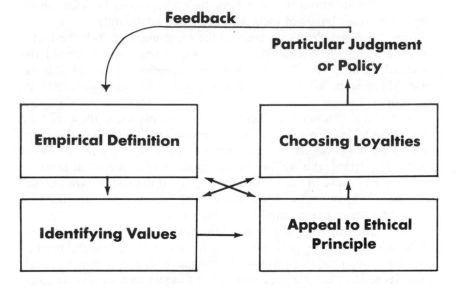

Figure 1.2

We have moved from first impressions to explaining various aspects of what is happening in the situation. Each newspaper has declared its loyalties. It now has a mechanism to assess further its values and principles. Eventually, when a case arises, it might change its policy regarding names. At least the editorial staff will have clarified for itself how responsible decisions are reached.

But we are still left with the initial question: Which newspaper made the right decision? This returns us to a central inquiry raised by this exercise: Is there a universal ground for making ethical decisions, an overarching theory from which we can choose among competing alternatives? Or, is ethical decision making a process of adjusting to the mores and commitments of a given community? Potter's circular model, with its potential for continual expansion, takes both aspects seriously (see Figure 1.3). Community mores are accounted for when elaborating on the values people hold and when separating out our loyalties before making a final choice. But the sociological matters are tempered in the Potter Box by appeal to an explicit ethical principle. Without such an appeal, a conclusion is not considered morally justified.

Under the circumstances, both papers made a morally defensible decision. Both modes of argument are consistent and coherent. In this particular case, either choice can be made with integrity and defended. Both aim toward a good widely held in our society, though these goods are defined differently. Often one media company will adopt a morally enlightened option and the other will choose to break promises, cheat, and deceive. Such immoral behavior cannot be justified by serious attention to the Potter Box cycle. Happily there are situations in which

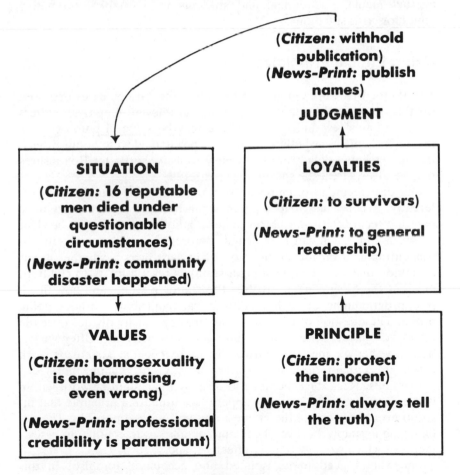

Figure 1.3

both options are ethically credible. The Potter Box process does allow competing goods to stand. These conflicts can then be addressed by appeal to ultimate values, metaphysics, or theology.[3]

For our purposes in this volume, the process by which choices are made is of the greatest importance. Media professions are demanding, filled with ambiguous situations and conflicting loyalties. The practitioner must make decisions quickly and without much time for reflection. Knowing the elements in moral analysis sharpens our vocabulary and thereby enhances our debates in media ethics. By understanding the logic of social ethics, we improve the quality of our conceptual work and thereby the validity of the choices actually made in media practice. The four dimensions introduced with the Potter Box, in effect, instruct media practitioners and students in developing normative ethics for crisis situations.

Using Ethical Principles

The Potter Box can help guide us through the various cases prepared for this book. In the Cinema situation, the relevant empirical matters are reasonably few and simple. There may be some dispute over the theater's clientele—whether or not the 16 who died were homosexuals. But the essential details are fairly easy to list. The Potter Box insures that we always treat the specifics very carefully.

Our disagreements often result from our seeing the actual events differently. When a newspaper purchases a building secretly, sets up a bar, and records city officials on camera, a host of details must be clear before a conclusion can be reached, before we can decide whether it was entrapment or not, an invasion of privacy or not, whether it was deception or not. When debating a station's responsibility to children, much of the disagreement involves the station's profits and how much free programming of high quality it can contribute without going broke. The question of controlling advertising usually divides over the effect we consider advertising to have on buyer behavior. Often we debate whether we must overthrow the present media system or work within it. Actually these quarrels are usually not genuine moral disagreements. Regarding the need to destroy the system or work within it, for example, both sides may appeal to a utilitarian principle that institutions must promote the greatest amount of good possible. The debate might simply be over facts and details, over conflicting assessments of which strategy is more effective, and so forth.[4]

Our values need to be isolated and accounted for also. In this straightforward Cinema episode, the values held regarding homosexuality probably determined to the greatest extent people's attitudes about what ought to be done. People having the most positive commitments to gay rights, for example, would see no reason not to publish the victims' names. But several other values entered and shaped the decision-making process. No exhaustive list of the values held by participants is ever possible, but attention to them helps prevent us from basing our decision on personal biases or unexamined prejudices. Our values constitute the frame of reference in which theories, decisions, and situations make sense to us.

Cases and commentaries, as they appear in this book, attempt to clarify the first two squares in the Potter Box. Case studies, by design, describe the relevant details and suggest the alternatives that were considered in each situation. The cases themselves, and the commentaries particularly, explicate the values held by the principal figures in the decision-making process.

Occasionally the commentaries extend even further and offer ethical principles by which the decision can be defended. Yet, on the whole, these norms or principles must be introduced by readers themselves. As the Potter Box demonstrates, appealing to ethical principles which illuminate the issues is a significant phase of the moral reasoning process. However, while the options can be outlined, the imposing of moral principles by teachers and authors is normally counterproductive in that it shortcircuits the analytical process. The purpose of sound moral reasoning is to draw responsible conclusions which yield justifiable actions. Therefore, several moral norms are introduced below. In analyzing the cases, these principles can be incorporated where appropriate and beneficial to given situations. Historically ethicists have established many moral principles. The five ethical guidelines described in the following pages have achieved a significant hearing and together represent a reasonably wide scope of time-tested alternatives.[5]

1. *Aristotle's Golden Mean*: "Moral virtue is appropriate location between two extremes."

The golden mean is a middle-level principle which emerged at the earliest beginnings of Western philosophy in fourth-century B.C. Greece. A moral norm of enduring quality, the theory of the mean—more exactly rendered as "Equilibrium and Harmony"—was developed before Aristotle by the grandson of Confucius in fifth-century B.C.

By his "Principle of the Mean" Aristotle meant that moral virtue is a mean between two extremes, the one involving excess and the other deficiency.[6] From Aristotle's predecessor, Plato, the Greeks inherited the four cardinal virtues: justice, courage, wisdom, and temperance. When doing his ethics Aristotle emphasized moderation or temperance and sharpened it. Just as wisdom is reasoning well, so moderation is living well. In moral virtue, excellence is regarded as a mean between excess and defect. Courage is a mean between cowardice and temerity; a liberal person follows a mean between stinginess and wastefulness; modesty is a mean between shamelessness and bashfulness; righteous indignation stands between envy and spite. Propriety is stressed rather than sheer duty or love. As a biologist, Aristotle noted that both too much food and too little spoil health. One begins operating with this principle by identifying the extremes—doing nothing and exposing everything, for example, in a question of how to report some event.

The basic idea is prominent in several diverse areas. In journalism, the sensational is derided and the virtues of balance, fairness, and equal time are recognized. When faced with a decision of whether to prohibit all raising of tobacco and to allow unregulated promotion, the Federal Trade Commission (FTC) took the golden mean—banning cigarette ads from television and placing warning labels on cigarette packages. The Strategic Arms Limitation Treaty (SALT) and Strategic Arms Reduction Talks (START) are a classic political example. Those who want an arms build-up without restrictions on the one hand and those who favor dismantling of nuclear weapons on the other are bound to be unhappy with SALT and START negotiations. But in extremely complicated situations, Aristotle would contend, the golden mean is the most fair and reasonable option.

The point for ethics is that virtue stands between two vices. That such vices are not always easy to locate is true enough. In considering action regarding a hostile editor, a reporter cannot say, "The two ends of the scale are to murder him or burn down his house, so I will take the mean and merely pummel him senseless in a back alley." Finding excess and defect involves honesty and imagination before their mean, that is, responsible behavior, becomes clarified. Moreover, some issues are not amenable to a center. A balanced diet positioned between famine and gluttony is undoubtedly wise, but occasionally our health requires drastic surgery also. There were slaves in Greece; Aristotle opted for treating them well and fairly but not for the radical change of releasing them altogether.

Bear in mind, though, Aristotle does not advocate a bland, weak-minded consensus or the proverbial middle-of-the-road. While the word "mean" has a mathematical flavor, a sense of average, Aristotle explicitly denies that a precise equal distance from two extremes is intended. He speaks of the "mean relative to us," that is, to the individual's status, his particular situation, his strong points and weak ones.[7] Thus, if we are generally prone to one extreme we ought to lean toward another this time. Affirmative action programs thereby can be justified as appropriate since they help correct a prior imbalance in hiring. The mean is not only the right quantity, but at the right time, toward the right people, for the right reason, and in the right manner. The distance depends on the nature of the agent as determined by the weight of the moral case before him. Think here of the Greek love of aesthetic proportion in sculpture. The mean in throwing a javelin is 4/5 of the distance to the end, in hammering a nail 9/10 from the end.

2. *Kant's Categorical Imperative*: "Act on that maxim which you will to become a universal law."

Immanuel Kant, born in 1724 in Königsberg, Germany, influenced eighteenth-century philosophy more than any other Western thinker. His writings established a permanent contribution to epistemology and ethics. Kant's *Groundwork of the Metaphysic of Morals* (1785) and *Critique of Practical Reason* (1788) are central books for every serious student of ethics.

Kant gave intellectual substance to the golden rule by his categorical imperative which implies that what is right for one is right for all. As a choice for measuring the morality of our action, Kant declares: "Act only on that maxim whereby you can at the same time will that it should become a universal law."[8] Check the underlying principle of your decision, he says, and see whether you want it applied universally. The test of a genuine obligation is that it can be universalized. The decision to perform an act must be based on a moral law no less binding than such laws of nature as gravity. "Categorical" here means unconditional, without any question of extenuating circumstances, without any exceptions. Right is right and must be done even under the most extreme conditions. What is morally right we ought to do even if the sky should fall, that is, despite whatever consequences may follow.

Kant believed there were higher truths (which he called *noumena*) superior to man's limited reason and transcending the physical universe. Conscience is inborn in every person and it must be obeyed. The categorical imperatives, inherent in man, are apprehended not by reason but through conscience. By the conscience one comes under moral obligation; it informs man when he ought to choose right and shun evil. To violate one's conscience—no matter how feeble and uninformed—brings about feelings of guilt. Through the conscience, moral law is embedded in the texture of human nature.

The moral law is unconditionally binding on all rational beings. Someone breaks a promise, for example, because it seems to be in his or her own interest. But if all people broke their promises when it suited them, promises would cease to have meaning and societies would deteriorate into terror. Certain actions, therefore, are always wrong: cheating, coveting, dishonesty, for example. Benevolence and truth telling are always and universally right. These moral duties are not abrogated by the passage of time nor superseded by such achievements as the Bill of Rights. Even if one could save another's life by telling a lie, it would still be wrong.

Kant's contribution is called deontological ethics (*deon* from the Greek word for duty). The good will "shines like a jewel," he writes, and the obligation of the good conscience is to do its duty for the sake of duty.[9] All ethics for Kant is actually reducible to reverence for duty, and his work is like a hymn on its behalf. For Kant, categorical imperatives must be obeyed even to the sacrifice of all natural inclinations and socially accepted standards. Kant's ethics have an austere quality, but they are generally regarded as having greater motivating power than subjective approaches that are easily rationalized on the basis of temporary moods. Kant's dictum encourages obedience and faithful practice.

3. *Mill's Principle of Utility*: "Seek the greatest happiness for the greatest number."

Utilitarianism is an ethical view widespread in American society and a notion well-developed in philosophy. There are many different varieties, but they all hold in one way or another that we are to determine what is right or wrong by considering what will yield the best consequences for the welfare of human beings. The morally right alternative produces the greatest balance of good over evil. All that matters ultimately in determining the right and wrong choice is the amount of good promoted and evil restrained.

Modern utilitarianism originated with the British philosophers Jeremy Bentham (1748–1832) and John Stuart Mill (1806–73). Their traditional version was hedonistic, holding that the good end is happiness or pleasure. The quantity of pleasure can be equal, Bentham would say, for a child's game of kickball as for writing poetry.[10] Mill contended that happiness was the sole end of human action, and the test by which all conduct ought to be judged.[11] Preventing pain and promoting the pleasurable are for Bentham and Mill the only desirable ends.

Later utilitarians, however, have expanded on the notion of happiness. They have noted that if pleasure is upheld as the one object of desire (in the sense of "wine, women, and song"), then all men do not desire it (Puritans do not) and it cannot be the only desired goal. Thus, these utilitarians argue that other values besides pure happiness possess intrinsic worth—values such as friendship, knowledge, health, and symmetry. For these pluralistic utilitarians, rightness or wrongness is to be assessed in terms of the total amount of value ultimately produced. The press' role in Watergate, for example, did not yield a high amount of pleasure for anyone except enemies of Mr. Nixon. Yet in a utilitarian perspective, the overall consequences were valuable enough to be considered proper action by most people, even though pain was inflicted on a few.

Worked out along these lines, utilitarianism provides a definite guideline for aiding our ethical choices. It suggests that we first calculate in the most conscientious manner possible the consequences which would result from our performing the various options open to us. In making this estimation we would ask how much benefit and how much disvalue would result in the lives of everyone affected, including ourselves. Once we have completed these computations for all relevant courses of action, we are morally obligated to choose the alternative that maximizes value or minimizes loss. Knowingly to perform any other action would result in taking an unethical course.

The norm of utility actually becomes a double principle. It instructs us (1) to produce the greatest possible balance of good over evil and (2) to distribute this as widely as possible. Hence utilitarianism is often defined as promoting the greatest good of the greatest number. In this sense, the principle directs us to distribute a good consequence to more people rather than to fewer, when we have a choice.[12]

Two kinds of utility are typically distinguished: act and rule utilitarianism. For act utilitarians the basic question always involves the greatest good in this case. One must ask whether my doing this particular act in this circumstance will result in a balance of good over evil. Rule utilitarians, also attributing their view to Mill, construct moral rules on the basis of promoting the greatest general welfare. The question is not which act yields the most utility, but which general rule does. The principle of utility is still the standard, but at the level of rules rather than specific judgments. The act utilitarian may conclude that in one specific situation civil disobedience obtains a balance of good over evil, whereas rule utility would seek to generate a broadly applicable moral rule such as "civil disobedience is permitted except when physically violent."[13]

While happiness is an end hard to argue against, utilitarianism does present difficulties. It depends on our making accurate measurements of the consequences, when in everyday affairs a blurred vision often emerges from the results of our choices, at least in the long term. Moreover, the "greatest public benefit" principle applies only to societies where certain nonutilitarian standards of decency prevail. In a society of ten people nine sadists cannot justly persecute the tenth person even though it yields the greatest happiness. In addition, utilitarians view society as a collection of individuals, each with his or her own desires and goals; the public good is a sum total of private goods. These ambiguities, while troublesome and objectionable, do not by themselves destroy the utilitarian perspective. At least for our purposes in this volume, no moral norms can be considered free of all uncertainties, and the obvious difficulties with utilitarianism have been addressed by its adherents. Occasionally in resolving the cases below, utility is the most productive principle to include in the lower right-hand quadrant.

4. *Rawls' Veil of Ignorance*: "Justice emerges when negotiating without social differentiations."

John Rawls' book, *A Theory of Justice*, is widely quoted in contemporary work on ethics, and from his perspective fairness is the fundamental idea in the concept of justice.[14] He represents a return to an older tradition of substantive moral philosophy and thereby establishes an alternative to utilitarianism. He articulates an egalitarian perspective that carries the familiar social contract theory of Hobbes, Locke, and Rousseau to a more fundamental level.

In easy cases, fairness means quantity. Everybody in the same union doing similar work would all fairly receive a 10 percent raise. Teachers give the same letter grade to everyone with three wrong. All the children should have two cookies each at a birthday party. Eliminating arbitrary distinctions expresses fairness in its basic sense. However, Rawls struggles more with inherent inequalities. For example, players in a baseball game do not protest against different positions or decry the fact that pitchers touch the ball more times than outfielders do. We sense that graduated income taxes are just, though teachers pay only 22 percent and editors, advertisers, and film producers perhaps find themselves in the 50 percent bracket!

When situations are inherently unequal, blind averages are unfair and intuitional judgments too prone to error. Therefore, Rawls recommends his now classic "veil of ignorance," asking that all parties step back from real circumstances into an "original position" behind a barrier where roles and social differentiations are gone.[15] Participants are abstracted from such individual features as race, class, sex, group interests, and other real conditions and are considered as equal members of society as a whole. They are men and women with ordinary tastes and ambitions, but each suspends these personality features and regains them only after a contract is in place. Behind the veil, no one knows how he or she will fare when stepping out into real life. The participants may be male or female, ten years old or 90, a Russian or a Pole, rookie or veteran, black or white, advertising vice-president or sales representative for a weekly. As we negotiate social agreements in the situation of imagined equality behind the veil of ignorance, Rawls argues, we inevitably seek to protect the weaker party and to minimize risks. In case I emerge from the veil as a beginning reporter rather than a big-time publisher, I will opt for fair treatment for the former. The most vulnerable party receives priority in these cases and the result, Rawls would contend, is a just resolution.

Because negotiation and discussion occur, the veil of ignorance does not rely merely on intuition. Such individual decisions too easily become self-serving and morally blind. Nor is the veil another name for utility, decisions based on what is best for the majority. Again, the question is virtuous action, not simply action that benefits the most people.

Two principles emerge from the hypothetical social contract formulated behind the veil. These, Rawls declares, will be the inevitable and prudent choices of rational men and women acting in their own self-interest. The first principle calls for a maximal system of equal basic liberty. Every person must have the largest political liberty compatible with a like liberty for all. Liberty has priority in that it can never be traded away for economic and social advantages. Thus the first principle permanently conditions the second. The second principle involves all social goals other than liberty and allows inequalities in the distribution of these goods only if they act to benefit the least advantaged party. The inequalities in power, wealth, and income upon which we agree must benefit the worst-off members of society.[16]

Consider press coverage of Edward Kennedy and Chappaquiddick. Normally such coverage is justified on the basis of the public's right to know superseding one person's right to privacy. But put Ted Kennedy and a newsperson such as Roger Mudd behind the veil of ignorance, not knowing who will be who when they emerge. Undoubtedly they would agree that the reporting of issues is always permissible, but that Chappaquiddick itself, many years after the incident, is undue harrassment in the absence of any new material.

On a broader matter, place politicians and journalists behind the veil and attempt to establish a working relationship agreeable to all after the veil is parted and space/time begins again. All stark adversary notions would disappear. It would not be agreed that elected officials as a class be called the enemy or liars since those who emerge as politicians would resent such labels. Independence for the journalist, some toughness and persistence seems reasonable, but in the original position a basic respect for all humans would replace an unmitigated and cynical abrasiveness among reporters.

5. *Judeo-Christian Persons as Ends*: "Love Your Neighbor as Yourself."[17]

Moral norms of nearly all kinds emerge from various religious traditions. The highest good in the Bhagavad-Gita, for example, is enlightenment. Of all the options, however, the Judeo-Christian tradition has dominated American culture to the greatest extent, and its theological ethics has been the most influential.

The ethics of love is not solely a Judeo-Christian notion. Already in the fourth century B.C., the Chinese thinker Mo Tzu spoke in similar terms: "What is the Will of Heaven like? The answer is—To love all men everywhere alike."[18] Nor are all Judeo-Christian ethics a pure morality of love; some ethicists in that tradition make obedience or justice or peace supreme. But the classic contribution of this religious perspective, in its mainline form, is to contend that ultimately humans stand under only one moral command or virtue: to love God and mankind. All other obligations, though connected to this central one, are considered derivative.

"Love your neighbor" is normative, and uniquely so in this tradition, because love characterizes the very heart of the universe. Augustine is typical in declaring that the supreme good is divine love.[19] The inexhaustible, self-generating nature of God Himself is love; therefore, human love has its motive and ground in the highest reaches of eternity. Man is made in the image of God; the more loving humans are, the more like God they are. The Judeo-Christian norm differs from other ethical formulations at this very point; love is more than a raw principle, stern and unconditional, as in Kant's categorical imperative. It remains personal at its very roots, and while rigorously dutiful, it is never purely legalistic. As Emil Brunner notes in summarizing the biblical exhortations:

"Live in love." Or, still more plainly: "*Remain* in love." . . . It is the summons to remain in the giving of God, to return to Him again and again as the origin of all power to be good and to do good. There are not "other virtues" alongside the life of love. . . . Each virtue, one might say, is a particular way in which the person who lives in love takes the other into account, and "realizes" him as "Thou"[20]

The Old Testament already spoke of lovingkindness. But the Christian tradition introduced the more dramatic term *agape*—unselfish, other-directed love, distinct from friendship, charity, benevolence and other weaker notions. To love a human being in agapic terms is to accept that person's existence as it is given; to love him or her as is.[21] Human beings thus have unconditional value apart from circumstances. It is unloving, in this view, to give them only instrumental value and use them merely as a means to our own ends. Especially in those areas which do not coincide with a person's own desires, love is not contradicted. In this perspective, one ought to love his neighbor with the same zeal and consistency with which he loves himself.

Loving one's neighbor in this tradition is far from sentimental utopianism. It is thoroughly practical, issuing in specific help to those who need it. "Neighbor" designates the weak, poor, orphans, widows, aliens, and disenfranchised in the Old Testament. Even enemies are included. This love is not discriminatory: no black or white, no learned or simple, no friend or foe. While not denying the distinctions that characterize creaturely existence, agape stays uniquely blind to them. Love does not estimate rights or claims and then determine whether the person merits attention. The norm here is giving and forgiving with uncalculating spontaneity and spending oneself to fulfill a neighbor's well-being.

To Whom Is Moral Duty Owed?

The Potter Box forces us to get the empirical data straight, investigate our values, and appeal to an appropriate principle. Those steps accomplished, the process faces us with the question of our ultimate loyalties. Many times while doing ethics, direct conflicts arise between the rights of one person or group versus those of others. Policies and actions inevitably must favor some to the exclusion of others. Often our most agonizing dilemmas revolve around our primary obligation to a person or social group. Or, we ask ourselves, is my first loyalty to my company or to a particular client?

To reach a responsible decision, we must clarify which parties will be influenced by it and which ones we feel especially obligated to support. When analyzing the cases in this volume, we will ordinarily investigate five categories:

1. *Duty to ourselves*. Maintaining a sense of integrity and following our conscience may finally be the best alternative in many situations.
2. *Duty to clients/subscribers/supporters*. If they pay the bills and if we sign contracts to work for them, do we not carry a special obligation to this class? Even in the more amorphous matter of a viewing audience that pays no service fee for a broadcast signal, a station's duty to them must be addressed when deciding which course of action is the most appropriate.
3. *Duty to one's organization or firm*. Often company policy is followed much too blindly, yet loyalty to an employer can be a moral good. Whistleblowing is one aspect here also, that is, revealing persons or procedures who are harming the company's reputation. Reporters might even defy court orders and not give up records, under the thesis that in the long run the sources on which the media system depends will dry up. Thus duty to one's company might conceivably take priority over duty to an individual or to a court.
4. *Duty to professional colleagues*. A practitioner's strongest obligation is often held toward colleagues doing similar work. Reporters tend to prize first of all their commitments to fellow reporters and the standards of good reporting. Some even maintain an adversary posture against editors and publishers, without violating the standards of accepted etiquette. Film artists presume a first obligation to their professional counterparts, and account executives to theirs. These professional loyalties, almost intuitively held, also must be examined when determining what ought to be done.
5. *Duty to society*. This is an increasingly important dimension of applied ethics and has been highlighted for the media under the term "social responsibility." Questions of privacy and confidentiality, for example, nearly always encounter claims about society's welfare over that of a particular person. The "public's right to know" has become a journalistic slogan. Advertising agencies cannot resolve questions of tobacco ads, political commercials, and nutritionless products without taking the public good fully into the equation. Violence and pornography in media entertainment are clearly social issues. In all such cases, to benefit merely the company or oneself is not morally defensible. In these situations, our loyalty to society warrants preeminence.

Throughout this volume the media practitioner's moral obligation to society is stressed as critically important. Admittedly the meaning of that responsibility is often ill-defined and itself subject to debate. For example, when justifying one's decision, particular social segments must be specified: the welfare of children, the rights of a minority, or the needs of senior citizens. As emphasized throughout this introduction, in spite of the difficulties, precisely such debate must be at the forefront when considering the loyalty quadrant in the Potter Box. No longer do the media operate with a crass "public be damned" philosophy. Increasingly the customer is king and belligerent appeals to owner privilege have been lessened. However, these gains are only the beginning. They need to be propelled forward, so that a sincere sense of social responsibility and a genuine concern for the citizenry become characteristic marks of all contemporary media operations in news, advertising, and entertainment.

The version of the Potter Box described in this chapter furthers this book's overall preoccupation with social responsibility. Consider the upper tier of the Potter Box (empirical situation and ultimate loyalties) that stresses the social context and social order. The Potter Box as a schematic design is not just eclectic, a random gathering of several elements in justifying a decision or policy. The lower half (values and ethical principles) deals more with analytical matters than it does with sociological ones in everyday experience. But the lower tier feeds into the higher. Also the two levels are integrated at crucial junctures so that social situations initiate the process and the choice of cultural loyalties forces one toward the final decision. Thus the loyalty component especially provides a pivotal juncture in moral discourse and indicates that conceptual analysis can hardly be appraised until one sees the implications for institutional arrangements.

The line of decision making that we follow, then, has its final meaning in the social context. Certainly precision is necessary when dealing with ethical principles, and their relation must always be drawn to the values held and empirical situation described. But the meaning becomes particularly clear when the choice is made for a particular social context or a specific set of institutional arrangements. Considered judgments, in this view, do not derive directly from normative principles, but are woven into a set of obligations one assumes toward certain segments of society. In this scheme, debate over institutional questions is fundamental and ethical thinking is not completed until social applications and implications have been designated. In social ethics of this kind, the task is not just one of definition but an elaboration of the perplexities regarding social justice, power, bureaucracies, and cultural forms. Social theory assumptions are central to the task and not peripheral.[22]

Who Ought to Decide?

During each phase of moral reasoning, some actor or group of actors is directly involved in deciding, determining values, selecting moral norms, and choosing loyalties. The cases following cannot be read or discussed fruitfully without constant attention to the question of who must be making the decision. Applied ethics always takes seriously at every step the matter of who should be held accountable.

There are usually numerous decision makers involved. In simple cases, it is an organizational matter where an editor or executive decides rather than a reporter or sales representative. In more complicated areas, can producers of entertainment dismiss their responsibility for quality programming by arguing that they merely give the public what it wants? Are only parents to be held accountable for the television programs that children watch or do advertisers and networks carry responsibility also? If so, in what proportions? Does the person with greatest technical expertise have the greatest moral obligation? Vice versa, we must be wary of paternalism in which laypeople and informal social networks are downgraded in the decision-making process. When is the state, through the courts, the final decision maker? Absolutizing the authority or responsibility of any person or group is morally disastrous, yet clarifying accountability is an important endeavor and helps to curb the human penchant for evading one's own liability.

For all the emphasis in this volume on social ethics, the individual practitioner does not become lost. Only the individual is truly personal and therefore an authentic moral agent. It is true that a firm or institution, when infused and animated by a single spirit and organized into a single institution, is more than a mere sum of discrete entities and has a personality of its own. It is also true that such institutions can in a sense be held accountable for their deeds and become the object of moral approval or disapproval. But only in a limited sense. Such institutions are real enough, but they lack concreteness. Those we seek to call into account while reasoning morally are not organizations or generalities, but precisely individuals. These alone are existing and responsible agents and these alone can be praised or blamed.[23]

Certainly there is corporate obligation, and it is a meaningful notion. When individuals join an organization, and as long as they remain members, they are co-responsible for the actions taken by that organization. What is to be observed, however, is that guilt finally rests upon individuals. We wish in this volume to have all persons judged according to the measure of their responsibility and involvement.

It should be obvious that this is not a plea for a heavy-handed individualism; that would stand directly at odds with the social ethics of the Potter Box process. The point is that responsibility, to be meaningfully assigned and focused, must be distributed among the individuals constituting the corporation. Individuals are not wholly discrete, unrelated, atomistic entities; they always stand in a social context with which they are morally involved. But individuals they nevertheless remain. And it is with each person that ethics is fundamentally concerned. Gross attacks and broad generalizations about entire media systems usually obscure more than they enlighten. On most occasions such assessments are not normative ethics but hot-tempered moralism. The cases and commentaries in all three sections, filtered through the Potter Box model, steer media practitioners toward socially responsible decisions.

Notes

1. Henry D. Aiken, *Reason and Conduct* (New York: Alfred A. Knopf, 1962), pp. 65–87.

2. The name "Potter Box" is a designation of Dr. Karen Lebacqz, Pacific School of Religion. The original version is described in Ralph B. Potter, "The Structure of Certain American Christian Responses to the Nuclear Dilemma, 1958–63" (Ph.D. diss., Harvard University, 1965). Potter assumes this framework in Ralph B. Potter, "The Logic of Moral Argument," in *Toward a Discipline of Social Ethics*, ed. Paul Deats (Boston: Boston University Press, 1972), pp. 93–114.

3. This is actually labeled the "ground of meaning" level in the original version. As Potter describes it in his dissertation, "Even when ethical categories have been explicated with philosophical exactitude it is possible for one to ask, 'Why ought I be moral?' or 'Why ought I to consider your expressions of ethical judgment and your pattern of ethical reasoning to be convincing?'" Further inquiry "drives men ultimately to reflect on their more fundamental ideas concerning God, man, history, and whatever is behind and beyond history." Potter, "Structure of Certain American Christian Responses," p. 404–5.

4. While taking the empirical dimension seriously, this does not imply a commitment to neutral facts and what is called "abstracted empiricism" in C. Wright Mills, *The Sociological Imagination* (New York: Oxford University Press, 1959), ch. 3, pp. 50–75. W.I. Thomas' "definition of the situation" is actually a more sophisticated way of explicating the empirical dimension of moral questions. See W.I. Thomas, *Primitive Behavior: An Introduction to the Social Sciences* (New York: McGraw-Hill, 1937), p. 8.

5. Ethical egoism has not been included in the list despite its immense popularity. The authors stand with those who doubt its adequacy and coherence as an ethical theory. Furthermore, the view that everyone ought to promote his or her own self-interests does not synchronize with the social responsibility thrust of the Potter model. However, there are several formulations of ethical egoism and students interested in pursuing this option should see Edward Regis' significant attempt to present a conception that overcomes the standard objections. Edward Regis, "What Is Ethical Egoism?" *Ethics* 91 (October 1980): 50–62. For a history of the debates in this area, see Tibor R.

Machan, "Recent Work in Ethical Egoism," *American Philosophical Quarterly* 16 (1979): 1–15.

6. For example, *Nicomachean Ethics*, in *Introduction to Aristotle*, ed. Richard McKeon (New York: Modern Library, 1947), (1104a) p. 333, (1106a) p. 340, (1107a) p. 341, (1138b) p. 423.

7. Ibid., 1107a, p. 340.

8. Immanuel Kant, *Groundwork of the Metaphysic of Morals*, trans, H.J. Paton (New York: Harper Torchbooks, 1964), pp. 69–71, 82–89.

9. Ibid., p. 62.

10. Bemtham suggests a scheme for measuring the quantity of pleasure in human acts in Jeremy Bentham, *An Introduction to the Principles of Morals and Legislation* (New York: Hafner, 1948), chs. 3–7.

11. John Stuart Mill reached this conclusion in the last chapter of his *A System of Logic* (London: J.W. Parker, 1843). He attempted eighteen years later to expand and defend this conviction. See John Stuart Mill, *Utilitarianism* (London: J.M. Dent & Sons, 1861).

12. For a significant discussion of these and related issues, see Samuel Gorovitz, ed., *Utilitarianism: Text and Critical Essays* (Indianapolis: Bobbs-Merrill, 1971), pp. 59–401.

13. The Potter Box can function without this distinction, but a working knowledge of act and rule utility increases the Box's sophistication. Students are therefore encouraged to read additional descriptions of these two forms of utilitarianism, such as William Frankena, *Ethics* (Englewood Cliffs, N.J.: Prentice-Hall, 1962), pp. 29–35. A twentieth-century act-utility is presented in George E. Moore, *Principia Ethica* (Cambridge, England: Cambridge University Press, 1954), ch. 5. Richard Brandt and J.O. Urmson are prominent rule-utilitarians. Cf. Richard Brandt, "Toward a Credible Form of Utilitarianism," in *Morality and the Language of Conduct*, ed. H.N. Castēneda and G. Nakhnikian (Detroit: Wayne State University Press, 1963), pp. 107–43; and J.O. Urmson, "The Interpretation of the Moral Philosophy of J.S. Mill," *The Philosophical Quarterly* 3 (1953): 33–39.

14. John Rawls, *A Theory of Justice* (Cambridge: Harvard University Belknap Press, 1971), ch. 1, pp. 3–53.

15. Ibid., ch. 3, pp. 118–92.

16. For critique and elaboration of the two principles, see Norman Daniels, ed., *Reading Rawls: Critical Studies of A Theory of Justice* (New York: Basic Books, 1976), Part III, pp. 169–281.

17. A rationalized and secularized account of this principle was developed by Kant who contended that we ought to treat all rational beings as ends in themselves and never as means only. The Judeo-Christian version is included here because of its vast influence on the popular level. William Frankena judged Judeo-Christian ethics to be even more important to Western society than utilitarianism.

18. Cf. E.R. Hughes, *Chinese Philosophy in Classical Times* (London: J.M. Dent and Sons, 1942), p. 48.

19. Augustine, *The Confessions*, trans, J.G. Pilkington (New York: Liver-right Publishing Corp., 1943), (2.2) p. 40, (4.10–4.13) pp. 71–75, (7.12) p. 150, (9.1) p. 188, (10.1) p. 218, (10.29) p. 249, (13.1–13.4) pp. 340–43. God's love is a basic theme throughout Augustine's writings. For a summary, see Frederick Copleston, "St. Augustine: Moral Theory," in his *A History of Philosophy*, vol. 2 (Westminster, Maryland: Newman Press, 1960), pp. 81–86.

20. Heinrich Emil Brunner, *The Divine Imperative*, trans. by Olive Wyon (Philadelphia: Westminster Press, 1947), pp. 165 and 167.

21. For a comprehensive review of this concept, see Gene Outka, *Agape: An Ethical Analysis* (New Haven: Yale University Press, 1972).

22. The precise role of philosophical analysis and social theory is debated even among those who generally follow this decision-making paradigm. Potter himself emphasized philosophical analysis as the primary element in moral deliberation, highlighting, in effect, the principial quadrant as the key to a tough-minded social ethics. James Childress follows the spirit of Potter's apparent focus on philosophical ethics in the analytical tradition. See James Childress, "The Identification of Ethical Principles," *Journal of Religious Ethics* 5 (Spring 1977): 39–66.

The desire for precision does war against the power of a comprehensive method. But the issue is not over the desirability of philosophical rigor versus the benefit of social theory. Both are indispensable forms of knowledge for ethical reflection. The question is which domain galvanizes the total process of reaching a justifiable moral decision. Which particular emphasis achieves the superior disciplinary coherence for applied ethics? Stassen argues for a "focus upon social theory which includes philosophical analysis but extends beyond it" (Glen H. Stassen, "A Social Theory Model for Religious Social Ethics," *The Journal of Religious Ethics* 5, Spring 1977, p. 9). This volume provides a streamlined version of Stassen's adaptation of Potter, a schematic model that seeks to be both useful and rigorous.

23. Henry Stob, *Ethical Reflections: Essays on Moral Themes* (Grand Rapids, Mich.: Eerdmans, 1978), pp. 3–6.

PART 1

News

Democratic theory gives the press a crucial role. In most mainline democracies, education and information are the twin pillars on which a free society is said to rest. Informed public opinion is typically heralded as a weapon of enormous power and, indeed, the cornerstone of legislative government. The free press is central to Jefferson's understanding of politics, for example, and he characteristically referred to an independent information system as "that liberty which guards our other liberties."[1]

Because of this privileged position—commonly called the enlightenment function—outside critics and inside leaders have persistently urged the press to responsible behavior. Thomas Jefferson himself lamented how such a noble enterprise could degrade itself by publishing slander and error. Joseph Pulitzer worried that without high ethical ideals newspapers would fail as a public servant and even be-

come a danger. Early in the seventeenth century, the French moralist LaBruyére chided newswriters for trivia, for demeaning their high obligation: "They lie down at night in great tranquility upon a piece of news... which they are obliged to throw away when they awake." John Cleveland a few years earlier cautioned against respecting diurnal maker, "for that would be knighting a Mandrake... and giving a engineer's reputation to the maker of mousetraps."[2]

Thus modern complaints about journalism seem merely to echo complaints that are centuries old. Yet the number of today's cavilers and the bitterness of their attacks set the present decade apart. Open news remains our national glory in a complicated world and expectations of journalistic performance are higher than ever before. In fact, the intense and widespread carping may have yielded a modest dividend in this decade. Never before have the media been so aware of their need for responsible behavior. A self-conscious quality hangs heavily over newsrooms and professional conventions. Aside from the bandits and the pompous who remain untouched by any attacks, some movement is evident. How can we fulfill our mission credibly? Should Pulitzer Prizes be given to reporters who deceive to get the story? Why not form an ethics committee? Do journalism schools teach ethics courses or not? Such well-intentioned questions crop up here and there. As the horsemen of old, one sees a stirring in the mulberry trees. Ezekiel's dry bones are revivifying. Only a little, perhaps, but a splendid little. As always, the proverbial smoke means at least a small fire somewhere. The cases in Part One represent the primary issues and problems that are being debated at present among those with a heightened awareness of journalism's ethical responsibility.

The fresh interest in ethics and whatever profit may be gained from working through these cases are threatened by the press' visceral commitment to independence. "Where the press is *free*," cried the prince of freedom, Thomas Jefferson. And others chime: "You cannot chain the watchdog." "The First Amendment guarantees the news media's independence." "Allowing controls by anyone makes us a mockery." Such is the common rhetoric. And in an environment where freedom is prized above all, accountability is not often understood clearly. Accounting, properly requested and unreservedly given, is alien territory. The belief in a free press is sincerely held and of critical importance. Yet it often plays tricks on the press' thinking about ethics. Ethical principles concerning obligation and reckoning do not find a natural home within a journalism hewn from the rock of negative freedom. While advocating press freedom, Part One promotes an accountable news system and attempts to provide content for that notion.

Ethical questions concerning truthfulness, privacy, social justice, confidentiality, and the other issues in this section must be considered in an environment of stress. Restriction tends to make a newsperson feel stifled, yet the contemporary cultural climate demands that journalism use restraint. The five chapters in this section cannot solve the problem, but the analysis and resolution of the moral dilemmas presented here address matters of high priority on the journalist's agenda.

Notes

1. Thomas Jefferson, Address to Philadelphia Delegates, 25 May 1808, located in Andrew J. Lipscomb, ed., *The Writings of Thomas Jefferson* (Washington, D.C.: The Thomas Jefferson Memorial Association, 1903), Vol. 16, p. 304. For similar highly quoted passages see his Letter to Marquis De Lafayette, 4 November 1823, and his Letter to Dr. James Currie, 18 January 1786, located in Paul L. Ford, ed., *The Writings of Thomas Jefferson* (New York: G.P. Putnam's Sons, 1894), Vol. 4, p. 132. The Lafayette letter is also located in Lipscomb, Vol. 15, p. 491).

2. LaBruyère and Cleveland are quoted in William Rivers, Wilbur Schramm, and Clifford Christians, *Responsibility in Mass Communication*, 3rd. ed. (New York: Harper & Row, 1980), p. 2.

Chapter One

Business Pressures

William Peter Hamilton of the *Wall Street Journal* apparently argued at one time: "A newspaper is private enterprise owing nothing whatever to the public, which grants it no franchise. It is emphatically the property of the owner, who is selling a manufactured product at his own risk."[1] That is an extreme statement, yet over the last two centuries many American publishers and broadcasters have tended to approve its spirit. Based on the principles of classical democracy and traditional capitalism, the individual's right to publish has been a strongly held convention.

However, the mood may be shifting somewhat, at least in theory. Increasingly now, enlightened owners and executives realize their special obligation precisely because news—and not widgets—is their business. In First Amendment perspective, journalism is in fact a business, but of a particular kind.

In actual practice it becomes extraordinarily difficult to separate the media's financial interests from the public's legitimate news interests. While American media are constitutionally protected from government constraint, the news is under the perpetual risk of corporate control.

Granted, no inevitable conflict may exist between the public's need for unpolluted information and stockholders' profits. Earning a respectable income, for example, and deciding to stop a dead-ended investigation could both be appropriate; moral questions emerge when the two are connected as cause and effect. Without a press pool to help pay expenses for a charter, a minor party candidate could not conduct a modern campaign. Serving in two roles, as executive for Columbia Broadcasting and board member for Columbia University, may each be permissible in itself.[2] Not every owner or executive is automatically suspect.

Nonetheless, ever since mass communications took on a big business character at the turn of the twentieth century, built-in commercial pressures vie for mastery. Upton Sinclair, the angry critic, cried out in 1920: "The Brass Check is found in your pay envelope each week ... the price of your shame—you who take the fair body of truth and sell it in the market-place, who betray the virgin hopes of mankind into the loathsome brothel of Big Business."[3] As the ominous trend continues toward concentrated ownership of media properties, cost-conscious publishers threaten to overwhelm the press' noble mission.[4] The five cases that follow demonstrate how media practitioners are often caught in conflicting duties to the owners, to their readers or viewers, and to their own professional conscience. Together with examples in Part II regarding advertising control, these cases illustrate some of the conundrums which occur regularly in today's news business. No wonder the public remains enormously concerned over whether media enterprises spend money honorably.

The first case, "Hispanics Versus Suburbia," revolves around the expanding percentage of ethnic minorities in American cities. High-minded talk about social welfare and minority hiring clashes directly in this instance with the newspaper's profitability. Regrettably, the publisher reduced the issues to budgetary concerns only.

In the Miami *Herald* case, the question is whether a specific newspaper ought to use its money to maintain an existing business climate favorable to its own sales position. A media company decides to use its financial power to benefit itself directly, to use position, in effect, for expanding that position.

Lobbying represents a somewhat more complex problem on the corporate level. The focus of the argument centers on the manner in which media firms flex their political muscle. The issue at stake is whether lobbying by its very nature is designed essentially to promote the press' own cause or to serve society's wider needs.

The fourth case in this chapter addresses a common conflict of interest, where journalists are paid money by the agency being covered. This case involves "freebies" in general terms. Concrete situations such as the Super Bowl in football could have been selected just as easily. Every January hundreds of sportwriters enjoy a week of gala Super Bowl activity funded by the National Football League. The ethical issues—whether reporting for the leisure section or on sports or on politics—are fundamentally the same. The Ethics Code of the Society of Professional Journalists is more explicit in this regard than on any other matter: "Nothing of value should be accepted."

The fifth case considers potential conflicts between newspaper employment and activity in community affairs. It focuses on the owner's outside commercial affiliations as the most morally problematical.

Since biblical times, sages have warned against serving two masters. Nearly all professions, politics most notably, confront the same problem. Yet the issues cut especially deep in reporting. As some observers have noted, handling profits responsibly is the cornerstone of media ethics.

1. Hispanics Versus Suburbia

As a conscientious publisher of a large-city newspaper, you want to print news that is meaningful to your city's residents. Your goal is information that citizens want to know because it illuminates their social, economic, and political affairs. Your newspaper, however, is losing urban readers and gaining them in the sprawling suburbs. Over the years, your paper has followed these population shifts by content and advertising designed for your suburban reader. You ask yourself, "Are we still fulfilling our obligations to our city? Ours historically is a city paper, and maybe we should try to regain our next-door readers." Because you presume the necessity of your newspaper surviving economically, you seek the advice of your advertising and circulation experts. "The money lies in the suburbs," you are told. "If you gear a daily towards the poorer city residents, you risk alienating your suburban buyers. And that means losing substantial advertising revenue."

You inquire about a Spanish-language edition for the city's burgeoning Mexican-American population. "I'm afraid we would lose too much money on that one," comes the reply. "The Los Angeles *Times* studied such a possibility a few years ago and concluded that it would be financially unfeasible because the Hispanics still suffer from economic deprivation."[5]

Walking through the newsroom, you notice, as you have so many times before, the large proportion of white reporters and editors. This proportion reflects the present readership but hardly resembles the city's population as a whole. Despite the city's large percentage of ethnic minorities, and your newspaper's policy of funding minority scholarships and training programs, only five percent of the full-time editorial staff is nonwhite. You feel embarrassed that your newspaper has not solved either the circulation or hiring dilemmas. You point with pride to a few gains in both areas. Ten years ago you had only one minority staff person and now there are twelve. Your paper has run a series periodically on the Hispanics and other non-whites that was rated sensitive and intelligent by most readers. You do not tolerate blatantly segregationist practices and most stereotyping has been edited out. You conclude that nothing can be done to alleviate the problems fully.

The publisher struggled with the demographic dilemmas within a very explicit financial framework. One year earlier he had invested $1.5 million to add an edition for readers in the southwest suburbs. With $96 million in net profits last year, the paper did have the capital for continued expansion. A news bureau was opened recently on the north side and a special edition envisioned for Caucasian readers who were flocking to the new housing sites in that area. The specific question for him was whether a Spanish-language edition should also be initiated for the 700,000 Hispanics which now comprised 25 percent of the city's population. The editor concluded that such a paper would not make sense financially because the Mexican-American audience does not have enough purchasing power to attract the massive advertising on which the paper depends.

The publisher satisfied himself that his decision was not racist. "We are only talking about a certain demographic profile," he argued. "Race does not matter. The audience can be red, yellow, or brown. It just happens that our major advertisers have requested a certain type of person who happens to be more affluent, white, and suburban."

The publisher thus based his rationale solely on economic criteria. Certainly he has a demographic dilemma, with the demands of the stockholders pushing in one direction and the city's population in another. But he lays out his agenda in profit-and-loss terms only. There is no evidence from his argumentation or conclusion that he thinks about the moral dimension of his changing readership. As the chief officer for this firm, he could have used this occasion to show moral leadership, but he only asks about the paper's solvency.

Heads of institutions are regularly tempted to use the structure to limit the range within which they consider issues. In this case, the profit-based character of his newspaper sets the parameters of the publisher's thinking. He missed a chance to shape company policy in a morally enlightened manner.

2. Antigambling Corporate Gift

Voters in Florida were being asked to legalize casino gambling in Miami Beach and other nearby resort communities. Hotel owners were contributing heavily to a campaign to sell the idea to the voters. Alvah E. Chapman, president of the Miami *Herald*, was concerned. He believed the introduction of gambling would damage the area's economy, change its image, and threaten a lifestyle worth preserving. Chapman was also worried about the effect casino gambling would have on his newspaper. "I was concerned," he said, "that the Las Vegas South image in Miami would make it difficult to attract and hold the bright, competent newspaper professionals who are so vital to the future and present success of the Miami Herald Publishing Company."[6] Chapman sensed that his paper's prospects were directly linked to Miami Beach's future as a commercial and cultural center.

Chapman decided to fight the proposal with money. The Miami *Herald* contributed $16,000 to anti-casino groups. Three other Knight-Ridder dailies in Florida contributed $9,000. Chapman and his family, plus James L. Knight, the *Herald's* board chairman, made personal contributions of more than $10,000. Chapman led a fund drive among other media owners. In all, $180,000 was raised from media sources to be used by "No Casinos, Inc.," a citizens' committee sponsored by Governor Reubin Askew.

Before the November referendum, Chapman's action became the subject of a complaint before the National News Council. The charge: financial backing by the media would taint its news coverage. Ironically, the complaint was filed by Jim Bishop, whose syndicated column appeared in the *Herald* and who headed up the organization working for passage of the casino proposal. Chapman told the News Council that he made his contributions with the confidence that the independence of the paper's editorial and news operations was so deeply established and widely understood that there was little danger of public misunderstanding.

According to the News Council staff, reporters and editors assigned to the story believed they had been put in an "uncomfortable position"

by the *Herald's* contribution to the governor's campaign. According to
the investigative staff, the reporters decided to "strive even harder
than they normally did to be fair," and, again according to the Council's staff, "they succeeded admirably."[7] Because of the corporate
donation, the top news executives kept themselves totally remote from
the coverage, a stance that would have been unthinkable in the case of
any other major story.

The News Council concluded that on the question of whether such a
financial contribution affected the news coverage, the *Herald* "acquitted itself with distinction." But the Council left open for further debate what it called the "more fundamental question of the appropriate-
ness of such financial involvement by a newspaper on one side of an
emotional and controversial issue before the voters."[8] The Council
was concerned that such corporate activity would undermine a newspaper's credibility—a disservice to the public faced with a referendum.
Indeed, a statewide poll conducted by the *Herald* underscored the
Council's concern. It showed that both those favoring casinos and
those opposed to them believed, by a substantial margin, that newspapers contributing financially to the referendum could not be fair in
their news columns.

This case is primarily a problem in business ethics. Presidents of media
corporations are ordinarily not journalists even though their corporations have journalism as their business. If Chapman were the president
of a company that manufactured fishing nets a decision by its president
to make contributions to a campaign against gambling would hardly
have received attention as a serious moral dilemma.

Chapman made a number of judgments about fact, some judgments
about competing values (regarding life style and the quality of his paper), and a number of decisions concerning what kinds of action would,
under these circumstances, be morally justifiable.

He judged in the first instance that the impact of legalized casino
gambling would change the area's economy, its image, and its life
style. He was convinced also that it would change the conditions under
which his corporation and his newspaper conducted their business.
When he evaluated those changes which seemed inevitable, he made
some key value judgments and concluded that the legalization of casino gambling would threaten certain values that he held for the community and for the corporation. He then made a decision to take
action, opposing the legalization of gambling in order to preserve a

certain community life style and to protect what he perceived as his corporation's self-interest. He further decided to use not merely his personal resources but also the resources of the corporation in an attempt to influence public thinking and policy.

His next choice was one of strategy—*how* to influence the vote. It is not clear what alternative strategies he considered. He might have used the editorial page of the Miami *Herald*, and he might have sought to control the content of news columns. He could have sought to conduct his corporation's own campaign. In fact he chose to join forces with an existing organization, No Casinos, Inc. Perhaps there were alternative strategies toward moral ends. It would be useful in examining this case to brainstorm which possible strategies might arguably be better.

Chapman, as president of the Miami Herald Publishing Co., actually faces a serious set of competing obligations. In the first place he has a contractual obligation to investors to protect and advance both their short-run and long-run financial interests. Secondly, he has an obligation to readers to disseminate unpolluted news and opinion. If he makes a contribution to an agency designed to influence public policy, he risks polluting the news and if he does not contribute he risks at least long-run loss to the corporation. If he could make an anonymous donation, he could contribute financially without influencing the paper's content since the editorial staff would not be aware of his position. But since he did not choose anonymity, he risks biasing the news and editorial columns.

But what did Chapman's decision to contribute to No Casinos, Inc. actually do to the *Herald's* coverage? Reporters and editors at the *Herald* believed they were put in an "uncomfortable position" by the contribution. They decided to "strive even harder than they normally did to be fair." Thus the News Council concluded that the contribution was a decision to risk effects judged in this case to be innocent.

The bottom line is whether this media corporation should have made financial contributions to support one side in a matter of public policy. It seems obvious that siding with a partisan group does influence news coverage. Even if management does not directly interfere with reporters, the subtle pressures toward uniformity will be even greater than usual. While that effect in the *Herald's* case may not have been detrimental, in general the risk of biased coverage is very high. A well-informed public is too important a matter to allow corporate interests this kind of power. The National News Council has left that question open for further debate—a fact, incidentally, which seems irresponsible on the Council's part.

3. Lobbying: Putting the Press on Congress

The Houston *Chronicle* was in a fix. Owned by a charitable foundation, it was facing a 1969 law that essentially forced foundations to di-
vest themselves of majority control in profit-making businesses. Divest-
iture would mean an erosion of the paper's financial base. It would
most likely make it necessary to sell the paper to a chain. The principle
of local and independent control, argued two Texas Congressmen, is
more socially important than the principle of charity-business separation embodied in the 1969 law. Representatives Bill Archer and J.J.
Pickle thus cosponsored HR 4640, a bill to "exempt holdings in independent local newspapers from taxes on excess business holdings of
private foundations." An identical bill was introduced in the Senate.
Both bills came to Congress at the request, of course, of the *Chronicle*.

Should a media channel get involved in lobbying for special treatment?

- Washington *Post* executive Katherine Graham led publishers around Capitol
  Hill lobbying against a bill that would permit AT & T to produce and distribute over its wires a computerized "Yellow Pages" that could potentially
  steal classified advertising away from newspapers. Graham and her colleagues contended that it was dangerous to put so much power in the hands
  of a monopoly. The potential threat to their own businesses could hardly be
  a secondary concern either.
- A "landmark" newspaper lobby produced the 1970 Newspaper Preservation
  Act, a bill permitting competing papers to combine certain functions like
  pressroom and business departments, ostensibly for the purpose of preserving competitive news desks. The bill also blocked antitrust suits against 44
  newspapers in 22 cities and enhanced the cash value of those papers when
  some did go up for sale.
- When a gas rationing plan was drafted in December 1979, the American
  Newspaper Publishers Association (ANPA) and other newspaper representatives lobbied hard to be included in the special category of vital
  businesses which could obtain extra gasoline coupons at the standard rate.
  (Otherwise, should rationing ever be necessary, newspapers would have to
  bid on the open market for extra coupons like everyone else.) Publishers at
  Energy Department hearings around the country claimed that newspaper
  distribution could be vital in a crisis, among other reasons to keep people informed about how gas rationing works. The final version of the plan gave
  publishers the special consideration they requested.

Lobbying does not provide foolproof protection, of course. Consider
the Houston *Chronicle* case. When the House subcommittee scheduled
a hearing, the Houston *Post* mustered forces. Its president, who was

also the lieutenant governor of Texas, announced he would testify against the bill.

Archer and Pickle could see the crossfire coming with them in the middle. They suggested to their colleagues that the bill be shelved. "We're not going to get in the middle of a fight between two major newspapers," said Archer's administrative assistant.

Neither paper printed stories about the thrust and parry. Said a Washington correspondent for the *Chronicle*: "I think we have a policy of not getting into that. . . . To a certain extent, readers resent having to read about the paper itself."[9]

The news business usually justifies lobbying on the basis of consequences. The Houston *Chronicle* needs special treatment, it is said, or this paper must sell to a big chain with sufficient capital. AT&T would become too monopolistic. Without the Newspaper Preservation Act, too many cities would have only one paper. During gas rationing, newspaper distribution is vital for keeping the public informed. In nearly every case, the grounds presented for privilege or exemption were the favorable results.

The American Newspaper Publishers Association, in fact, resists the word "lobbyist." Their governmental affairs staffers are not registered with Congress as lobbyists. Their purpose is broader, the ANPA contends, than pushing their own interests. Given the many bad court decisions regarding the press, the aim is to monitor legislation and offer advice on ill-conceived policies. On the surface, the motivation seems largely a defensive one, that is, to ensure that the news industry does not naively live in ignorance of governmental activity. The Gannett Company, for example, does not employ a former deputy press secretary, and the American Newspaper Publishers Association does not have the former head of the Federal Communications Commission (FCC) on retainer "to do advocacy work," but "to collect legislative information." The National Association of Broadcasters (NAB) insists that its lobby's only concern is the stability and freedom of the American way of broadcasting. The Washington Counsel for the American Society of Newspaper Editors mails out analyses of legislation and occasionally sends "alerts" to members; any action that follows is the choice of individual publishers.

However, using the same ethical principle employed by the media industry—that of consequences—several negative results become apparent. Press lobbying on its own behalf is not as innocent as the industry presumes.

First, does lobbying in Congress not lead to distorted and unfair coverage of congressmen? When Senator Leahy of Vermont supported a lobbying effort against police searches of the newsroom, the Burlington (Vt.) *Free Press* lauded him in an editorial ("Leahy Meets Civil Liberties Issue Head-on"). William G. Mullen of the National Newspaper Association insists that "there's never an implied threat, or even an inferred threat that someone would take out after a member of Congress editorially."[10] Yet it is not patently obvious how the media's business interests can be kept so distinct from the contents. In smaller units where the publisher and editor, owner and manager are the same person, the separation becomes virtually impossible.

Frank Leeming, publisher of the Kingsport (Tenn.) *Times-News*, admits that quick response from local congressmen is partly due to their dependence on his paper for public attention. However, Leeming adds, congressmen understand that their assistance will not win them any favors from him. But critics are not impressed by these disclaimers and many media practitioners are uncomfortable also. Lobbying certainly makes the task of honest and unbiased reporting more difficult.

A second consequence of heavy lobbying may be the loss of media credibility. The press is a business and lobbying is considered legitimate for businesses. However, the reporter's unique relationship to the government sets them off from their counterparts. In the public eye, the press often stands for fearless investigation of government officials. The press typically styles itself as the "Fourth Estate," a check and balance on the other branches in the name of the citizenry. To what extent is the Fourth Estate designation meaningful when newspapers and broadcasters ply with these politicians over their own commercial advantage? While there may be no provable conflict of interest, the media do operate on a double standard here. Working journalists prize their objectivity and seek to protect their independence at all costs. Even appearances are important in the reader/audience and journalist relationship. If they are concerned on this level, why should not the corporate posture be carefully guarded also? Demanding special treatment when laws are designed, playing the political games out of self-interest, looking for tax breaks and expanded profits—all these pursuits through lobbying inevitably tarnish the media's reputation as democracy's lifeline.

A third negative result may be a weakening in news coverage of lobbying activity of all kinds. Whenever legislation is considered now in Washington, the sky is filled with Lear Jets of company officials who might be affected. The voices of every special interest, especially the powerful ones, seem to dominate the legislative process at present. Certainly the news media will continue to report bribes, illegal influence peddling, and immoralities among lobbyists. But a sharp edge on the overall issues is dulled when media businesses operate identically to other corporations.

Such negative consequences of lobbying are even more likely than the affirmative ones promoted within the press. Therefore, lobbying designed merely to protect the economic power of the news business should be eliminated. The four examples introduced in this case are all of this type. The fact that the Houston papers carried no reports of their lobbying suggests that they could not justify it to their readers. It is theoretically possible that certain lobbying by media institutions could be done in the public interest rather than in their own. But the dividing line between arrogant self-advancement and the public need is too easily obscured by rhetoric.

4. All Expenses Paid

The four-day, all-expenses-paid vacation had not quite lived up to expectations. But, on balance, the reporter enjoyed herself and it was a pleasant change from the office routine. There had been highlights, too: an unforgettable sunset, the relaxing cruise around the bay on the tourist launch, and interesting people.

Those things, and others like them, offset the disappointing ones. Her plane had been an hour late in arriving; even so she beat the hotel's limousine to the airport by fifteen minutes. When she had finally checked into her room, hot and sweaty, there were no towels. The hotel had been profuse in its apology, but still took a half hour in sending up towels. The hotel's staff, in fact, consisted of equal parts of courtesy and inefficiency. She waited an hour for dinner one evening, and then was served cold soup and warm juice. The sun's force on clear days and the penetrating chill of damp breezes on rainy ones surprised her.

Yet, on balance, it had been a good trip. And a free one. The reporter began to write: "You have never truly seen a sunset until you enjoy one at . . . ."

We must see more of the story. If the reporter did not include the annoyances and inefficiencies, the story was a bad one. They were a real part of the situation and not to report them is to deceive. A deliberate choice to withhold relevant information deprives the reader of an accurate account.

The problem is obviously to record faithfully both the good and bad associated with such a trip. To expect reporters on free trips to report carefully on both sides is to assume that reporters are willing to "bite the hand that feeds them." That is more than one should normally expect of mere mortals. Thus agreeing to free trips is tantamount to accepting the proposition that it is morally permissible to write deceptive pieces.

The question, then, turns on company policy regarding free trips for travel writers. To examine the matter of policy one must inquire about the reasons for having a travel section at all. Since people are interested in traveling, the paper's self-interest encourages coverage of this subject. If the public's fascination with travel stories were purely one of entertainment, no journalistic question would be involved at all. There would be no need for balance or accuracy, and the more fanciful and entertaining the story the better. But some people are interested in reading about travel in order to determine where to go and most effectively how to do so. Hence readers sometimes turn to travel sections for important information on which at least some people will depend rather heavily. The informing role of travel writing places special moral responsibility on the paper and on reporters.

What then should the paper's policy be regarding the acceptance of free trips? The ethical problem is immediately apparent because the acceptance of free trips may involve a conflict of interest whereas their refusal does not.

In the final analysis nothing in life is free. The agency or organization that picks up the tab expects some return on its investment. The sponsoring organization pays the bill in order to get relatively inexpensive and very effective publicity. That converts the role of the reporter from journalist to public relations agent. The organization offering the free trip is fully aware that reports in travel columns can be much more influential than can a paid commercial advertisement. In light of those circumstances it seems clear that the newspaper's policy should flatly prohibit participation. If the paper cannot pay for the reporter's trip, the reporter should stay home.

But for some papers such a policy would, in effect, eliminate stories on travel. The consequence would be to deprive readers of information in which they have a justifiable interest. The question then becomes whether it is possible to adopt a strategy which will meet the legitimate public need for information about travel while accepting the gift of trips from outside organizations. Can ways be found for minimizing the likelihood of deceit?

Two things can be done. First, the editor can insist that reporters who take trips must report as accurately as possible without considering the effect on possible future trips. Editors are more likely to be successful, of course, if the reporter is not just a travel specialist, but a carefully trained journalist.

Second, an editor can notify the public that the trip was in fact paid for by some outside organization. The specific name of the party need not be reported, but the article should identify the kind of enterprise it was (a travel agency, hotel, airline). That information enables the reader to assess the story more intelligently.

The decision to accept outside sponsorship of such trips, nevertheless, does run the risk of biased reporting that deceives the public. On the other hand, not to accept trips for which the paper cannot pay is a decision that in effect deprives certain social groups. Thus the absolute policy of forbidding free trips is not always in the public interest.

It might be useful to examine a case where a free trip involves more serious journalism. Suppose Acme Electric is contemplating construction of a nuclear generating facility in your area. Your paper has been reporting carefully in the news columns about the benefits and risks of that facility. The utility, rightly or wrongly, believes that the reporting has not given an accurate picture of the alternatives. The utility operates a nuclear facility in a distant state and has asked the paper to send a reporter to that area to get firsthand information on the operation of the facility and on the public attitudes toward it. The paper cannot pay the bill. The utility offers to pay it. Should the paper send a reporter at utility expense?

"Yes" seems to be a reasonable answer. The paper should send its best informed reporter, and it should make clear that the trip was underwritten by Acme Electric. In this case, the public has an overriding need for the most accurate information available. If that news story cannot possibly be obtained without accepting the gift, the paper should take Acme's financial assistance and find strategies for avoiding a deceptive report.

5. Employment and Civic Duties in Lewiston

In 1978 the Lewiston (Idaho) *Morning Tribune* took a look at the community interests of its staff. Staff member Cassandra Tate summarized the issue in the newspaper article that resulted: "Should the journalist exercise the rights and responsibilities of citizenship by participating in civic and political affairs? Or should he/she remain above the fray, a neutral observer? There is a danger of conflict in the first course, the potential for social isolation and sterility in the second."[11]

As would be expected, the *Morning Tribune*'s publisher had the lengthiest list of civic involvements. A.L. "Butch" Alford, Jr. was president of the Idaho Board of Education and a director of the Lewiston Roundup Association, the Lewis-Clark Boys Club, the Nez Perce National Historical Park Advisory Committee, and the Twin County United Way. He also served on the St. Joseph's Hospital Lay Advisory Board, the Bonneville Power Regional Advisory Council, and Potlatch Corporation's Foundation for Higher Education. He was active in the Lewiston Chamber of Commerce, a director of the Idaho First National Bank and of the University of Idaho Foundation.

Meanwhile, the newspaper's editorial-page editor, Bill Hall, had returned to the paper after 16 months as press secretary for Idaho Senator Frank Church. Night managing editor Perry Swisher was serving on the Governor's Blue Ribbon Committee on Taxation, the Idaho Manpower Board, and the Idaho Advisory Committee to the United States Commission on Civil Rights. He also was advisor to the Lewiston Downtown Beautification Committee and the Public Safety Building Committee. Executive editor James E. Shelley had a position as campaign coordinator for a Democratic senate candidate in 1972. Reporter Thomas W. Campbell was chairman of the Lewiston Historic Preservation Commission, a Democratic precinct committeeman and a member of the Civic Theater board. Part-time writer Diane Pettis was a member of the County Planning and Zoning Commission. Business writer Sylvia Harrell chaired the Lewiston Planning and Zoning Commission. Her husband worked for Potlatch, the area's largest industry and a frequent subject of pollution stories.

A similar list could be drawn up for the staffs on most newspapers, particularly the smaller ones. And the *Morning Tribune* follows standard policy—staff members do not report on their own activities. But, of course, those who draw the assignments are aware they are reporting on the performance of their friend and coworker or, in cases where editors or publishers are participants, on the performance of their bosses. For example, a young reporter, uninvolved in the community, encountered difficulties in covering the Roundup, Lewiston's annual rodeo, because the publisher served on its board. Said Gary Sharpe: "I don't know how many times I've been confronted by a person aware of Butch's membership on the board who says, 'I think Butch would like to see this in the paper.' "

As one concrete result of the study, reporter Campbell was told he could no longer write about politics if he did not resign as a Democratic precinct committeeman. Campbell took exception: "They're saying I won't give a fair interview to the Republicans because I'm a Democratic precinct committeeman. I'm saying that doesn't make one bit of difference."

Said Publisher Alford of the story on external involvements of his staff: "It's the first time in my association with the paper that we've thought to look at ourselves. . . . I hope as a result of our editorial coverage of ourselves we can see the weaknesses in our own process."[12] Alford's newspaper departed from tradition in publishing an open examination of its own operation. Alford also broke another tradition. Copies of his complete income tax return were filed with the newsroom secretary and could now be examined by anyone.

Most of the conflicts in this case come from potential role conflicts. The role of journalist as practitioner may well contradict at times the journalist's role as citizen. The good to be achieved as journalist is the publication of news as free from bias as possible. The good as citizen, on the other hand, is the social service that comes from responsible citizenship. The question, then, in part, is whether journalists should sacrifice their role as contributing citizens in order to be journalists, or whether the conflicts in this case are more apparent than real.

It can be reasonably argued that organizational memberships themselves are not a significant source of biased journalism. In the present case, it is likely that a reporter who is a Democratic precinct committeeman could not be entirely fair in an interview with a Republican candidate. That, however, would not be the consequence of his committee membership. He may show bias whether he is on the committee or not. Hence, resignation from that job would be essentially cosmetic, since he would surely remain a Democrat with perhaps strong political views.

It is possible in precisely the opposite direction that the reporter with active political interests is much more likely to be well informed about political matters than a politically disinterested reporter. It may be that even with a Democratic bias, reporter Campbell could do a better job interviewing either Democrats or Republicans than would someone who had no political interests. Cassandra Tate is quite incorrect if she thinks that human beings can "remain above the fray, a neutral observer." Since humans are valuing creatures, neutrality is not possible.

The moral obligation, then, cannot be to produce value-free journalists. The objective, as the Potter Box suggests, is to make clear at all times what values are operating.

Since bias-free reporting is not possible, another distinction becomes necessary. Note Alford's membership on United Way. This suggests that a bias in favor of the ideals for which an institution stands must be distinguished from a bias toward the organization itself. Bias in favor of charitable giving is a proclivity that can be tolerated; but favoritism toward the United Way organization, its directors and paid employees, cannot. Corruption or misuse of public funds by that organization should be reported vigorously, and indeed can be if the journalist's bias is simply toward charitable giving and not in favor of the United Way as an institution. Moreover, Alford's affiliation with United Way ought not diminish publicity for other charitable organizations.

What kind of policy, then, should journalists adopt regarding memberships in community organizations? Some would even discourage membership in all organizations: religious, civic, country club, corporate, and so on. However, such a policy risks the isolation of journalists from community affairs. The damage would include the loss of leads on important stories, as well as frustration over the inability to pursue personal, non-journalistic value commitments in some active, organized way. Thus a policy preventing all organizational memberships has little to commend it.

On the opposite end of the spectrum, media companies could ignore the question of organizational memberships altogether. They might do that on the ground that biased reporting does not stem from memberships per se, but from underlying value systems, making journalists' memberships in organizations a superficial matter. Using Aristotle's golden mean as an ethical guideline here, it is not desirable to preclude all outside involvements, nor is it acceptable for the staff to have no restrictions at all. That leaves the problem of finding strategies for minimizing the conflicts that arise from community memberships.

In this regard the *Morning Tribune*'s policy of not allowing reporters to cover their own activities is sound. Commendably, the *Morning Tribune* took a second step, alerting readers to the staff's external activities.

The boss' affiliations are another matter. His presidency of the Idaho Board of Education and membership on the Historical Park Advisory Committee would not likely create unmanageable conflicts. But several of Alford's positions in commercial firms are clearly problematical. Potlatch is the largest local industry and often under public scrutiny for pollution. He is also a director of First National Bank and on the advisory council for Bonneville Power.

These commitments are very questionable. A reporter's interest in pleasing the boss would inevitably conflict in these situations with the reporter's concern for sound news reporting. But the hazards can be minimized. In the case of Alford, he can make it unmistakably clear to the staff that he is a newspaper owner first and a member of Potlatch Foundation second. He should also convey that to Potlatch as a condition for serving. If the *Morning Tribune*'s staff is made up of competent journalists, the message will quite likely get across. If, however, the staff see themselves primarily as employees and only secondarily as responsible journalists with primary obligations to the public, the point will not get through. Thus, Alford's clarifying his commitments—even in the best of all circumstances—can only reduce the likelihood of damaging results. It would enable his employees to be better "watchdogs" if he would sever entirely his connections with Potlatch, First National, and Bonneville Power.

On the more fundamental level, Alford must face the question whether he is caught up in a business mentality which subtly weakens his service to the community. William Allen White, an outstanding editor and publisher, once complained, "Too often the publisher . . . is a rich man seeking power and prestige. He has the country club complex . . . and the unconscious arrogance of conscious wealth. Therefore it is hard to get a modern American newspaper to go the distance necessary to print all the news about many topics."[13] Within the free enterprise system, owners of media institutions consider themselves entitled to order whatever policy they choose, provided such policies are legal. Ethically sensitive publishers and broadcast executives follow stronger guidelines, however, deliberately adopting specific safeguards against the bewitching power of business allegiances.

Notes

1. Fred S. Siebert, Theodore Peterson, and Wilbur Schramm, *Four Theories of the Press* (Urbana: University of Illinois Press, 1956), p. 72.

2. The question is whether one's dual obligation in this instance prevents the fulfilling of both contracts. See Joseph Margolis, "Conflict of Interest and Conflicting Interests," in *Ethical Theory and Business*, ed. Tom L. Beauchamp and Norman E. Bowie (Englewood Cliffs, N.J.: Prentice-Hall, 1979), pp. 361–72.

3. Upton Sinclair, *The Brass Check: A Study of American Journalism* (Pasadena, Calif.: published by author, 1920), p. 436.

4. For a useful overview of concentration in various media, see Benjamin M. Compaine, ed., *Who Owns the Media?* (White Plains, N.Y.: Knowledge Industry Publications, 1979).

5. See Felix Gutierrez and Clint C. Wilson II, "The Demographic Dilemma," *Columbia Journalism Review* 17 (January/February 1979): 53–55.

6. National News Council Report, "Should the Media Use Dollars to Sway Public Issues?" *Columbia Journalism Review* 17 (March/April 1979): 73.

7. Ibid., p. 74.

8. Ibid.

9. Bill Keller, "How News Business Lobbyists Put Their Press on Congress . . . But With Mixed Feelings," *The Congressional Quarterly*, 2 August 1980, p. 2179. For additional details included in this case, see pp. 2176–84.

10. Ibid., p. 2183.

11. Cassandra Tate, "Conflict of Interest: A Newspaper's Report on Itself," *Columbia Journalism Review* 16 (July/August 1978): 44–48.

12. Ibid.

13. Commission on Freedom of the Press, *A Free and Responsible Press* (Chicago: University of Chicago Press, 1947), pp. 59–60.

Chapter Two

Truthtelling

The press' obligation to truth is a standard part of the rhetoric. Virtually all the ethics codes begin with the newsperson's duty to tell the truth under all conditions. High-minded editors typically etch the word on cornerstones and their tombstones. Credible words are pivotal to the communication enterprise.

When Pontius Pilate asked "What is truth?" he posed the question people of every kind have struggled to define. And as ideas and world views shift, so do the definitions of truthfulness. News people must live within the larger ambiguities about truth today in Western scholarship and culture. And their situation is complicated by budget constraints, deadlines, reader expectations, editorial conventions, and self-serving sources. Journalism is often referred to as history in a hurry and providing a precise, representative account can rarely occur under such conditions. All the while, advancing technology generates unceasing newscopy and the journalistic gatekeeper must choose from a mountain of options, often without the time to sift out the moral intricacies.

The cases that follow introduce several dimensions of the truthtelling issue. While every conceivable aspect is not offered, truth is enlarged beyond a simple facts-only definition. One way to broaden our scope, for example, is to consider the antonym of truthfulness and to account for newsgathering as well as newswriting. The opposite of truthtelling is deception, that is, a deliberate intention to mislead. Outright deceit occurs infrequently in the newswriting phase; only rarely, if ever, does a reporter or editor specifically and consciously give the wrong story. But deception in newsgathering is a persistent temptation, because it often facilitates the process of securing information. The first case in this section, "Maggots in a Nursing Home," has been selected because it is not an exotic example involving big money and overstepping the limits of legality. It is news gathered under false pretenses for a noble end, and depicts a project virtually any newspaper or station might conceivably consider.

Case number two, "Sexism and Mayor Byrne," represents one of journalism's most persistent agonies. Social groups suffering from discrimination are particularly sensitive to stereotyping. In that situation, even determined effort from the media to avoid prejudicial language is not considered sufficient. Many instances of blatant sexism could have been chosen, but they present no moral dilemma; sexist language dehumanizes and is therefore wrong and unprofessional. The accounts contrasted in this case indicate the subtleties even among those of good purpose.

Situation number three concerns historic Wounded Knee in South Dakota and introduces the issue of fairness in covering legitimate civil disobedience. Though civil disobedience is a violation of the law, it is committed as an act of conscience and therefore normally has received special privilege from standard democratic theorists since John Locke. The action of the American Indian Movement in case three is considered legitimate in the description below, in order that the analysis can concentrate on the issue of fair coverage.

The fourth case, "Tony Holds a Sawed-Off Shotgun," exemplifies the increasing use of media spectacle by those who are mentally deranged and irresponsibly violent. This case questions our conventional definitions of newsworthiness. Here a person's life is at stake and the moral problem is how to protect that life most effectively.

Case five, dealing with posed photographs, is tested in terms of journalism's long-standing commitment to accuracy and realism. This ambiguous example is selected for debate rather than as an obvious instance of fakery. Such fabrication we assume to violate professional and ethical standards so strongly that no debate is even possible. Case five is complicated by the photographer's failure to tell his editor that the picture was set up.

Case six, "Science Convention in Philadelphia," suggests two levels of difficulty—a reporter's obligations as employee, and the relative importance of soft and hard news. These two facets represent the structure within which most news gathering is done today. Both layers make the possibility of a truthful account very elusive and often only hard won by those reporters who handle their employee status and customs regarding hard news in an enlightened way.

6. Maggots in a Nursing Home

Some employees of the county nursing home had been calling the newspaper, reporting cases of patient neglect. The charges were often vague. The city editor of the Midwestern daily sensed that he was dealing with a small faction feuding with other employees and their supervisors. The vindictiveness threaded through the complaints made him wary of the sources. But some of the accusations had the ring of truth.

Then one day, a caller made a charge that was both specific and shocking. A woman patient with a gangrenous leg was so neglected that maggots were found under the dressing. The caller said the leg smelled so badly that some orderlies refused to change the bandages.

A reporter telephoned a doctor. If the report were true, the doctor responded, he would not let any relative of his live at the county nursing home. A second doctor who was contacted downplayed the incident. Maggots and gangrene go together, he said. The appearance of maggots did not in itself prove extreme delinquency.

The city editor was in a quandary. Even with medical opinion divided, the discovery of maggots seemed too newsworthy to ignore, particularly in light of other charges employees had made. Yet medical opinion was mixed and the sources might be using the newspaper for punishing their enemies. A story seemed necessary, but how should it be pursued? An inspection of the facility would yield nothing concrete, of that the city editor was certain. He wanted a true picture, free of both sensation and self-serving language. Finally he sent a young reporter to apply for a job as orderly at the nursing home. The reporter, who had a common last name, used a first initial and middle name for his byline. On his job application, he used his full first name and middle initial.

The reporter was hired on the spot, went through a brief training program, and was put on the night shift. At the end of two weeks, he began writing a series on the nursing home. Though not particularly damning, it was graphic. He noted the constant smell of urine and the idiosyncrasies of the patients. He described the employees and the work they did and neglected to do.

Before publishing the series, the city editor and the reporter told the nursing home director what they had done. The director was shaken by the news but submitted to an interview. When the series appeared, the city editor was satisfied that the picture it painted was as near the truth as could be hoped.

The public had been informed. But readers were outraged by the tactics used in getting the story. The newspaper received more than 60 letters to the editor, almost all of them negative. Although no names had been used in the series, letter writers charged that the privacy of both patients and employees had been invaded, that old age was held up to ridicule, and that the method used in gathering information was deceitful.

The vast majority of media professionals would approve this city editor's decision. In fact, similar practices have become widely used in the newsgathering process. Reporters hired as clerks have encountered corruption first-hand in welfare and unemployment programs. Across the country, newspapers and broadcasters, posing as consumers, have exposed cheating repair shops by having them "fix" cars or appliances rigged with minor defects. A Chicago daily recently sent reporters with necks "hurt" in car accidents to lawyers, thus uncovering those willing to file fraudulent damage suits. The Pulitzer board refused to honor the Chicago *Sun-Times* for its famous "Mirage" case when the newspaper staff surreptitiously operated a bar in order to investigate the city's inspection system. But the board's refusal largely stemmed from the fear that the *Sun-Times* was guilty of entrapment. More innocent misrepresentations are normally considered a necessary means for achieving a valuable end.

In other words, this deceptive practice is usually justified on utilitarian grounds. How else, the question goes, can such corruption be exposed? The city editor of the Midwestern daily, for example, concluded that sending reporters to the nursing home would accomplish nothing. The leaked information was too narrow and vituperative to be of any value. Documented records from nursing home administrators would not indicate the true level of patient care. In this line of reasoning, hiring out a reporter under disguise appears to be eminently defensible, even essential. The enormous social value far outgains the few negative consequences. Embarrassing officials and some of the staff, invading privacy to some extent are unimportant compared to better care for severely neglected patients and the onward march of truth.

However, the moral issues are more complicated than this typical framework assumes. Even accepting the principle of utility, have all the consequences actually been considered? If the short-term results are calculated, the amount of good effects surpasses the bad. But what about the long-term consequences? The hostile avalanche from newspaper readers is a significant clue here. The newspaper assumed it had served the public with valuable information. Many readers were outraged instead. Their response signals that over the long-term the Midwestern daily's credibility, and that of the media generally, might be undermined. Such a negative consequence changes the equation; it is no longer obvious that the sum benefit outweighs the total harm. All such tricks, in Donald Warwick's lament, "strengthen the growing conviction that you can't trust people you don't know. If a mugger doesn't hit you, a credit checker doesn't spy on you, or a salesman doesn't take you to the cleaners, a social scientist will dupe you."[1] The result is a climate of distrust and a heavy toll on social faith.

Appealing to a different ethical system sheds another light on the nursing home maggots. Kant's categorical imperative treats all deception as immoral behavior; under no circumstances would anyone wish deception to become a universal practice. It is arguable that an explicit class, such as law enforcement officers, could be permitted some minor forms of deception in order to capture criminals. But trust, in the Kantian outlook, is absolutely essential for individuals to be human and for a society to function. Anything that erodes the public trust damages irreversibly the social fabric. In her persuasive book, *Lying*, Sissela Bok contends that "trust is a social good to be protected just as much as the air we breathe or the water we drink."[2] From a creative synthesis of such moral philosophers as Aristotle, Augustine, and Immanuel Kant, Professor Bok advocates that cultures ought to be weighted toward veracity and against deception. She warns that "deceit and violence . . . are the two deliberate forms of assault on human beings."[3] Even if done for noble ends, the deceived feel violated to their inner core.

In a modified version of the categorical imperative, one could permit a modicum of deception in situations of extreme crisis. The Dutch rightfully lied to Nazi soldiers seeking Jews. A murderer pursuing your children need not be told the truth. But these are extraordinary occurrences. Most practitioners would never see one case in a lifetime that warranted an exception. On this view, the Midwestern daily chose the expedient route of duplicity, rather than more difficult but honorable ones based on informed consent. There is no concrete evidence that the newspaper hired out its own reporter under duress, as a last unfortunate resort, after exhausting every resource and exploring all other possibilities.

An undercover reporter would probably not have been necessary in this case if the newspaper kept a regular eye on the community's elderly. The hard questions then shift to publishers who do not provide large enough staffs to report systematically on jails, juvenile centers, nursing homes, mental hospitals, veterans' facilities, and so forth. The long-range solution here involves the beat system, and the manner in which news beats are established reflects a complex interaction between business ethics and public morality. Publishers may deliberately underfund the news operation, but more likely perceive that the public does not relish this kind of threat to their cliches and consciences. Nor would the majority of advertisers—community-minded as most are—choose to support such stations and papers. Thus journalists with a keen sense of human decency must frequently struggle against unfavorable odds.

7. Sexism and Mayor Byrne

Jane Byrne accomplished two near miracles in April 1979: she became the first woman mayor of Chicago, and she beat the fabled Cook County Democratic machine to do it. Byrne was a protege of Chicago mayor Richard J. Daley. He appointed her to cabinet level posts in the city administration and she paid her dues with lots of hard work for the Democratic slate. Some critics say that Byrne was little more than Daley's token female in a male-chauvinist regime, but she was nonetheless there and she was no wall prop.

Her independence was put to the test under Daley's successor, Michael Bilandic. Byrne had evidence that city officials stood to profit under legislation raising the taxi rates in Chicago. Bilandic understandably denied the allegations and fired Byrne when she refused to quiet down.

Then came the mayoral primary. Byrne cast her name into the lot as a non-machine Democrat who wanted to clean up the city, eradicate waste, and return government to the people. She was perceived as a candidate with high ideals and absolutely no chance of denting the power of Chicago slatemakers. Bilandic was the party choice and seemed comfortably in command until a January snowstorm that city crews were slow to clear. Traffic snarled for days, Bilandic's image plummeted, and the city machine stumbled under the weight of its patronage overload. To the surprise of the city if not the country, Byrne defeated Bilandic in the primary and easily won the mayoral election.

The Byrne administration began with high promises and great hopes, but before long the acerbic mayor had the tough Chicago press aiming for the jugular. The climax in a deteriorating relationship came in June 1980, when the *Tribune* gave front-page play to a report that Byrne had shelved a study she herself had commissioned on the efficiency of city government. The study criticized waste and incompetence in City Hall and the *Tribune* saw self-serving politics suppressing the progress of the people's city. They blew the horn. Her Honor took the *Tribune* report personally. Her press office quickly issued a release accusing the paper of "innuendoes, lies, smears, character assassinations, and male chauvinist tactics since Jane Byrne became mayor.'"

On the same Saturday night that the *Tribune* hit the streets, Byrne called the city desk to announce she would throw the *Tribune*'s reporter out of City Hall's press room on Monday morning. On Sunday Jay McMullen, Byrne's husband and press officer, called Robert Davis, the reporter in question, telling him to remove his personal belongings from City Hall immediately. The *Tribune* was paper non grata in the halls of power; Byrne indicated that City Hall employees would be instructed not to speak with *Tribune* personnel.

Reaction was fast and furious from both sides. *Tribune* managing editor William Jones said: "There is no vendetta and the mayor knows it. The *Tribune* will continue to publish the news without first seeking approval from the city administration." On the editorial page the *Tribune* lamented:

If the city's image is being hurt, it is the mayor herself who is hurting it, by her past record of impulsive and often inconsistent behavior, by her inability to obtain and keep qualified administrators, and now by a vindictive step that is bound to make her administration the laughing stock of the country. . . . We hope that the mayor will reconsider her stand, because an attack on freedom of the press goes far beyond the cast of characters involved; it is a nationwide threat, especially to publications smaller than the *Tribune* and less able to resist the arrogance of power.[4]

In the news hole the paper reported Byrne's reactions to reporters' questions about the incident. She "picked up her purse and hurried into an elevator, refusing to comment," the paper said.

On Monday the mayor backed down. Bob Davis was at his desk, a momentary celebrity. Nevertheless Monday's *Tribune* carried an editorial noting "this continued round of thoughtless and unproductive public outbursts by the chief executive. . . . Mayor Byrne's antics would be more frightening if they were not so absurd."

Mike Royko, syndicated columnist for the Chicago *Sun-Times*, was a minority voice on the mayor's side, sort of. Why all the fuss, he asked?

The *Tribune* can go on implying, without proof, that Byrne is a tool of the crime syndicate, that she may be mentally unbalanced and that she might destroy Chicago. It can go on dreaming up nonexistent scandals and fishing around for something—almost anything—that will make her look bad. And it can go on pompously pretending that all it is doing is covering the news fairly and impartially. That's really the fascinating thing about this silly flap—the thinness of the news media's skin.[5]

Royko defended the mayor in the metro press, but he was not alone on her side. In the Summer 1980 issue, *Matrix* (published by Women in Communication) featured a story on the mayor that never mentioned the *Tribune* trouble. Claiming "repeated and continuing incidents of sexist treatment," the *Matrix* writer claimed that the Chicago papers had not attempted to understand the mayor. Contrary to her press image, Byrne has attributes of "forthrightness and honesty in saying what she thinks, regardless of the consequences. She has been known to take positions that no man would espouse, but she sticks with them because she has drawn a line in her mind on what is morally right and won't cross it."[6] Her enemies are "ethnic groups who feel slighted," and her troubles stem from her liberal views in a conservative city, *Matrix* said. For the future, "there's no telling what goal the mayor can achieve. It is tempting to say that she could be the first woman vice-president, but the latent sexism in that prediction is too apparent. And Jane Byrne probably would impose no such limitation upon herself."[7]

Several dimensions of this Chicago case warrant consideration: Did Mayor Byrne actually pose a "nation-wide threat" to press freedom, as the *Tribune* claimed, when she told Robert Davis he was no longer welcome at City Hall? Did the *Tribune*, as Mike Royko charged, suggest without proof that Mayor Byrne "was a tool of the crime syndicate?" Did the mayor's rejection of the efficiency study indicate an ongoing wastefulness in her administration? Does it represent a conflict of interest that Jay McMullen, Mrs. Byrne's husband and press secretary, was at the time on leave from the *Tribune*'s competitor (the Chicago *Sun-Times*)?

The specific moral issue, however, concerns unfair treatment of Mayor Byrne as a human being. Is the *Tribune* guilty of sexist bias as she charges? In contrast, has *Matrix* given the public a true account? What kind of portrait best emulates the ethical principle regarding respect of persons?

Women have been stereotyped regularly in the press. The problem has long historical roots. During the women's suffrage movement, for example, news accounts often distorted the issues and editorials regularly denounced their "petty whims," spoke of "appalling consequences," and even used labels such as "insurrection." Sample twentieth-century writing of almost any kind (including journalism) and the failures are obvious: over-emphasis on clothes and physical appearance, the glorification of domesticity, empty heads or at least nonintellectualism. Even in recent years, Edward M. Miller used blatant sexism to defend the rules for women issued by the Associated Press Managing Editors association (APME). Women, in his view, do well on people stories but cannot unravel complicated financial ones. Miller considers them excellent copy editors because of their disposition and "repetitious work does not seem to bother them."[8]

Because the media generally reflect cultural mores and male-female inequality does exist, a thorough content analysis of all the *Tribune* copy regarding Mayor Byrne is warranted. She very quickly dismisses her male critics as chauvinists who refuse to admit that women can be successful politicians. Negative press coverage she likewise rejects as sex bias. Such claims are too sweeping to be believable, yet so many failures have occurred on so many levels that the *Tribune* must insure that all anti-feminist bias has been purged from its stories. It is pertinent to ask whether the *Tribune* has provided any institutional safeguards for covering City Hall. Under maximum conditions, one's behavior should be justifiable even to the accused. But would the Mayor ever be able to admit, "they disagreed with my policies, but they did treat me fairly and represented my viewpoint accurately." Given the emotional overtones surrounding sexism, such an expectation may be too strong. Additional measures by the *Tribune*, however, could indicate its unalterable commitment to respecting all persons. Should women reporters not be assigned to City Hall, for example, and editors be given specific warning about Robert Davis's reports and Bob Wiedrich's columns? Susan B. Anthony spoke prophetically in 1900: "As long as newspapers and magazines are controlled by men . . . women's ideas and deepest convictions will never get before the public."[9] Admittedly dictionaries cannot be rewritten overnight and these corrections must be etched out of inherited usage. However, newspapers such as the *Tribune* could adopt specific guidelines for the treatment of women, such as the list of ten compiled by Pat Corbine, editor of *MS*.[10]

The *Matrix* article attempts to balance the record. The author, Grace Kaminkowitz, focuses on "a job well done" and dismisses criticism by a patronizing press and politicians. But that slant fails too. It builds from a "gee-whiz, this woman did it first" mentality. A letter to *Matrix* from Michelle Sipe responding to Kaminkowitz points directly to the subtleties:

I can't agree with Ms. Kaminkowitz in applauding Mayor Byrne for a job well done. We can't make examples of women in jobs . . . simply because they are women and we may need that morale boost. I think it's commendable that Mayor Byrne believes and fights for ERA—but it is not commendable that she lets every criticism of her behavior in office be labeled as sexism. . . . You have totally ignored the person that is mayor of Chicago . . . . She has no business in City Hall and we have no business commending her for being a woman in a tough spot because she puts herself there time and time again. We don't want to encourage women to continue in jobs just because they have them.[11]

8. Ten Weeks at Wounded Knee

One of this century's leading civil libertarians, Zechariah Chafee, Jr., once wrote: "Much of our [national] expansion has been accomplished without attacking our neighbors. . . . There were regrettable phases of our history, such as breaches of faith with the Indians, but these are so far in the past that they have left no running sores to bother us now. . . . We have not acted the bully."[12]

If a distinguished Harvard law professor, a man considered a champion of oppressed minorities, can write so casually about the plight of American Indians, little wonder a tight circle of American Indian Movement (AIM) leaders thought they needed a major event to publicize their concerns. And what better event than an old-fashioned "uprising" complete with teepees, horses, rifles, war paint, and television cameras.

On 27 February 1973, some 200 Indians seized the hamlet of Wounded Knee on the Pine Ridge Sioux Indian Reservation in the southwest corner of South Dakota. Tension had been growing steadily for three weeks, ever since a group of Indians clashed with police in Custer, South Dakota, protesting the light charge (second degree manslaughter) returned against a white man accused of stabbing and killing an Indian there. Thirty-six Indians were arrested in that melee, eight police were injured, and a chamber of commerce building was burned.

But the problem at Wounded Knee was of different magnitude. Indians had taken hostages (11 townspeople who later declared they were not being held against their will and refused release to federal authorities), and were prepared to hold their ground by violence if need be. They sensed considerable public support as they traded on sympathy for Chief Big Foot's warriors who were slaughtered there in 1890 by the U.S. Seventh Cavalry. That morbid raid had been the last recorded instance of open hostilities between American Indians and the U.S. government—until February 1973.

As the siege began, news crews rushed to cover the developing story. On February 28, Indians demanded that the Senate Foreign Relations Committee hold hearings on treaties made with Indians and that the Senate begin a full-scale investigation of government treatment of Indians. George McGovern, a liberal democrat and South Dakota senator at the time, flew home to try negotiations, but to no avail. Meanwhile, FBI agents, federal marshals, and Bureau of Indian Affairs (BIA) policemen surrounded Wounded Knee, hoping to seal off supplies and force a peaceful surrender.

But the siege turned violent. On March 11, an FBI agent was shot and an Indian injured as gunfire erupted at a roadblock outside town. On the same day AIM leader Russell Means announced that Wounded Knee had seceded from the United States and that federal officials would be treated as agents of a warring foreign power. A marshal was seriously wounded on March 26, and two Indians were killed in gunfire as the siege wore into April. Finally on May 6, with supplies and morale nearly expended, the Indians negotiated an armistice and ended the war.

An incredible 93 percent of the population claimed to follow the strike through television. Indian attorney Roman Roubideaux did not think they were seeing the real story:

The TV correspondents who were on the scene filmed many serious interviews and tried to get at the essence of the story, but *that* stuff never got on the air. Only the sensational stuff got on the air. The facts never really emerged that this was an uprising against the Bureau of Indian Affairs and its puppet tribal government.[13]

Television critic Neil Hickey summarized the feelings of many:

In all the contentiousness surrounding the seizure of Wounded Knee last winter, a thread of agreement unites the disputants: namely, the press, especially television, performed its task over a quality spectrum ranging from "barely adequate" to "misguided" to "atrocious." For varying reasons, no party to the fray felt that his views were getting a decent airing.[14]

The lack of sufficient evidence foiled prosecutors at the subsequent trial of AIM leaders Means and Dennis Banks. Defense attorneys Mark Lane and William Kunstler argued that Indians were not guilty since they were merely reclaiming land taken from them by treaty violations. But the real defense was an inept offense. In September 1974, U.S. District Judge Fred Nichol accused the FBI of arrogance and misconduct and the chief U.S. prosecutor of deceiving the court. After an hour's lecture to the government, he dismissed the case.

The occupation at Wounded Knee was deliberately staged for television. AIM leaders knew that the legends of Big Foot, and the recent popularity of Dee Brown's *Bury My Heart at Wounded Knee* would virtually guarantee a good press. Yet no one can reasonably contend it was not a newsworthy event. The Indians at Pine Ridge had just witnessed what they perceived as a breakdown in the judicial system at Custer. The American Indian Movement had tried other forums for airing their argument that 371 treaties had been violated by the United States government. The Ogalala Sioux were Western Plains horsemen pushed off their land during Western expansion. And while the tribal militants actually precipitated the siege—though numbering only a small percentage of the Pine Ridge population—traditional grievance procedures through the Bureau of Indian Affairs had been tried and had failed to date. While producing several excesses, sympathy for the event was aided by heavy doses of folklore and liberal guilt. Yet it was based on a defensible civil disobedience. Joe Ledbetter, a painter in Custer, did not represent the prevailing opinion: "Them Indians learned from the niggers. They got the same tactics." Assuming the distinction between psychotic behavior and understandable frustration, media coverage seems warranted.

The moral issue is the degree to which the conflicting voices were fairly represented. In fact, the ten weeks of siege produced so many aggrieved parties that fairness to all protagonists became totally impossible. How accurately did reporters cover the law officials ordered to the scene, for example? After the event, FBI agents and marshals were hissed by hostile crowds near Wounded Knee and ordered to leave lest another outbreak occur. And how could the press treat fairly the Bureau of Indian Affairs? Its policies became the lightning rod of attack, catching all the fury born from 200 years of exploitation. An inept Justice Department, abuses from ranchers and storekeepers, racism from area whites, and inadequate congressional leadership also contributed their share, but received only a minor part of the blame. How does one measure out accusations where appropriate, and yet recognize legitimate achievements in a raucous setting? The Bureau contended, for example, that it was not responsible for every conceivable abuse, and that it had sponsored nearly all vocational training and employment on the reservation.

But the hardest questions concern fair treatment of the Ogalala Sioux grievances. According to the ethical principle that human beings should be respected as ends in themselves, the moral ideal entails an account that clearly reflects the viewpoint of these aggrieved. And even a minimum definition of fairness certainly includes all avoidance of stereotypes. A young Ogalala Sioux bitterly scourged some members of the press in this regard for giving their stories the stilted cast of "wild West gunfights between the marshals and Indians." On 30 December 1890, the New York *Times* warped its news account of the original Pine Ridge battle with biased phrases about "hostiles" and "reds." The story concluded: "It is doubted if by night either a buck or squaw out of all Big Foot's band is left to tell the tale of this day's treachery. The members of the Seventh Cavalry have once more shown themselves to be heroes of deeds of daring."[15] Eighty-five years later, many newspapers and broadcasters had still not eliminated cliches, prejudices, and insensitive language.

Fairness, as a minimum, also entails that the coverage reflect the degree of complexity inherent in the events themselves. Admittedly when events are refracted through the mirrors of history, separating fact from fiction becomes impossible. Moreover, the Pine Ridge Indians themselves disagreed fundamentally about the problems and the cure. Richard Wilson, president of the Tribal Council, despised the upstarts of AIM: "They're just bums trying to get their braids and mugs in the press." He feared a declaration of martial law on the reservation and considered the militant Means and Banks to be city-bred leaders acting like a "street gang," who destroy the tribe in the name of saving it.

"No more red tape. No more promises," said Means in response. "The federal government hasn't changed from Wounded Knee to My Lai and back to Wounded Knee." Raymond Yellow Thunder, after all, had been beaten to death earlier by whites and the charges limited to manslaughter by an all-white jury in Custer. Investigations demanded by Congress, the Justice Department, and Senator McGovern had been to no avail. The average annual wage at Pine Ridge was $1,800, with alcoholism and suicide at epidemic rates. Why not action now?

Why were the AIM occupiers, speaking for thousands of Indians, unable to get a hearing for themselves? Maybe the BIA had instituted a corrupt, puppet government after all. Where is the truth in all the highly charged rhetoric?

Some reporters did break through the fog with substantive accounts. NBC's Fred Briggs used charts and photos to describe the trail of broken treaties which reduced the vast Indian territory to a few small tracts. CBS' Richard Threlkeld understood that AIM really sought a revolution in Indian attitudes. ABC's Ron Miller laid vivid hold of life on the Pine Ridge reservation itself by "getting inside the Indian and looking at what was happening through his eyes." But, on balance, journalists on the scene did not fully comprehend the subtleties of tribal government nor the historical nuances. Reporters covering Wounded Knee complained that their more precise accounts were often reduced and distorted by heavy editing at home. In any case, after 71 days, the siege ended from weariness, not because the story was fully aired or understood. During that period the press largely became an accomplice of the guns and spectre, a victim of media politics rather than an agent whereby a political complaint was sensibly discussed.

Maybe the principle of fairness can only operate before and after spectacle of this kind, when the aggrieved knock on doors more gently. If that is true, owners of news businesses in the Wounded Knee region carry an obligation to develop substantial and balanced coverage of Indian oppression over the long term, even though such coverage may threaten some of their established interests. Often reporters sensitive to injustice receive little support and thus have no choice but to break stories of injustice when they fit into traditional canons of newsworthiness.

9. Tony Holds a Sawed-Off Shotgun

Richard O. Hall, a 42-year-old mortgage company executive in Indianapolis, spent 63 hours with a sawed-off shotgun attached to his neck. Part of that time was on camera, Hall standing numbly in the glare of the television lights while his captor, Anthony G. (Tony) Kiritsis, told viewers how Hall's mortgage company had cheated him in a land transaction.

In some ways, the media helped keep Hall alive and may have caught unnecessary criticism for so doing. But on two occasions the media endangered Hall's life by following the principle that the public ought to be informed. The media were Kiritsis's conduit for making public his grievances against the mortgage company. During the ordeal, the mortgage company aired a public apology to Kiritsis and one radio news director allowed Kiritsis air time to tell his side of the story. The news director, Fred Heckman, gradually assumed the role of a mediator. Heckman later said his conversations with Kiritsis and the fact he permitted him the microphone "set up a trust that eventually was credited as a major part in saving not only Dick Hall's life, but that of Kiritsis." But, as critics pointed out, Heckman, in giving Kiritsis a platform, contributed to his becoming a folk hero. Many viewers saw him as a good but frustrated man who had been swindled by a loan company when in fact the courts were later to judge him insane.

Heckman concedes the point. He explained his position at a workshop of the Radio-Television News Directors Association:

I didn't like it. There was a twenty-year development of credibility and integrity in the Indianapolis market that I had on the line and quite obviously some of it was lost. Yes, it did make Kiritsis a folk hero. . . . To a great extent I was probably the one responsible for that and I didn't like it, but felt that there was no other way, no other course to take.[16]

One of Heckman's most outspoken critics was Steven Yount, director of news and public affairs for WIRE-AM/WXTZ-FM, Indianapolis. He charged that in general the Indianapolis media surrendered their independence "by basing news reports on a police request that we not report anything that would upset the kidnapper. We became part of a police effort to fool a kidnapper instead of being an independent bystander there to inform the public." Yount insisted it was the news media's responsibility "to gather and report facts," even if such reporting endangered the life of a hostage or angered the police.[17]

One news organization did report the truth, and that report could have heightened the danger to Hall's life. The truth concerned an offer of immunity made by the county prosecutor's office, an offer intended as a last-resort, ace-in-the-hole strategy reserved for an emergency. The emergency arose because of the way Douglas O'Brien, a newsman from Heckman's station, was describing the episode. At the scene he reported:

The Army bomb squad that's here has begun to try and think of ways to somehow get in without setting off the explosives. We're told (here some words were indistinct) that they may be able to. . . . If Kiritsis could be incapacitated somehow, they could get in and defuse the explosives that are in the room, if they are in fact there, and they do believe they are.

Announcer: Okay, but it hasn't really come to that and we'll anxiously await the next report from the scene.[18]

Kiritsis, who had his radio tuned to the station, interpreted the report to mean that the bomb squad was rushing the apartment. Ordering a brother and a friend to leave a nearby apartment, he angrily threatened to blow up Hall and himself. Officials decided the time had come to offer Kiritsis immunity. George Martz, a Marion County deputy prosecutor, broadcast the offer of immunity from state prosecution if Kiritsis would release Hall unharmed. Martz added that he understood that immunity from federal prosecution was "in the making."

Hearing the broadcast, a reporter at the Associated Press (AP) bureau called the U.S. Attorney for Southern Indiana. The attorney, speaking for the record, said immunity would not be offered. "The Justice Department won't bargain with gunmen." A reporter at AP's Washington bureau got the same answer from Justice Department officials. Should AP run the story? AP staffer Darrell Christian said the staff "had a severe conscience qualm. . . . What if we ran the story, Kiritsis hears it on TV and blows Hall's head off?"

AP decided to move the story. However, the decision was not made in Indianapolis, but rather by AP's managing editor in New York. This occurred, said Christian, "because no one here wanted to take responsibility involving two lives." When Kiritsis surrendered, it was unclear whether he had actually heard about the denial of federal immunity.

This case raises a number of fundamental issues. An analysis could begin by simple identification of the several decisions which were made. Then the issues involved in each of those decisions could be located and evaluated.

The following seem to be the central decisions: (1) Some journalists had to decide whether to put Kiritsis and Hall on camera. (2) Heckman had to decide whether to provide air time to allow Kiritsis to tell his side of the story. (3) Heckman had to decide whether to assume the role of mediator. (4) Someone had to decide whether to report an offer of immunity by the county prosecutor. (5) Reporter O'Brien had to decide whether to broadcast speculations by the army bomb squad about whether they could get in the building and incapacitate Kiritsis. (6) Someone at the Asssociated Press had to decide whether to report the fact that no immunity to Kiritsis would in fact be given by federal prosecutors.

As in all decisions to act, the moral dimension of human choice lies in the possible impact these decisions will have on human well-being. The choices are complex because of the difficulty in predicting the likely outcome. Many people are involved here and some will be affected more seriously than others. Some will be hurt badly and others helped. The case has so many possible ramifications that a complete examination would require several chapters. Therefore, the focus will be on numbers one, two, and five, with brief attention to the other decisions made.

Decision one is clearly the most complex in terms of both factual assessment and moral judgment. Should Kiritsis and Hall be allowed to go on camera? The very existence of the mass media makes such decisions inevitable. In a sense the media's own definition of newsworthiness tends to make them a pawn in the hands of people like Kiritsis. We do not know what specific facts led to the decision to air this event, though its very nature made the story a natural victim of these circumstances. If Kiritsis demanded that he be put on the air with the threat of executing Hall were he not, he would put both journalists and the authorities in a real moral bind. How could they assess the seriousness of his threats? How could they predict his actions if they did put him on the air or if they did not? He might have executed Hall before an audience. More important is the question as to who should decide when one is obviously dealing with a seriously deranged individual. Journalists by and large are not well equipped either by experience or by training to make predictive judgments concerning the behavior of such a person. Nor are the police well equipped to make such judgments. Both must depend upon consultation with professionals who deal with the mentally deranged.

Should they decide to put Kiritsis and Hall on camera? For Hall's sake it seems that they should decide on the basis of whatever the responsible public authorities determine. If the authorities in charge concluded that going on television might save Hall's life, the station should put him on. There is a positive moral obligation not only to avoid harm but also to prevent harm to a fellow human being if doing so does not subject us to the risk of comparable harm. In this case the station does not risk serious loss. The journalists do indeed become pawns, not in the hands of the police, as Yount suggested, but in the hands of Kiritsis who by holding Hall hostage manipulates both the media and the police. These same considerations apply to news director Heckman and his decision to provide air time for Kiritsis.

That brings us to Yount's criticism of Heckman, a response frequently heard. However, claiming that the media became a part of the police effort to fool the kidnapper is a criticism which does not recognize the fundamental realities of the situation. By Kiritsis' action the media were no longer able to remain independent bystanders. Kiritsis made them participants whether they wished to be or not. Yount's insistence that the news media's responsibility was only "to gather the facts" gives no guidance whatever in this situation. In this case, getting the facts interferes clearly with the responsibility for Hall's life. Anything that risks the life of an innocent human being is immoral by almost any standard.

Regarding decision five, reporter O'Brien had to decide on the spot whether to broadcast speculations by the bomb squad. Remote, on-the-scene, live broadcasting places a very heavy responsibility on reporters at the scene. Those responsibilities are unavoidable. Live broadcasts put reporters in a position of having to make far-reaching news judgments and to make them quickly. For that reason it is arguable that remote facilities should not be taken to such a scene at all! Yet to be there as a reporter is *ipso facto* to become a participant. In this case, since lives are at stake, and since O'Brien could report enough later to straighten out the entire situation, O'Brien should here decide what to broadcast not by typical criteria of newsworthiness, but by criteria applicable to his role as a participant. Once the crisis is over and he no longer participates, he can report the event without endangering life. It was morally irresponsible for him as a participant to broadcast speculations about the bomb squad since that quite predictably would further upset an already desperate and deranged kidnapper. He clearly compounded the risk to Hall. The same may be said, of course, of the AP decision to report the fact that no immunity would be given to Kiritsis by federal prosecutors. The public gained nothing by being told the facts *then*. Those facts could keep until the crisis was over.

10. Foot Photo Ends a Career

Sixty-one year old Norman Zeisloft had served for 17 years on the photo staff of the St. Petersburg (Florida) *Times* and *Evening Independent*. On May 14, Zeisloft was assigned to a baseball game between Eckerd and Florida Southern colleges. "It was quite a nothing event," he recalled.[19]

Zeisloft spied three teenage fans with their bare feet up on a railing and it sparked the idea of writing "Yea, Eckerd" on their soles. The fans agreed and Zeisloft etched the words with a felt-tip pen on the bottom of one man's feet. "It was just a whimsical thing," Zeisloft recounted, "just for a little joke . . . to make people smile."

But Phil Sheffield, a Tampa *Tribune* photographer, stood nearby.

Almost instinctively, Sheffield said, he photographed Zeisloft as he put pen to sole. Also watching were the director of public relations and a photographer for Florida Southern.

Meanwhile, Zeisloft found his pen too dry and the spectator's feet too dirty. He turned to following the game. The fan then left the stands, washed his feet, and returned with "YEA, ECKERD" on his soles. Zeisloft took the photo and it appeared two days later in the *Evening Independent*.

Over in Tampa, Sheffield developed his shot of Zeisloft at work and posted it on the *Tribune* bulletin board. From there a xerox copy circulated "as a light-hearted thing" to a former staffer now at the Minneapolis *Tribune*, and then to important people such as Stephen Isaacs (editor of the Minneapolis *Star* and chairman of the Pulitzer Prize international reporting jury), and Norman Isaacs (chairman of the National News Council). Isaacs passed it on to his longtime friend, Eugene Patterson (president of the St. Petersburg papers and chairman of the Pulitzer Prize Board recently involved in the Janet Cooke incident).

"It's one thing journalism can't afford," Norman Isaacs said of the incident. "It's of the same genre as Janet Cooke, when the honor of journalism takes second place to getting a story or picture." Patterson was "deeply embarrassed." Zeisloft received a hearing and was fired on June 24, his first day back from vacation. "To me," Zeisloft responded, "it seemed like cruel and unusual punishment to be fired after 17½ years of faithful service on the basis of one photo that was designed merely to bring a chuckle to our readers."

In this particular instance, the posed photograph does not deceive in any meaningful sense. Not surprisingly, the *Evening Independent* did not receive one phone call or letter about it. No reader could reasonably feel cheated or misinformed as a result. Zeisloft showed no intention to distort the news deliberately. In addition, the intense rivalry between the Tampa and St. Petersburg papers may have pushed the situation out of all reasonable proportions.

However, in reaching a conclusion about this seemingly innocuous case, a larger issue must be considered—that of posed photographs generally. Officially Zeisloft was terminated because he submitted a staged photograph without informing his editor. Certainly a number of questions arise. Are such posed photographs even avoidable? An editor may not approve of certain poses, say by political rivals from the same party smiling together to show a nonexistent party unity; how does that differ from photographers staging their shots to meet certain professional criteria regarding good photos? Is the selection of an angle for a photograph, for framing it, for lighting it, different in some significant respect from selecting the lead or the slant to a written story? How does this incident differ from sending photographers to ribbon-cutting ceremonies at store openings or fancy promotions with the local mayor, for the business sections of papers and to please advertisers? Is a picture taken by photographers any more or less their creation than stories created by reporters?

The last question, in effect, became decisive for Zeisloft's superiors. They contended that just as reporters writing a story ought always guard against misrepresentation, so photographers must not fabricate events. The moral obligation in both cases is to avoid deceit with stories or pictures; both should carry the inherent meaning and present an accurate account. To assume otherwise makes photographers second-class members of the newsroom who need not operate with the same professional standards as writers. Otherwise they are subtly demanded as merely providing "art" or diversion for the printed copy. As Robert Haimon, executive editor of the St. Petersburg papers, explained: The one important obligation in "the journalistic community" is "to tell the truth, the whole truth, and nothing but the truth. There is simply no room for people who don't tell the truth." That principle was so compelling in Haimon's mind that terminating Zeisloft became the only option.

Within months of each other, two other photographers were fired because of questions about the credibility of their pictures. The United Press International dismissed a photographer at its Buffalo, New York, bureau for a photo made of two negatives, but not identified as a composite. *Geo* magazine released a veteran contract photographer for taking pictures of pandas in a two-acre research pen, the caption alleging that they came from the wilds of China. A high view of truthtelling is thereby applied as vigorously to news photography as it should be to written copy.

11. Science Convention in Philadelphia

Early in 1972, the American Association for the Advancement of Science (AAAS) met in Philadelphia. Some 35 of the participants, comprising the total membership of Scientists and Engineers for Social and

Political Action, came solely to attract mass media attention for their anti-establishment cause. Also present at one session during the five days were former Vice-President Hubert Humphrey and former Lyndon Johnson aide William Bundy. Humphrey was considering the possibility of challenging Richard Nixon in the fall presidential campaign.

For the most part, the convention progressed without incident. Scientists presented over 1500 papers and conducted 120 symposia. When Humphrey spoke, however, he was greeted with paper airplanes and a tomato that nearly hit him. Bundy was heckled. These brief demonstrations were planned by the Scientists and Engineers for Social and Political Action, who had demonstrated at the preceding annual conventions in Chicago and Boston.

The attending science reporters had to choose between highlighting the disruptions to make their stories more exciting, or writing more accurate accounts which de-emphasized the demonstrations as only one episode in a full week. Most reporters opted for the sensational. Donald Drake, medicine and science reporter for the Philadelphia *Inquirer*, began his story: "Shouted insults and belligerent questions leveled at one of the principal planners of the Vietnam War broke up a science meeting Thursday after fist fights almost broke out three times." Drake later confessed,

I wrote the story that way because I knew, without asking, that that's what the desk would want and I wanted good play for the story. I didn't want to see a wire story substituted, nor did I want to argue with an editor after an exhausting week. And finally I felt that the facts, using conventional journalistic criteria, supported the lead regardless of whether it was the right lead.[20]

Donald Drake is blameworthy. By his own admission, his story conveyed the impression that the Annual Meeting of the AAAS was almost destroyed by an uprising of radicals. Average readers were given a distorted picture. Along with others who covered this yearly gathering of scientists—the world's most diverse and significant—the *Inquirer* concentrated on a single event and thereby twisted its meaning out of all reasonable proportion. Compounding the misrepresentation, editorial writers for the *Inquirer* took the clue from their own newsroom, wondering how science could show such a "juvenile display of bad manners." The scientists who demonstrated repeated the same tactics they had used at the two previous AAAS conventions; the outburst was not spontaneous rage within the entire assembly. These dissenters did not aim to establish a serious challenge to institutional science—at least the reporters Drake queried later agreed on that. Yet they gained access to the headlines, while those papers and symposia dealing with nuclear energy, recombitant DNA, and new forms of life did not.

It is materially relevant that Drake is a company employee. Like the vast majority of reporters—and such professional counterparts as nurses and engineers who also have employee status—he is obligated by contract to company policy. As noted in other cases in this book, such commitments often involve conflicting duties. However, in this instance, Drake cannot argue that he fulfilled his obligations, and his superiors failed in theirs. There was no newspaper directive regarding coverage of scientific and educational events, no demand on the kind of stories that should be filed. Drake was a respected and experienced reporter, not a rookie needing close supervision. The editor and publisher maintained the conventional expectations, a definition of newsworthiness that Drake actually imbibed by writing "what the desk would want." The editor and publisher apparently had not articulated a more substantive definition of news. Yet, in this situation, Drake failed to meet high professional standards, as he himself admitted: "In effect, I gave them what they wanted. In doing so I became a hack, a whore, not only to my profession but to my paper. . . . Only a hack or whore writes just to satisfy his city desk and the sin is compounded when this is done in the absence of specific instructions."[21]

In their gatekeeper function, reporters and editors preside over an important national resource, news space. In a typical newsday, only one of a thousand items can be printed or broadcast. Once selected, what prominence the story deserves and the particular focus it warrants must also be determined. These matters of human judgment are too easily done by reflex, according to established conventions of newsworthiness rather than by careful evaluation. The pressures are always strong to overemphasize physical confrontation, the eccentric, and the deviant. For the *Inquirer*'s editor and publisher, the momentary violence became the most important news story. Television news particularly tends to hallow the "visually satisfactory." A presidential candidate, for example, legitimately complained that he had issued several white papers on foreign policy during one day of his campaign. Ignoring them, the nightly news of the commercial networks covered only his brief visit to a home for mentally retarded children. Such journalistic criteria, while occasionally attacked, seem deeply embedded in American newsgathering. That fact does not absolve Donald Drake, however, from having violated a seasoned reporter's conscience and better judgment, his own.

Notes

1. Donald Warwick, "Social Scientists Ought to Stop Lying," *Psychology Today*, February 1975, p. 39.

2. Sissela Bok, *Lying: Moral Choice in Public and Private Life* (New York: Pantheon Books, 1978), p. 26.

3. Ibid., p. 18.

4. See the *Chicago Tribune*, 23 June 1980, p. 2, section 4.

5. See the *Chicago Sun-Times*, 24 June 1980, p. 2.

6. Grace Kaminkowitz, "Jane Byrne, Mayor of Chicago," *Matrix* 65 (Summer 1980): 17.

7. Ibid.

8. Edward M. Miller, "APME's Guidelines a 'Sexist Document'? An Editor's Reply," *Columbia Journalism Review* 10 (September/October 1971): 62–63.

9. Quoted in Joan Behrmann, "How the Press Treats Women," in *Questioning Media Ethics*, ed. Bernard Rubin (New York: Praeger, 1978), p. 119.

10. Maurine Beasley and Sheila Silver, *Women in Media: A Documentary Source Book* (Washington, D.C.: Women's Institute for Freedom of the Press, 1977), pp. 163–69. Practical suggestions for avoiding sexist language are compiled in Casey Miller and Kate Swift, *The Handbook of Nonsexist Writing* (New York: Harper & Row, 1981).

11. Michelle Sipe, "Letters: Unqualified Mayor of Chicago?" *Matrix* 66 (Winter 1981): 30.

12. Zechariah Chafee, Jr., "Why I Like America" (Commencement Address at Colby College, Waterville, ME, 21 May 1944).

13. Neil Hickey, "Only the Sensational Stuff Got on the Air," *TV Guide*, 8 December 1973, p. 34. For details on which this case and commentary are based, see the other three articles in Hickey's series: Dec. 1, "Was the Truth Buried at Wounded Knee?" pp. 7–12; December 15, "Cameras Over Here!" pp. 43–49; December 22, "Our Media Blitz is Here to Stay," pp. 21–23.

14. Ibid.

15. Arnold Marquis, "Those 'Brave Boys in Blue' at Wounded Knee," *Columbia Journalism Review* 13 (May/June 1974): 26–27; and Joel D. Weisman, "About That 'Ambush' At Wounded Knee," *Columbia Journalism Review* 14 (September/October 1975): 28–31.

16. Walter B. Jaehning, "Journalists and Terrorism: Captives of the Libertarian Tradition," *Indiana Law Journal*, 1977–78, p. 735.

17. Ibid.

18. Ibid., p. 726.

19. Jim Gordon, "Foot Artwork Ends Career," *News Photographer*, November 1981, p. 32. Details of this event and all quotations are from this article, pp. 31–36.

20. Donald C. Drake, "A Science Writer Looks at Newspapers," *Grassroots Editor* 13 (November/December 1972): 9.

21. Ibid.

Chapter Three

Reporters and Sources

Well-informed sources are a reporter's bread and butter. Journalists rely on them for their livelihood. This dependence creates some genuine perplexities. A news medium could pledge to reveal frankly all its sources of information and that would be significant for the public. However, printing names usually results in the sources drying up or in their speaking guardedly. Several tactics are used in confronting this dilemma so that audiences are served and sources remain content. A Washington *Post* editorial captured some of the struggle in a recent description of "Source's" family tree:

Walter and Ann Source (nee Rumor) had four daughters (Highly Placed, Authoritative, Unimpeachable, and Well-Informed). The first married a diplomat named Reliable Informant. (The Informant brothers are widely known and quoted here; among the best known are White House, State Department, and Congressional). Walter Speculation's brother-in-law, Ian Rumor, married Alexandre Conjecture, from which there were two sons, It Was Understood and It Was Learned. It Was Learned just went to work in the Justice Department, where he will be gainfully employed for four long years.[1]

The complications here are not easily resolved. Walter Lippmann noted this journalistic bind more than 50 years ago in his *Public Opinion* and as a result, distinguished news from truth. News he saw as fragments of information that came to the reporter's attention; explicit and established standards guide the pursuit of truth.[2] The judicial process, for example, follows rigorous procedures when gathering evidence. Academics footnote and attribute sources so that knowledgeable people can verify or dispute the conclusions. Medical doctors rely on technical precision and expertise. However, in this instance, reporters cannot compete with these other professions. They have found no authoritative way of examining, testing, and evaluating their information, at least not in a public arena and not under risky, hostile conditions.

The difficulties result primarily because a multitude of practical considerations need to be jockeyed under deadline pressures. On occasion reporters must be adversarial, at least skeptical; friendliness and cooperation work better at other times. If newspeople become too intimate with important men and women, they lose professional distance or develop unhealthy biases protecting them. However, to the degree powerful sources are not cultivated and reporters establish no personal connections, the inside nuance and perspective may be lost. At times written documents supplemented by public briefings are superior to information painfully dug out by a conscientious reporter. On most other occasions the official source is blinded by self-interest. But who can predict? And all the while journalists must be vigilant against those who exploit them. Little wonder that as Watergate documents came to light, for instance, several "scoops" proved to be stories leaked originally by Mr. Nixon's staff.

Most news operations have developed specific guidelines to help prevent chaos and abuse. Certain conventions also hold journalistic practice together. It is typically assumed that all information must be verified by two or three sources before it can be printed. Most codes of ethics and company policies insist on attribution and specific identification whenever possible. A few news operations allow reporters to keep sources totally secret, but a majority openly involve editors as judges of the data's validity. The rules also include accurate quotation marks, correction of errors, and an account of the context. However, even with these safeguards, a responsible press must continually agonize over its treatment of sources in order to prevent lapses.

This chapter chooses five entangled aspects of the reporter-source relationship, all of them actual occurrences of some notoriety. The first case selects out of Watergate the question of tapping grand jury sources: members and documents. In case 13 the debate revolves around using stolen materials. While few journalistic events have the historic significance of the Pentagon Papers, the decision whether or not to accept valuable stolen materials has to be made frequently. The Abscam case provides a specific example of leaked sources and the journalist's responsibility in turning leaks into public information. Case four in this series treats the issue of familiarity and the boundary between exploiting friendship and building on it legitimately in gathering news. Myron Farber illustrates the problem of dealing with confidential sources, particularly when the pledge to secrecy impinges on the welfare of another human being. Cheap answers are not forthcoming, but at every point the ethical issues form a prominent part of the resolution.

12. Watergate and Grand Jury Information

After leading the pack on the Watergate story in the early going, Washington *Post* reporters Carl Bernstein and Bob Woodward ran into rough waters.[3] On 25 October 1972, a major coup had turned into a major disaster. They had written that H.L. (Bob) Haldeman, President Nixon's chief of staff, had been personally involved in controlling espionage and sabotage. The charge moved the Watergate break-in to the door of President Nixon. But then, through his attorney, their source for the report denied he had given such testimony before a grand jury. The White House used the opportunity to respond with a vigorous counterattack on the Washington *Post*.

In an effort to discover how they had gone wrong, Woodward and Bernstein revealed their primary source (an agent of the Federal Bureau of Investigation) to his superior. Back at the office the two reporters and *Post* executives discussed revealing all five sources of their erroneous information, but decided against it.

After that debacle, Woodward and Bernstein ran into more trouble; now the problem was not erroneous stories but no stories at all. They had hit a lull. The timing was bad. The *Post*'s executive editor, Benjamin Bradlee, became frustrated. The Nixon forces were shooting at him. Charles Colson, speaking to a group of New England editors, said, "If Bradlee ever left the Georgetown cocktail circuit, where he and his pals dine on third-hand information and gossip and rumor, he might discover out here the real America." Bradlee told an interviewer that he was "ready to hold both Woodward's and Bernstein's heads in a pail of water until they came up with another story." That dry spell was anguish.

Such was the pressurized atmosphere in the *Post* newsroom at the
time that Woodward and Bernstein and their editors decided to seek
information from members of the Watergate grand jury. They came to
the idea by happenstance. One night late in November a *Post* editor
told Woodward that his neighbor's aunt was on a grand jury, that from
remarks she had made it was the grand jury on Watergate, and that in
the words of the editor, "My neighbor thinks she wants to talk."

The two reporters checked the Federal Rules of Criminal Procedure
—grand jurors take an oath of secrecy. But it appeared that the burden of secrecy was on the jurors; nothing in the law directly forbade
questioning them. The *Post's* lawyers agreed with that interpretation
but urged "extreme caution" in approaching the juror. Bradlee, nervous, echoed that warning: "No beating anyone over the head, no
pressure, none of that cajoling."

All the consultation and advice were for nothing. The woman,
Woodward and Bernstein were to learn, was not on the Watergate
grand jury after all. But the episode had "whetted their interest." The
day after the abortive interview, Woodward went to the courthouse,
found the list of Watergate grand jurors and memorized their names;
he had been forbidden to take notes.

After typing up the list of jurors, Woodward and Bernstein had a
session with Bradlee, metropolitan editor Harry M. Rosenfeld, managing editor Howard Simons, and city editor Barry Sussman. They
went over the list, looking for members "least likely to inform the prosecutors of a visit." Eliminating civil servants and military officers, they
sought, through occupation, jurors "bright enough to suspect that the
grand jury system had broken down in the Watergate case" and "in
command of the nuances of the evidence." "Ideally," Woodward and
Bernstein wrote, "the juror would be capable of outrage at the White
House or the prosecutors or both; a person who was accustomed to
bending rules, the type of person who valued practicality more than
procedure." *All the President's Men* describes the mental state of those
in the room:

Everyone had private doubts about such a seedy venture. Bradlee, desperate
for a story, and reassured by the lawyers, overcame his own. Simons doubted
out loud the rightness of the exercise and worried about the paper. Rosenfeld
was concerned most about the mechanics of the reporters not getting caught.
Sussman was afraid that one of them, probably Bernstein, would push too hard
and find a way to violate the law. Woodward wondered whether there was ever
justification for a reporter to entice someone across the line of legality while
standing safely on the right side himself.

Bernstein, who vaguely approved of selective civil disobedience, was not concerned about breaking the law in the abstract. It was a question of *which* law, and he believed that grand jury proceedings should be inviolate. The misgivings, however, went unstated, for the most part.[4]

The procedure for interviewing the jurors was agreed upon. The reporters were to identify themselves and say that through a mutual but anonymous friend they understood he or she knew something about the Watergate case. They would then ask if he or she was willing to discuss it. If the answer was no, the reporters were to leave immediately.

A visit to about half a dozen grand jurors yielded nothing but trouble. One of the jurors reported the visit to a prosecutor, who informed Judge John Sirica. *Post* attorney Edward Bennett Williams met with Sirica. After the meeting, he told Woodward and Bernstein he thought they would get off with a reprimand. He was right. The chiding came in open court, in a room packed with reporters. But Sirica did not identify them or the *Post*. The reporters present were out for the story, questioning each other, seeking the identity. Woodward and Bernstein agreed they would make an outright denial "only as a last resort." A colleague caught up with them as they headed for the elevator. *All the President's Men* describes the scene and thinking of the two reporters:

He (the reporter) caught up with Woodward near the elevator and asked point-blank if the Judge had been referring to him or Bernstein.

Come off it, what do you think? Woodward answered angrily.

The man persisted. Well, was it one of them or wasn't it? Yes or no.

Listen, Woodward snapped. Do you want a quote? Are we talking for the record? I mean, are you serious? Because if you are, I'll give you something, all right.

The reporter seemed stunned. "Sorry, Bob, I didn't think you'd take me seriously," he told Woodward.

The danger passed. The nightmare vision that had haunted them all day—Ron Ziegler at the podium demanding that they be the object of a full federal investigation, or some such thing—disappeared. They tried to imagine what choice phrases he might use ("jury tampering"?), and they realized that they didn't have the stomach for it. They felt lousy. They had not broken the law when they visited the grand jurors, that much seemed certain. But they had sailed around it and exposed others to danger. They had chosen expediency over principle, and, caught in the act, their role had been covered up. They had dodged, evaded, misrepresented, suggested and intimidated, even if they had not lied outright.[5]

———

This case involves a long sequence of ethical choices. It reveals many of the pressures on the *Post's* staff. Bradlee's desire, for example, for a story, "any story," to take the heat off the *Post* could be examined as a nonethics of self-interest, principles be damned. The case is thus realistic in its reflection of conditions under which journalistic decisions are frequently made. Under most circumstances these pressures are much less strong than they were for the *Post* in this instance. However, knowledge of those circumstances does not help resolve the ethics of the case. Surely, the existence of pressures, even intense ones, cannot itself justify a reporter's conduct. At best the reality of pressure may help one sympathize with a reporter who, feeling it strongly, made bad moral judgments. But that is not ethics, in the sense of reaching justified decisions.

Perhaps the best way to begin examining a multi-sided situation is to identify some of the moral choices made along the way.

1. They decided to reveal the identity of a source to his superior "in an effort to find out how they had gone wrong." But they also decided not to reveal all five sources. The decision to reveal likely involved violation of promises, but the case does not tell us.
2. They decided to seek information from the grand jury. Clearly they were aware of potential legal problems, as evidenced by the check into the Federal Rules of Criminal Procedure and by the conversation in the planning session.
3. They decided to get the list of grand jurors by memorization rather than by taking notes. This is already a step in the direction of misusing the grand jury system and of violating the important moral principles on which it stands.
4. They decided to do everything possible to avoid being caught in interviews with grand jurors. This was not a case of deliberately violating the law toward the end of changing an unjust law; it was a case of violating the law in order to serve the interests of the newspaper at the moment.
5. In their approach to the grand jurors they decided to deceive by saying that "through a mutual friend. . . ." This lie was told in order to open the possibility of getting a juror to talk, to use jurors toward the *Post's* own ends.
6. They decided to lie if they were identified by fellow reporters as those reprimanded by Sirica. Admittedly, they would stoop to that only "as a last resort."

Certainly the nation can be grateful to Woodward and Bernstein for the final result of their investigation (Nixon's resignation). The morality of their investigation is seriously flawed, however. They did nothing that could not be justified by utilitarian principles. If they had known at the time that issues of overriding national importance were involved, their improprieties could be considered as outweighed by the enormous public benefits. Their lying and their serious tampering with the grand jury resulted in uncovering one of the biggest threats to American democracy in its history. That vital end could be used to justify the immoral means.

The ethical problem is that they employed these immoral means toward immoral ends, namely, the self-interest of protecting themselves and the *Post*. At the time they chose to lie and to violate the grand jury system they could not have known, and did not claim to know, the final dimensions of the story they uncovered. In this case, then, democracy was benefited, but not by their conscious intent to aid society. The benefit was an unforeseen, and unforeseeable, consequence of decisions to violate not only the law but basic moral principles. Their decisions cannot, therefore, be justified ex post facto in light of the fortunate results. Evil choices do sometimes, unwittingly, evoke good ends. But this does no more than place us in the awkward position of being glad that immoral people were at work on this case.[6] Journalists cannot morally follow in the *Post's* footsteps as a general rule. Lying must always be justified in terms of some higher value; truth telling need never be justified.

13. The Pentagon Papers as Stolen Documents

The Pentagon Papers, a confidential report detailing American involvement in Vietnam since World War II, had been commissioned by Robert McNamara when he was Secretary of Defense. The account of their publication, begun in the *New York Times* on 13 June 1971, reads like a spy story. The *Times* would say only that it received 7,000 pages of the document through investigative reporter Neil Sheehan sometime in March of 1971. (It was a former *Times* reporter, speaking on a radio show, who named Daniel Ellsberg as the man who supplied the document to the *Times*.)

The *Times* set about publication with a secrecy worthy of a security agency, according to *Times* writer Jules Witcover. Preliminary work was done in two rooms of the Jefferson Hotel in Washington, D.C. Then the operation was moved to a three-room suite in New York's Hilton, and eventually it commanded nine guarded rooms on two floors. Staffers working on the story were told to stay away from the *Times'* main office. In late May, key production people were told of the project. In a vacant office building, these employees set up a secret composing room to handle the special copy and included a paper

oofs. On June 10, the first segment of the
rom the hotel and punched on tapes. The
secret composing room. At 1:30 p.m. on
page of the *Times'* report was sent to the
xultation. . . . One of the great journalistic
with hardly a whisper of suspicion any-

)peared on Monday, June 14. That evening
:neral John N. Mitchell requested that the
;uing that the papers contained "information
efense of the United States" whose publica-
ited" by the Espionage Law. Two hours later,
the *Times* read a statement for Mitchell that it also published: "The
Times must respectfully decline the request of the Attorney General,
believing that it is in the interest of the people of this country to be informed of the material contained in this series of articles."[8] Later that
day, the *Times* was enjoined from further publication, pending a hearing on the government's plea.

On Thursday, June 17, the Washington *Post* obtained 4,000 pages of
the document. Plans were made for publication. Ben Bagdikian, then
assistant managing editor for national news, said the *Post's* management and lawyers were wary of publishing stories based on the document. The lawyers, posing a question of "propriety," said it would be
"wiser to establish the right to publish by allowing the *Times* case to
run its course, avoiding indication of a contempt for the court in that
case." But, Bagdikian said, "The editors and writers saw it strictly in
terms of freedom of the press and journalistic responsibility to the public—if it is authentic and significant, publish it."[9] The editors and writers prevailed. The *Post* began publication on Friday, June 18. It, too,
was enjoined.

While the cases of prior restraint were in the courts, partial copies of
the Pentagon Papers cropped up elsewhere: The Boston *Globe*, for
example, began publication and was enjoined. The St. Louis *Post-
Dispatch* began a series on Friday, June 25. Contacted by the Justice
Department, the *Post-Dispatch* executives said they did not plan to
publish an article on Saturday (because of the size of that day's edition) but would resume on Sunday. Before it could do so, it too was required to desist from further publication. Finally on June 30, the
Supreme Court in a 6–3 decision ruled in favor of the newspapers.

Three questions must be answered satisfactorily before publication of the Pentagon Papers can be justified morally. First, was it ethically permissible to publish classified material? The legal battles centered entirely on that issue and were finally resolved by the Supreme Court in favor of First Amendment guarantees regarding the free press. Nor would typical moral systems contradict this type of decision. Nearly all ethical frameworks permit civil disobedience under certain circumstances. Obeying legally constituted authority is promoted as a moral good under normal circumstances (and in this instance the Espionage Law invoked by the Attorney General had been duly enacted). However, this act of conscience against the state cannot be dismissed as immoral by any typical set of ethical principles.

Second, ought the New York *Times* and the other papers use stolen documents as their source? Daniel Ellsberg had taken the material without authorization. The decision to publish stolen goods is a fundamental ethical issue.

From a Kantian perspective, theft is always wrong. The categorical imperative suggests that we do not permit for ourselves what we do not wish to make a universal law. And obviously, from this viewpoint, societies cannot exist if stealing is allowed. A Kantian would point to the double standard involved, arguing that newspapers do not want government officials stealing their property so why should they condone theft for themselves? Justice Warren Burger reflected this ethical perspective:

To me it is hardly believable that a newspaper long regarded as a great institution in American life would fail to perform one of the basic and simple duties of every citizen with respect to the discovery or possession of stolen property or secret government documents. That duty, I had thought—perhaps naively— was to report forthwith to responsible public officers. This duty rests on taxi drivers, Justices, and the New York *Times*.[10]

An opposing point of view over stolen property can be built on a utilitarian basis. The various editors who published the Pentagon Papers appealed to the historic circumstances and enormous consequences of the material. Fifty-five thousand Americans had already died in Vietnam, tens of billions of dollars had been spent militarily, and the nation was acrimoniously divided. Thus, when A.M. Rosenthal, managing editor of the *Times*, gave his paper's rationale, he dismissed simplistic declarations and contended publication was within the *Times'*

constitutional rights and in the best interests of our country. . . . Can you steal a decision that was made three years ago and that has caused consequences that a country now pays for, good or bad? How can you steal the mental processes of elected officials or appointed officials? . . . I never thought that Americans would buy the argument that you can steal information on public matters.[11]

Third, were the contents of the Pentagon Papers treated fairly and accurately? Not all the documents were printed since they totaled more than 7000 pages and covered a 25-year period. Substantial sections were complex and academic. The *Times* staff chose the theme of duplicity, that is, American leaders were saying different things about the Vietnam War in public and private. Edward Jay Epstein did not score the *Times* very highly in meeting their editorial obligations:

To convert this bureaucratic study into a journalistic exposé of duplicity required taking certain liberties with the original history. Outside material had to be added, and assertions from the actual study had to be omitted. For example, to show that the Tonkin Gulf resolution resulted from duplicity, the *Times* had to omit the conclusion of the Pentagon Papers that the Johnson Administration had tried to avoid the fatal clash in the Tonkin Gulf, and had to add evidence of possible American provocations in Laos which were not actually referred to in the Pentagon Papers themselves.[12]

Clearly this case represents an important legal triumph for the press. The Anglo-American tradition, in principle, has condemned all kinds of prior restraint for nearly three hundred years. Ethical questions two and three above warrant consideration nonetheless. The media generally do not traffic in stolen property and this celebrated situation ought not to dim their conscience. As suggested before, a utilitarian defense is possible here but not compelling. Did the editors unequivocally serve the public interest or merely use a noble end to justify desultory means? And ethicists remain uneasy about the duplicity theme also, wondering whether that characterization honestly represents official Department of Defense decision making. Impugning evil motives is not permitted by any moral system that respects human beings. To justify their action, the *New York Times* would have to demonstrate that its presentation faithfully tells the Pentagon Papers story and does not piece together a story of its own.

14. A Leaking Abscam

A United States senator and nine representatives were informed that the Arab businessmen with whom they had been dealing were not Arabs at all; they were undercover agents of the Federal Bureau of Investigation. The Abscam (Arab scam) case was breaking. The elected officials learned by information leaked to the press that they were suspects on bribery charges. The secrecy of the two-year-old operation had not been officially lifted by the FBI itself, but the curtain had been rent by inside informers. The New York *Times* story was filled with details: how much each suspect was alleged to have accepted from the "Arabs" in return for promising political favors, where and when the transactions occurred, even the type of containers used (for one a brief case, for another a paper bag). The *Times* story, written by Leslie Maitland, said the results of the investigation would soon be presented to a federal grand jury, which, according to the account, "would be asked to consider bringing criminal charges against some of the officials." The attribution given in the first paragraph—"law-enforcement authorities"—was repeated dozens of times in the lengthy story.[13]

Three days later, one of the *Times* stories included the announcement that the Justice Department would "seek to determine if department employees deliberately disclosed information" on the Abscam case. Further, an editorial on that date took up the matter of naming names prior to indictment and formal charges. That editorial read, in part:

Our first reaction is to marvel at the scale of the greed attributed to the alleged bribe-takers. . . . Our second reaction—perhaps it should be our first—is to caution that none of the implicated individuals has been indicted, much less convicted of any crime. . . . It is unfortunate, though perhaps hard to avoid in so large an investigation, that political reputations may suffer before guilt or innocence can be legally established.[14]

The next edition of the *Times* carried a short article reporting that the American Civil Liberties Union (ACLU) accused the Justice Department of misconduct in leaking to the press "prejudicial details of bribery allegations." Ira Glasser, ACLU executive director, complained: "Justice by press release and summary political punishments are methods we should have learned by now to avoid." Another story in this edition noted that news reports "have attributed accounts of the investigation to 'law enforcement officials' rather than to either the Justice Department or the Federal Bureau of Investigation."

Two days later, a story by David E. Rosenbaum asked the question: Why would the law-enforcement authorities disclose information on an investigation to reporters before it was presented to a grand jury? The answers given:

One reason is the belief of some law-enforcement officers in the field that charges against politicians tend to be watered down or negotiated away by high-priced legal talent once they reach the Justice Department's headquarters in Washington. If the case is known to the public, it is felt, there will be pressure on the Department for strong action. More ominous, some law-enforcement officers may have a grudge against a politician and want to punish him with publicity even if an indictment is not warranted.

Another reason is the desire of some investigative units for public credit for their work and the belief that, unless they put the story out themselves, officials in Washington will receive all the glory.

In short, law-enforcement officers talk to reporters for the same reasons that politicians, publicists, corporate executives and others do. That is, they have a story to tell, and they want it to be based on their point of view, not someone else's.[13]

The exact motive of the Abscam leakers is not known, but one New York *Times* article might be a clue. The day after the original story, the *Times* reported that the U.S. attorney for New Jersey had recommended against prosecuting Sen. Harrison A. Williams, Jr. The prosecutor was reported to have said the evidence against Williams was insufficient.

———————

Because of the morally valid principle that we should assume innocence until guilt is proved, mere allegations of criminal conduct ought never be published. The New York *Times* editor concedes it is "unfortunate" and "hard to avoid" that political reputations may suffer before guilt or innocence can be legally established. That result is a good deal more than "unfortunate," and instead of being hard to avoid it is easy to avoid.

Three basic ethical principles are germane to this case. The first is the principle of protecting the innocent. In publishing allegations by unnamed sources against public figures, the *Times* harmed people who were possibly innocent. The *Times* damaged individuals before knowing whether they were guilty or innocent.

Second, the *Times* violated the ethical guideline that a person's right to a fair trial ought not be jeopardized. Given a current American propensity to assume guilt until innocence is proved, and given the current high level of public distrust of politicians, the likelihood of a fair trial is significantly reduced by publishing allegations of wrongdoing in high places.

The third moral principle relevant to this case is the Judeo-Christian principle that one should treat other people always as ends and never as means. The corollary is that no one should allow himself to be treated as a means to someone else's ends. By publishing the allegations leaked to the paper, the *Times* became a pawn in the hands of law enforcement agents who were merely using the *Times* as a means to their ends, whatever those ends might be.

The focus of this case then should not be on the motives of the law enforcement authorities in disclosing information. David Rosenbaum's speculations on the matter are interesting but not really germane to the *Times'* decision to publish the leaked information. Rosenbaum, however, does raise an important issue for the *Times*. He notes the belief of some law enforcement officers that charges against politicians tend to be watered down or negotiated away by high-priced legal talent before they reach the Justice Department. Pursuit of that theme would have given the *Times* a good story, and it could have been pursued in a morally responsible manner.

Suppose the *Times* editors, instead of publishing the details of the allegations against these officials, had published the fact that they possessed such details and would print them if they were significantly watered down for purposes of a public hearing. The *Times* had news of accusations made against top officials. Once the matter came to a public hearing, if the original accusations were slimmed down, the *Times* would be in a superb position to investigate the matter further and see what happened. By holding the details of the allegations, the *Times* could still have rendered a critical public service by comparing the first charges with the later ones.

What then ought the *Times* have contained in its release? It should have reported the fact of the leak, the general character of the allegations, some details of the alleged methods of payment (the brown bag and briefcase), and the fact that names were included. There is no reason initially to reveal the identity of the person who leaked the information, and there is no reason at first to publish the name of any official against whom the allegations were made.

15. A Television Reporter as Family Friend

Marjorie Margolies, a television reporter in Washington, D.C., found herself doubting her own motives while covering a story of a missing 12-year-old boy. Early in the story, she became an ally of the boy's family. The boy's mother, Rose Viscidi, knew that television publicity might help in the search for her son. She gave television interviews, offering friendship in return. Marjorie Margolies had gained an entree. She suspected that the nature of her work helped cultivate the friendship. "It is a fact of television newscasting," she wrote, "that we reporters are known to the public already—in effect, we've already been in their homes, as non-drinking guests at cocktail time."[16]

So she and her camera crew were well treated. "The Viscidis welcomed us—they fed us, gave us places to rest out of the hot August sun, and talked." Then came a report that 12-year-old Billy's body had been found—buried in the Viscidi's garden. Margolies recorded her reaction: "Oh, darn, the worst has happened—Billy's not coming back." But there was also a big side of me that said, "Geez. I've been with the story for so long and this has to happen on a day I was off it."[17]

She and her camera crew rushed to a hospital where Rose Viscidi's husband was being treated for a kidney infection. Reporters were barred. But Margolies decided she could still act as a friend. She persuaded an administrator to allow her to pay her condolences to Rose Viscidi (the administrator was subsequently fired). She found Rose sitting alone in a small room. "I bent down and patted her on the shoulders, and planted a kiss on her forehead. 'Do you have any idea how this happened?' I asked her—as a friend."

Developments in the case were to change Margolies' relationship with Rose Viscidi. Police suspected that another son, 15-year-old Larry, had killed his younger brother and buried his body in the garden. The Viscidis consulted a law firm and were advised to give no more information to the press. Margolies writes: "I was torn. I had grown to like Rose very much. But if I did my job as a reporter, the Viscidis would see me as a traitor. It was a no-win situation."

The news media, which had been focusing on the case of the missing boy, now concentrated on his 15-year-old brother. "Hordes of newspeople and photographers congregated on the Viscidi lawn and on the neighbors' lawns." Margolies wrote, "At times it took on the air of a picnic, people eating sandwiches and drinking Cokes. I felt uncomfortable."

Margolies and her camera crew, outmanned by members of the print media, attempted to capitalize on their strength—the impact of pictures.

We would wait hours for the chance to get five seconds of usable tape. Some might think this overkill—that especially in a story of this tragic nature we were intruding too deeply. A number of letters to me complained of this. They said we were all too hungry, but others said we were holding back information.

There were times when I would say to myself, "I wish I were not going out there again." But every time, we would come back with something news-worthy. There was incredible public interest in the story. It was news. And we had to report it.[18]

Margolies covered the funeral of Billy, being "careful not to disturb the services," but not before delivering a potted plant to the Viscidi home.

Officially, the story hit a lull. Neither the police nor the Viscidis were releasing information. The fact that the suspect was a juvenile further hindered the flow of information. Margolies developed sources and pieced together parts of the story. She explained:

When you are one-tenth of a television news team, you are expected to pro-duce. There is continual pressure either to produce on that story, or to go on to something else. I couldn't leave the Billy Viscidi story, so I spent every night—after a long day covering other assignments—calling, working sources, into the small hours of the morning.[19]

Margolies learned that the police were sure Larry buried his brother's body, but they were not so sure he did the killing. Billy may have smashed his skull in a fall and Larry, in shock, may have hidden the body to spare his mother grief. Margolies learned that Larry passed a lie detector test. She also learned that Larry was being given a truth serum. Larry's father inadvertently confirmed that report. Margolies told the prosecuting attorney she had the information and was going to use it. She did. The Viscidis concluded she was feeding information to the prosecutor. Margolies asked herself, "Was I crossing the line, in-flicting pain on this family with my revelations?"

Finally, police arrested Larry—identified only as "a juvenile." Wrote Margolies:

I resisted pressure to rush to the Viscidi house that evening to take shots. Another station did have someone out there, knocking on the door and attempting to get pictures of the family. It is a matter of taste—and that, I told my superiors, was something I wouldn't do. When the other channel aired its shots, I took some flak for not being on top of the story—when I clued them in on my scoop that Larry was with a psychiatrist taking a truth serum, they wanted me to camp outside the doctor's office and get some pictures. I refused. My bosses began to wonder whether I had gotten so involved with the family that I could not aggressively go after the story.[20]

When Larry was brought to court, the news media had assembled. Margolies called it a "madhouse scene." But she and her crew scored a coup—they got the only pictures of Larry leaving the courthouse through a back door. "I couldn't feel very proud," Margolies writes. "I felt like a vulture."

Daily the press and television crews stationed themselves for the entrance and exit of the Viscidi family. A bailiff provided Larry with a large bag to wear over his head. On one occasion Rose Viscidi shoved Margolies' soundman and sent him sprawling to the ground. The father, Burton, once passed Margolies' crew and said under his breath, "What do you want me to do—a little jig for you?" Eventually, a county court judge dismissed the manslaughter charge against Larry, holding that the death could as easily have been caused by an accident as by homicide.

And so the case ended. Six months of publicity came to a conclusion, or nearly so. There was one more interview. Rose Viscidi wanted to tell the family's side of the story. She mended her differences with Margolies, and she and her husband gave an interview. It was aired as a five-part series.

The most telling phase appears after the boy's body is discovered. In Margolies' own words: "Hordes of newspeople and photographers congregated on the Viscidi lawn and on the neighbor's lawn. At times it took on the air of a picnic with people eating sandwiches and drinking Cokes. I felt uncomfortable."

Well she might have felt uncomfortable. The reporters in this scene seemed oblivious to the grief of the Viscidis. The Viscidis were—to everyone but Margolies—merely objects to be reported on; they were not people. Because of Margolies' relationship to the family, she saw them as real people. She could identify with their needs and could be sympathetic to their feelings and frustrations. Thus, according to the principle that we should always treat others as ends and not merely as means, her attachment to the family inclined her to morally responsible conduct.

Her discomfiture stemmed from what she perceived as a confusion of roles, reporter (aggressive, analytical, above the fray) and friend (sympathetic, concerned, involved). It is therefore pertinent to ask whether the attributes usually associated with reporters are ethically responsible under some conditions and not so under others. When a journalist is functioning as a "watchdog" over a government agency, something of an adversary relationship exists. Under those circumstances a hard-nosed, aggressive, assertive, observer stance may be both necessary and good. When, however, those attributes become so ingrained that they spill over into the reporter's job of covering the story of a family's tragedy, they are altogether inappropriate. Under those conditions they only add to the family's grief.

Margolies was torn between the roles of reporter and friend. She gained access to Mrs. Viscidi at the hospital, but she did not use that occasion to get special information for the broadcast. In fact, she never used her friendship to get the story. At the end, the interview with the Viscidis benefited the family as well as the station. The friendship served both quite well.

Did she intrude too much into family privacy? There is no evidence in the case that she did. She wonders about that in connection with the information concerning the lie detector and truth serum. But using that information does not necessarily inflict pain. Moreover, there is reason for the public to know that the authorities are administering such tests to a juvenile.

Over all there are no bad moral choices by Margolies in this episode. It is a case where a reporter feels a deep internal, personal conflict in role. Since she did not use her friendship with the family to get private information, she did not behave unethically. The question, then, is: Should reporters allow themselves to become personally involved with the people on whom they report? Yes, when the situation is essentially one of family tragedy. No, when the situation is essentially adversarial, as in monitoring the performance of public officials.

But this only probes into the reporter's responsibility. It could be argued that prurient factions of the public are blameworthy also. At least some news directors perceived the viewing audience as clamoring for every detail. That thirst forced Margolies into a predicament. The institutional pressures were obvious too—either generate some footage and do your share or turn to another assignment. But such inhouse demands cannot obscure the public's apparent fascination with all facets—even though it is not a mad killer or rapist on the loose and thereby does not require up-to-the-minute details.

16. Myron Farber's Confidential Sources

Reporter Myron A. Farber had been with the New York *Times* nearly ten years when he was assigned to follow up a lead provided by Eileen Milling, a public relations consultant and writer who had begun an investigation of unexplained deaths at Riverdell Hospital in Oradell, New Jersey. Several surgical patients had died during post-operative care, allegedly after receiving doses of curare, a muscle-relaxing drug.

Farber faced some formidable obstacles in his investigation. The deaths had occurred in 1965, ten years in the past. Witnesses and relatives had moved away or themselves had died. Laboratory reports were on a technical level beyond a layman's ken, and some hospital files were missing. Nevertheless, after four months of digging, Farber filed his stories. They received frontpage play in the *Times* on 7–8 January 1976.

The stories presented evidence that a "Dr. X" had seen the victims shortly before their deaths, and that the drug curare had been found in his hospital locker by a suspicious medical colleague. Farber's stories led to the indictment of Dr. Mario E. Jascalevich, a 51-year-old Argentine-born surgeon, in May 1976. The case was brought to trial in early 1978.

What began as a routine newspaper investigation soon turned into a major test of reporters' First Amendment privileges. On 19 May 1978, trial judge William J. Arnold permitted defense attorney Raymond Brown to issue a subpoena for the notes held by Farber and the *Times*. Brown contended that the notes were essential to his client's defense. Complicating the proceedings was a book contract between Farber and Doubleday worth $75,000, of which Farber had already received a $37,000 advance. Brown contended that Farber stood to profit should Jascalevich be convicted and that he had concocted the allegations to advance his career.

Both Farber and the *Times* denied Brown's charges and refused to surrender notes, claiming that they contained information on sources who had been promised confidentiality. When Farber and the *Times* again declined to hand over notes for a private inspection by the judge, they were each cited for contempt. Farber was fined $1000 and sentenced to six months in the Bergen County jail, the sentence to begin after he complied with the subpoena; in the meantime he was to be confined to jail. The *Times* was fined $100,000 plus an additional $5000 for each day its editors resisted the court's authority. The *Times* finally turned over its files on August 18, but ten days later a New Jersey Superior Court judge accused the *Times* of sanitizing its files. The $5000-per-day fine was reinstated.

At the same time, Farber surrendered an incomplete book manuscript which he claimed would not establish the guilt or innocence of the accused. Farber was still not willing to compromise on the matter of his personal notes.

Appeals were filed with the New Jersey Supreme Court. The state shield law guaranteed protection, lawyers argued, but on September 21 the court ruled 5–2 against Farber and the *Times*.

In the meantime, the Jascalevich trial was grinding toward its thirty-fourth week, the longest murder trial ever held in the state. When arguments were finally over, the jury needed only a few hours to decide that the prosecution had not proven its case. Jascalevich was acquitted. Farber was released after spending a total of 40 days in jail. The *Times* made its last payment on the fine, which by now totalled $285,000.

The case against Jascalevich was closed, but the matter of reporter's privilege was still pending appeals to the United States Supreme Court. On November 28 the Court decided not to review the contempt convictions. The decision left standing the New Jersey Superior Court ruling that reporters do not have absolute privilege to keep sources confidential when defendants in a criminal trial need information for their defense.

The defense attorney's clever flamboyance, an inept judge, and Farber's unwise book contract prevented this case from being legally definitive or even illuminating. Its moral dimensions are not focused sharply either. However, two questions need to be considered whenever situations similar to this one arise: promise keeping and special privilege. How journalists treat confidential sources is an explosive issue in the law, generating various statutes to shield the press and stirring hot tempers at professional conventions. The moral domain warrants consideration as part of the answer regarding reporters and confidentiality.

We ought to keep our promises, a Kantian would suggest. A direct application of this rule to Myron Farber solves the ethical issue immediately—he made a vow to his sources of information and that pledge must be upheld regardless of circumstances. Farber himself appeals to this notion, at least in part, by telling the Superior Court judge: "If I give up my file I will have undermined my professional integrity and diminished the credibility of my colleagues."

However, that knee-jerk conclusion obscures an important detail—a man is on trial for murder and he stands trial largely because of Farber's investigation. Because certain crucial issues remain unanswered, Judge Arnold wants to determine whether Farber's materials ("all statements, pictures, memoranda, recordings, and notes of interviews") have any relevance to the case. The defense attorney has contended that Farber "collaborated with the State's prosecutor to concoct charges of murder against an innocent citizen for pecuniary gain and to advance their careers." Others speculate that Farber had been hoodwinked in a conspiracy to frame Mario Jascalevich.

Does not the crucial character of Farber's testimony make for an exception to one's fundamental obligation toward promise keeping? Certainly promise keeping needs no justification, and the breaking of promises does. The necessity of a fair hearing for someone accused of murder can qualify as such a rare exception. As Aryeh Neier, Executive Director of ACLU, argued: If Jascalevich can prove Farber's sources are *essential*, then Farber must tell. The sources "enjoy a right to anonymity as against the government, but not against a person placed on trial on criminal charges as a result of their accusations."[21] In this regard, Farber made a rash vow to his sources not to reveal their identity under any circumstances whatsoever. He thereby uncritically pledged too much. Farber should have communicated this possible exception to his sources at the very beginning. Otherwise he allows himself no opportunity to act on his conscience.

Actually Farber's adamant position is not based strongly on a categorical view of promise keeping. He really grounds his claims on a morally problematical appeal to special privilege. Ironically in wishing no exception to his confidentiality pledge, he seeks exception for his profession and the pursuit of its particular interests. Democratic societies depend on judicial fact finding and on the general obligation to testify. Farber remains silent on the grounds of journalistic privilege, contending, in effect, that he belongs to a special class immune from a responsibility born by the populace at large. The New York *Times* put it delicately in an editorial: "Frightened sources daily offer our reporters fact, confession, rumor or accusation on condition that their identity must remain secret. To betray one such source would jeopardize all. We cannot do the work that the community should prize the most if we are forced to reveal our informants and confidential notes."[22] Underneath the polite phrasing, however, the *Times* is contending that its reporter is not an ordinary citizen, but a professional journalist and thus entitled even to ignore subpoenas. Farber's frequent reference to his employer, "the nation's premier newspaper," gave his well-intended exclusivism a touch of arrogance. But few people outside the profession itself have been willing to confer a blanket exemption on the press as an institution. Nearly all Supreme Court justices, for example, interpret the First Amendment as conferring some measure of special status on the news media, yet the majority do not carry newsmen's privilege to the extreme of cavalierly disregarding the Sixth Amendment. Considerations in this case ought to reflect the plight of someone on trial for murder.

In many situations, pledges of confidentiality can be made with integrity and fully honored. However, journalists ought to promise with painstaking care. Sometimes sources seek confidentiality precisely because they fear a trial on serious charges. Promises, therefore, can be made too rashly. Reporters following their conscience in this complex arena may have to suffer occasionally, either by losing a story or two, or by going to jail if honoring a deliberate promise requires it. "For those journalists who insist they must make absolute promises of confidentiality in order to do their jobs, reporting will inevitably be a risky occupation. Let their badge of professionalism be a willingness to take those risks, rather than a willingness to seek special legal privileges."[23]

Notes

1. Editorial in the Washington *Post*, 12 February 1969. Quoted in John L. Hulteng, *The Messenger's Motives* (Englewood Cliffs, N.J.: Prentice-Hall, 1976), p. 81.

2. Walter Lippmann, *Public Opinion* (New York: The Free Press, [1922] 1949), Part 7, pp. 201–30.

3. Quotations for this case are taken from Robert Woodward and Carl Bernstein, *All the President's Men* (New York: Simon and Schuster, 1974), pp. 205–24.

4. Ibid., p. 210.

5. Ibid., p. 224.

6. This commentary focuses on the contribution of journalists in uncovering Watergate, though measuring the size of that contribution is debatable. Judge Sirica attempts to document that the judiciary (including special prosecutors) were primarily responsible for developing the case and securing the resolution. See John Sirica, *To Set the Record Straight* (New York: W.W. Norton, 1979).

7. Jules Witcover, "Two Weeks That Shook the Press," *Columbia Journalism Review* 10 (September/October 1971): 9.

8. Ibid., p. 10.

9. Ibid., p. 11.

10. Cf. Ben H. Bagdikian, "What Did We Learn?" *Columbia Journalism Review* 10 (September/October 1971): 47.

11. A.M. Rosenthal, "Why We Published," *Columbia Journalism Review* 10 (September/October 1971): 17–18.

12. Edward Jay Epstein, "Journalism and Truth," *Commentary* 57 (April 1974): 36–40.

13. Leslie Maitland, "High Officials Are Termed Subjects of a Bribery Investigation by FBI," *New York Times*, 3 February 1980, pp. 1, 26.

14. "Abdul's Sting," *New York Times*, 5 February 1980, p. A22.

15. David Rosenbaum, "The Federal Corruption Inquiry: Questions on FBI Techniques," *New York Times*, 8 February 1980, p. B6.

16. Marjorie Margolies, "The Billy Viscidi Story," *The Washingtonian*, vol. 14, no. 8, May 1979, p. 125.

17. Ibid., p. 126.

18. Ibid., p. 127

19. Ibid., p. 127.

20. Ibid., p. 128.

21. Aryeh Neier, "The Rights of Farber's Sources," *The Nation* 227 (16 September 1978): 229.

22. "Our Man in Jail," *New York Times*, 6 August 1978, p. E16.

23. Robert M. Kaus, "The Constitution, the Press, and the Rest of Us," *The Washington Monthly*, November 1978, p. 55.

Chapter Four

Social Justice

Charles Beard once wrote that freedom of the press means "the right to be just or unjust, partisan or nonpartisan, true or false, in news columns and editorial columns."[1] Historically the media have been conceived as reflecting the world on their own terms and telling the particular truth the owners preferred.

Very few still have confidence in such belligerent libertarianism. There is now substantial doubt whether the truth will emerge from a marketplace filled with falsehood. The contemporary mood among media practitioners and communication scholars is for a more reflective press, one conscious of its significant social obligations. But servicing the public competently is an elusive goal and no aspect of this mission is more complicated than issues of social justice. The Hutchins Commission mandated the press to articulate "a representative picture of the constituent groups of society." The commission insisted that minorities deserved the most conscientious treatment possible and chided the media of its day for tragic weaknesses in this area.[2]

Often a conflict is perceived between minority interest on the one hand and unfettered freedom of expression on the other. The liberty of the press is established in the First Amendment and this freedom continues to be essential to a free society. Practitioners thereby tend to favor an independent posture on all levels. Whenever one obligates the press—in this case to various social causes—one restrains its independence in some manner. Obviously the primary concern is government intervention, the argument goes, but all clamoring for special attention from the press ought to be suspect.

In spite of such debate over the precise extent of the news media's obligations to social justice, there have been notable achievements. Abolitionist editors of the nineteenth century crusaded for justice though the personal risks were so high that printing presses were thrown into rivers and printing shops burned by irate readers. A symbiosis between television and the black movement aided the struggle for civil rights in the 1960s. This chapter introduces five problems of social justice on a lesser scale, but involving typical issues of justice nonetheless. In all cases, a responsive press is seen to play a critical role. All five situations assume that genuine social concerns are at stake, and not just high-powered special interest groups seeking their own selfish ends. Each of the five pertains to the poor or disenfranchised—the malnourished in the first case, refugees in the second, an ethnic minority in the third, victims of bureaucratic agencies in the fourth, and the ghetto poor in case five. In all cases, the reporters involved sense some measure of obligation. Though press response is sometimes extremely weak, no cause is dismissed out of hand by journalists in these situations.

Social ethicists typically show a strong commitment to justice. We assume that principle here and try to apply it in complicated situations. The heaviest battles usually occur in this chapter over questions in the middle range, issues that media personnel confront along with the larger society. For example, do the media not carry a particular mandate from subscribers and audiences, in the same way a politician may sense a special obligation to represent the people who voted for him or at least live in his district? And further, does the press have a legitimate advocacy function, or does it best serve democratic life as an intermediary, a conduit of information and varying opinions? In a similar vein, should the press mirror events or provide a map that leads its audience to a destination? The kind of responsibility for justice that a particular medium is seen to possess often depends on how we answer these intermediate questions about the press' proper role and function.

17. Presidential Commission on World Hunger

On 26 April 1980, the Presidential Commission on World Hunger called a press conference. After months of deliberation, its bleak report was being presented to an aide of President Carter:

Millions of human beings live on the edge of starvation—in conditions of sub-human poverty that . . . must fill us with shame and horror. We see this now most poignantly in famine conditions, but it is a fact of life every day for half a billion people. At least one out of every eight men, women and children on earth suffers malnutrition severe enough to shorten life, stunt physical growth, and dull mental ability.[3]

The commission surrounded its study with chilling accounts of hunger and distress from Latin America to Africa and Asia. It emphasized that all other problems are academic if people cannot eat adequately. Sadly enough, the commission argued, even if food production should increase 100 percent by the year 2000, expanding populations and harvests going to those already fed will result in twice the number of malnourished by the turn of the century. Therefore, the commission recommended that eliminating hunger become the primary aim of the United States in the next two decades of its foreign policy.

The television networks were silent. One White House correspondent attended the briefing, but no story was filed with the nightly news. The national news magazines ignored it also and only six newspapers out of 1750 dailies were known to include wire service copy and none on page one.

When criticized for the network's callous refusal to carry this event, ace television news official Tom Jape might have retorted:

Issuing a government report is not news. This is a dead-letter study which will surely make no difference whatsoever in political and economic policy. President Carter did not even appear personally to receive it. Public awareness about world hunger may be dim, but repeating elegant phrases from this document reaches no one. The press is not responsible for making world hunger a national issue, government officials are. Meanwhile, as we report on the world scene, real poverty and hunger will be shown whenever they are newsworthy and relevant. But don't make pious demands that we hold up paper and ink.

Conventional definitions of news undoubtedly precluded press interest in the report. Studies have no visual impact. Had the president shown up, he may have been photographed with virtually no reference to the report's content. Hunger and poverty will be reported occasionally as actual events, in the context of fleeing refugees, or bloodshed by vicious dictators, or bloated bodies in the Sahara drought. But background, argumentation, political strategy, and ethical debates are scarcely considered news. More wire service lines appeared in 1977 on a South American boy flown to the United States for surgery than on massive hunger in his country. In 1976 more news space went to a live elephant sculpture in Kenya than to reporting starvation on the African continent.

Undoubtedly the president expected little to be done. In that sense the commission issued a dead letter. But could we not argue that the press had an opportunity here to put the president on public record and call him to action should nothing materialize? Otherwise the press' inaction becomes a self-fulfilling prophecy, a compliciter in a pious charade. The report issued a specific recommendation regarding policy— that eliminating hunger become the cornerstone of United States foreign relations since malnutrition is seen as a greater threat to world stability than Soviet aggression. Rather than pessimistically contending that nothing will happen anyhow, the press could monitor that recommendation and demand an explanation should it be rejected or fall into disuse.

No ethical system can reasonably hold the press accountable for world hunger. However, to argue as the television reporter did that only government officials are responsible is not defensible either. Assuming that individuals and agencies are answerable within the range of their capacity to effect just policies, the press certainly plays a role in making world starvation a national issue. Studies indicate that American citizens are not very knowledgeable about hunger and tend to rate their own country's performance much more strongly in this area than warranted by the facts. Journalists cannot be blamed for all the lack of information and for the ineffective public concern. However, they provide almost no comprehensive presentation of undernutrition, showing bits and pieces instead and spurning occasions such as a commission report to issue a full inquiry into the issues and government policy regarding them. Paulo Freire notes that social conditions can be transformed only to the extent that reality be codified in symbols that strike our critical consciousness.[4]

The *Christian Science Monitor*, although a slender paper averaging 25 pages, has been an exception to media neglect of world hunger. Its coverage is thoughtful and analytical. The Washington *Post*, while burying the commission report in a brief note on page 18, has achieved a notable record in well-researched front-page articles on hunger in various countries. Other notable exceptions can be cited too. The disturbing ethical question is why such coverage does not appear more regularly, given the magnitude of the problem.

18. Cuban Refugees in Arkansas

The walls of Cuba seemed to be tumbling down as Fidel Castro, in a reversal of long-standing policy, permitted dissident Cubans to board ships for passage across the 90-mile stretch of sea to Florida. Many came. So many, in fact, that handling these refugees became a colossal problem for the Immigration and Naturalization Service (INS) and the Federal Emergency Management Agency (FEMA).

Neila Petrick, a public information officer with FEMA, is part of the team assigned to make Fort Chafee, Arkansas, home for 18,000 Cubans. The team has two days to get ready. While the arrivals are all smiles on Friday, May 9, a certain restlessness sets in by May 26. On that day, 20 Cubans escape from the base while 100 stage a diversionary demonstration on the other side. Arkansas State Police easily round up the escapees.

The problem is a bureaucratic conundrum. Most of the refugees are unattached males. All must be screened and checked before they can be resettled. And this process cannot be sped up, especially when it becomes evident that Castro has used the boatlift to empty Havana jails. For some Cubans, days of waiting and uncertainty about the future find release in rioting and violence.

On May 30 Main Street at Fort Chafee is blocked by 300 Cubans threatening to go on a hunger strike in protest of the slow processing. All during the day, Petrick watches the situation deteriorate. Her job has been to get information to the media. Because the site is a military installation, security precautions are observed; journalists work through the press center. It is safer that way, though journalists themselves are restless for direct shoulder rubbing with the Cubans.

On Sunday, June 1, the phone rings at the press center. Petrick answers. A news team from Little Rock is filming without permission in front of the INS Center. Riot-minded Cubans are beginning to scream and throw rocks and bottles as the television cameras whirl. Petrick drives to the area, escorts the television crew back to the press center, and gives them a mild scolding. They have their story, however—action film—and they leave the base immediately. But their departure is ill-timed. Soon after, 300 Cubans rush the front gate and spill onto the state highway. Police begin the roundup as local residents watching the action load their shotguns in case the scene goes berserk.

Fortunately police contain the outbreak. But at 4 p.m. the call is issued for civilians to evacuate the base. Adrenalin is running fast. So is Petrick—running to her car outside the press center while rifle fire peppers her strides. When she reaches Fort Smith and safety, she learns that 70 people are injured, five hurt badly with gunshot wounds. Cubans have burned four buildings and have threatened the lives of a dozen civilian employees.

On Wednesday, the fires out and the action over, a television crew back on Main Street catches two men fighting over cards. One cuts the other, and that footage becomes national news in the evening. The impression is clear: chaos still rules Fort Chafee. But a day later when a tornado hits Nebraska and a bus filled with senior citizens drives off a cliff in Missouri, journalists exit posthaste. The Cubans have had their day on film.[5]

Aristotle's golden mean is one moral principle by which to proceed in complicated situations. Following Aristotle, the two vices to avoid are reasonably simple to identify in civil disturbances such as this one at Fort Chafee. On the one hand, reporters could cover every detail regardless of consequences, and provide no coverage whatsoever on the other. Those who argue for avoidance contend that television inspires or intensifies disturbances by its very presence; protest groups are usually considered to be performing for the cameras. The opposite extreme revolves around journalistic responsibility for recording all newsworthy events, disturbance or not.

UPI personnel are urged "to apply the rule of common sense in all cases," thus searching, in spirit at least, for the golden mean. And in 1976, CBS issued a set of "News Standards" also based on the golden mean. The primary concern behind the CBS guidelines is to enable its news people to report accurately and with restraint, that is, as reporters and not as participants. Presumably CBS camera crews would have been required to follow the guidelines below at Fort Chafee. If applied, the question is how the results would contrast with the Little Rock news team and the Wednesday television crew.

CBS News Standards: Demonstrations, Riots, and Other Civil Disturbances

1. Use unmarked cars, whenever possible, to transport equipment and personnel to the scene of the disturbance.
2. Position your equipment as unobtrusively as you can, taking advantage of the flexibility permitted by such equipment as shot-gun mikes, wireless mikes, color light amplifiers and miniaturized cameras and recorders.
3. If, in your judgment, your presence is clearly inspiring, continuing, or in-

tensifying a dangerous, or potentially dangerous disturbance, cap your cameras and conceal your microphones regardless of what other news organizations may do.

4. Use lights only when essential for the coverage of important aspects of the story. Turn them off, of course, if it appears that they are inspiring, continuing, or intensifying a dangerous, or potentially dangerous disturbance.

5. Operate as quietly as possible, keeping your conversation with each other at a minimum.

6. Be restrained, neutral and noncommittal in your comments and behavior despite the verbal and/or physical abuse to which you may be subjected by the participants.

7. Avoid coverage of i) self-designated leaders if they appear to represent only themselves or ii) any individual or groups who are clearly performing.

8. Cover the disturbance *exactly* as it happens with no staging whatsoever; make no request or suggestion of any kind that will in *any* way influence the participants to do or refrain from doing *anything*.

9. Obey *all* police instructions but report immediately to the president or a senior vice-president of Columbia News Division (CND) any such instructions that, in your judgment, seem to be intended, primarily, to manage or suppress the news.

10. Be careful about your physical safety. Although we try not to be deterred from our coverage of a story by threats of violence, overriding policy dictates that the health and safety of CND personnel take priority over the possible loss of a story.

11. Report the disturbance soberly, factually, and unemotionally. To this end:

a. Live coverage of a disturbance is prohibited unless specifically approved in advance by the president or a senior vice president of CND.

b. Do not broadcast a report of a disturbance until the seriousness of the situation, the extent of the damage, and the number, intensity, and mood of the participants have been appraised cautiously and with restraint.

c. Avoid the use of inflammatory catchwords or descriptive phrases such as "police brutality," "angry mob," "explosive violence," and so forth.

d. Do not characterize a disturbance as a riot unless that term is clearly justified by the size and intensity of the disturbance.

e. Do not report, as factual, rumors (for example, of sniping), "eyewitness" reports, or statements by participants unless and until their accuracy has been separately and authoritatively confirmed.

f. The facts, as reported, must be in proper perspective. If, for example, we are reporting a demonstration by 100 students on a college campus which has a total of 3,000 students, *both* figures should be included in the report.

g. Provide context for the story by reporting as quickly and competently as you can, the identity and background of the participants and the issues and circumstances which preceded or led to the disturbance.

h. Balance statements by participants or their supporters with contrary statements (if any) by other responsible sources.
i. Do not give the exact location of a disturbance or potential hot spot unless it is clearly and materially relevant to the story.

CBS reporters, interpreting this policy statement, undoubtedly would not have filmed the rock throwing on Sunday June 1 nor the two-man fight on Wednesday. This restraint would have pleased Neila Petrick and the executives at CBS news. Defending this policy to residents who live in the Fort Chafee area might be much more difficult. Curious about unending rumors and armed with the "public right to know" doctrine, local viewers could call CBS either lazy or sympathetic to law breakers. Along what lines could CBS answer this audience? About its only recourse would be to insist that sensationalism of this kind diverts attention from the essential. Local viewers concerned about this particular affair likely would not find that answer satisfactory.

19. Fight in a Dormitory Lounge

An argument breaks out in the lounge of a dormitory at a Midwestern university. A group of black students want to watch "Good Times," a show with a black cast, on the lounge's one television set. Some white students insist on watching "Happy Days" with its all white cast. Words grow heated and lead to blows. One student is taken to the hospital for treatment of a minor injury. Two students are charged with disorderly conduct.

The city editor of the local medium-size daily is unsure how to handle the story. The incident is minor, but the newspaper's policy book calls for publishing when an ambulance is required and hospital treatment involved. He fears that mentioning the fight was between whites and blacks would only stir up racism. The consequences of the incident were so minor that the facts themselves seemed like adequate coverage: one person slightly injured and two others charged. The editor shrugged and decided to go with the who and what, skipping the why. Why fan the flames?

Nonetheless, the facts of the story had rather surprised the editor. He still held a 1960s stereotype of college students as champions of blacks. Hearing about the fight gave him a different point of view. Realizing he had chosen not to share that altered perception with the readers, he later regretted his decision to omit the racial angle from the story.

There are two major decisions in this case. One involves the actual decision to publish and the other is the choice to withhold key information. The public need served by publishing this story is that of having accurate impressions regarding the extent of racism in the community. There are, to be sure, other relevant factors. The fact that college students were in this situation capable of violence resulting in personal injury is of some interest. It is also intriguing that the students took a television program seriously enough to fight over it. The key here is the fact that so small a matter as selecting an entertainment program could trigger this kind of violence. The fact that it did says a good deal about deep-seated racial hostilities about which the public ought to know.

The paper's policy of publishing stories that require an ambulance or hospital treatment is a curious one. The fact that a human being is sufficiently injured to want hospital care has little to do with the public need to know anything. It might be helpful to report periodically on the numbers of injured persons requiring ambulance and hospital, but the reporting of each individual case appears to be irresponsible use of valuable news space. Clearly, if it were not for the racial angle, a scrap in a college dormitory resulting in slight injury to one person and two charges of disorderly conduct is a waste of people's time.

The important issue in this case surfaces when the city editor expresses surprise that the incident carried racial overtones. How can he be this far out of touch with racial attitudes in his community? Why does he not have a clue about racial conditions on this campus? As it was handled, the story did not present a true picture of what actually occurred in the fight and did not place it in a meaningful setting. Obviously the newspaper had failed in its public obligation to cover this issue on a systematic basis. Now the editor reduces the question to the narrow one of including racial identities. There is no evidence that the editor uses this incident to redress the paper's glaring weaknesses here.

20. Investigating Public Agencies

The police detective was passing his outrage on to the reporter. He pointed to the file on his desk. "See how thick the file on that kid is!" he exclaimed. "And look where it all ended. A nice girl is dead and this young creep is in the lockup. But too late."

The reporter took notes. The file did, indeed, seem to indict the community's social service and juvenile agencies. The young man behind bars was charged that morning with the sex-motivated slaying of a 20-year-old college woman, and he had provoked quite a dossier in his

18 years. In trouble at age 12, he had been referred to the county mental health agency for counseling. Then came arrests and contact with juvenile agencies, then probation, then the county detention center, and finally a state prison facility. Then came parole, including referral back to the mental health center for therapy. "Everyone of those people in the agencies had to smell this coming," the detective fumed. "But they just mealy-mouthed around and wrote up reports with big words in them."

The reporter nodded. "What sort of case do you have against him?" she asked. "I can't give you details," said the detective, "but it's a good case—a damn good case."

Back at the office, the reporter talked with the city editor. She wanted to do a case-study story on the man, a detailed look at what the agencies had done and had not done. At first the city editor objected. "The kid's still presumed innocent, you know. His case has not even gone to a grand jury yet. And we do not report past criminal records—most of his arrests were as a juvenile, too."

"That's just it," the reported persisted. "We hardly ever examine the performance of juvenile courts and juvenile probation officers—or the mental health center either."

The city editor shook his head. "It smacks of sensationalism."

"No," the reporter argued, "it's not a crime story, really. I'm talking about a public service story. The community should be aware of how these things are allowed to happen. It's a social issue, not a crime story."

"Why don't we wait till after the trial?" the city editor suggested. "It would still be the same story."

"No, it wouldn't," said the reporter. "By the time the case comes to trial, the murder will have left people's minds. They are stirred up now. They'll read every word. Besides that, the detective is really hot right now—he'll let me get into the records. Later he might think better of it."

The city editor liked the reporter's motives. "OK," he said. "Go to it. But be thorough."

The editor made the morally responsible choice in this case by letting the reporter see what she could get on the story. He did not decide to publish the story, nor was it a decision on which story to write. There are obviously two stories. One involves the individual's life history, and the other concerns the performance of public agencies who deal with juveniles.

This case points to a very real problem. It is extraordinarily difficult for the public to know about the performance of key public agencies— especially those which deal primarily with juveniles, and at the same time preserve anonymity and confidence of minors. Since that problem is very real and very complex, it puts enormous pressure on the journalist. When, as here, there is an opportunity for examining the performance of these agencies, the temptations are all the greater and the possible gain all the more significant.

In this particular circumstance, journalists should pursue simultaneously and vigorously four important goals or values. The first is that of informing the public about public agencies and about individual crimes. The second is the protection of juvenile anonymity. The third goal is that of monitoring public agencies. The public needs to know how the agencies perform. The fourth goal is a critical one for all citizens, namely to guard the Sixth Amendment rights of the accused. The problem in this case, then, is to find strategies which would enable the pursuit of all four goals at once. Most everyone would agree that the goals are valid. Disagreements would come over strategies and tactics for pursuing them together.

It seems obvious that the reporter should not publish a case study on this man before the trial. That would be a serious violation of the journalist's moral obligation to protect the Sixth Amendment rights of the accused and to avoid potentially damaging pretrial publicity, including the prior record of the accused. If the reporter is correct in arguing that by the time the case comes to trial the murder will have left people's minds, then so be it. She is almost surely wrong in that judgment, however. Regardless of the verdict, this man's story will be timely when the verdict is announced and in the case of a guilty verdict, may be more timely at that point than before the trial. She should, therefore, before the trial, get all the information on him she can obtain responsibly.

Should the paper publish this man's life story after the trial is over, including identification by name? Probably so, if it can be done discretely. It is a story about a life turned sour, about the forces which impinged on that life, about its tragic consequences. For the local audience, after a guilty verdict, the name would add poignancy to the story without doing significant harm to the convicted. If the verdict is not guilty, there is probably no live story at all. Only the fact of juvenile records would be relevant material and these do not involve the accusation of murder.

Should she gather and publish the second story, the public service story on the performance of public agencies? Yes. Though it will be a

difficult one to do well, the public needs to know about those particular agencies. The case of this 18-year-old provides an important sense
of immediacy (and perhaps a lever for gaining access to agencies) for the
public service story. In order to avoid a wholesale indictment of all
public agencies dealing with juveniles on the basis of one failure, the
life story of this individual could well *not* be published unless the
second story can be written and published simultaneously.

In order to write either story it is important that this reporter gather
information prior to the trial, that is, immediately, while the detective
may be inclined to provide it. The really difficult issue here is that of
possible violation of the moral and legal rights of an accused individual
to get access to his past record. The fact that it involves a juvenile adds
yet another ethical dimension. Laws governing access to juvenile court
records, while they may help cover incompetence in juvenile judges,
are socially significant since they are designed to help in juvenile re-
habilitation. Our society has simply not found a tactic by which we can
monitor trials by juvenile judges and still preserve the privacy of juveniles. Though that is another matter, lawyers who practice before juvenile judges likely carry the heaviest moral obligations to monitor judicial performance.

That raises the difficult question of whether the reporter has a special obligation to the irate detective. She wants to gain access to records that in some jurisdictions are protected by law and in virtually all
jurisdictions are regulated by law enforcement agencies. She herself
recognized that it is the detective's state of mind which might prompt
him to give her access to documents now—an act which upon further
consideration and in a calmer moment, he might be unwilling to
perform.

Thus important moral considerations arise in the relationship of the
reporter to the detective as a key source of information. What kinds of
conduct are acceptable in her strategies for encouraging the detective
to give her access to restricted records? Should she, for example, stop
short of bribing the detective? Yes, since the public need is not that
powerful and overriding. Should she ask the detective for the documents? To do so would be to encourage him to violate the rules of his
agency (and perhaps to violate the law). If he gives them to her and
she uses them, he may later be identified as the source of the leak and
thus risk loss of his job and possible prosecution under the law. To
what extent ought she go in encouraging him to incur that risk? If she
thinks his state of mind (anger) is such as to blind him to the risk he
would be taking, she does have an obligation to let him cool off or to
remind him of his risk. Such a claim would be based on the proposition

that we not only have a moral obligation to others to prevent harm, but we also have an obligation not to entice others unwittingly to incur risk of harm to themselves.

Thus she and the detective should agree before documents exchange hands just what obligation each has to the other. In order to enable him to assess his degree of risk, she should tell the detective whether she would go to jail, if that were called for, to protect his identity as her source. The point is that the detective is a key person in her search for information and that she has special obligations to him.

If the reporter does gain access to the records, then she has an obligation to the accused to treat them as confidential documents. She and the paper must not use them in such a way as to jeopardize a fair trial for the accused.

There is no genuine moral dilemma in this case. Though this case involves different moral goals and principles they do not fundamentally clash. Strategies can be identified that enable the simultaneous pursuit of several worthwhile goals for the meeting of several moral obligations.[6]

21. Ownership of Cable Television

The city of Hawthorne anticipated a new cable television system within two years. The city council had debated the matter for several months now and had called for bids from cable companies who might be interested in the franchise. Bob Evans of the local radio station WCCR covered all phases of the discussion. Community interest was substantial and the city council seemed determined to negotiate an enlightened contract. Enough information carried through to the public, so that over 75 percent of those interviewed in a survey knew the basic details: $8.00 per month service charge, 32 video channels and four audio; they knew the purpose of a local origination channel. When the city council selected the two finalists, Armco and Warners, the majority knew the names and national headquarters of each.

Two questions which surfaced during the council's proceedings and hearings continued to bother Bob Evans. For one thing, all prospective cable companies had refused to cooperate in a regional plan without an increase of 40 percent in the monthly charge. Company representatives contended that in population areas of less than 1,000 per square mile, it is not cost efficient to provide cable service. Including the small towns in outlying areas would increase their equipment price so much as to make the investment unprofitable.

Secondly, Evans became curious why the operators preferred to lay cable only according to market demand and not insist that it reach every home in the city. Apparently companies realize their profit margin with 2/3 of the city, and find that reaching the remaining 1/3 is cost inefficient. In a private conversation one company executive complained about the "poor in the ghetto" who cannot afford the eight dollars per month, or, at least, "will not pay their bills promptly."

Meanwhile, Evans had become an interested student of cable technology. He was especially intrigued by third generation cable systems built on fiber optics and capable of 200 channels or more that would provide a complete range of information and cultural services. This two-way, broad-band cable structure, as Evans envisioned it, would become as basic to the city of the future as water and electricity are now. Through these 200 channels, library material, police protection, retail shopping, public affairs, banking, mail delivery, voting, meter reading, and medical diagnosis would all be available.

Evans began wondering whether the distribution patterns of the current cable proposals were equitable. He understood the realities of marketplace economics, but began asking whether Hawthorne's projected cable system was not just an added convenience for those already information-rich, and whether failure to include the ghettos and rural areas now would breed further inequities when the system was updated and expanded in the future.

He was aware that a few North American cities had chosen the path of municipal ownership for cable. In these systems every home was treated equally and all had hook-up potential. He noted also that the average price in municipal systems was two dollars below the Hawthorne proposals. Evans realized that municipal bonds would be necessary for equipment and that their payment would undoubtedly increase taxes at some point. He also rated the city administration as only slightly above average in competence and effectiveness. However, on balance, Evans considered a publicly owned system as more just, and he developed in his own mind a regional commission through which the citizens themselves would own and operate the franchise.

As part of a series on cable television in cities of similar size (350,000 population), Evans included one story on a neighboring municipal system. But he felt compelled to do more. Frequent appeals to his station management, however, were rebuffed. Station executives saw no useful purpose in advocating public ownership; they found it virtually impossible to appreciate Evans' concerns and were afraid that promoting this option would be heard by their listeners not as a cause of social justice but of socialism.

Six weeks later, the city council adopted the Armco proposal. No discussion of the public ownership alternative had surfaced. Evans remained attracted to a nonprivate option though he found himself discussing it only in personal conversations with friends.

Bob Evans correctly laments the dominance of engineering criteria to determine cable television policy. It gradually became clear to him that the city council was selecting a cable franchise in the same manner that they choose a contractor for building a new sewage system—on the basis of price, performance, and service. While not denying the relevance of such technical matters, Evans caught hold of the larger social dimensions and began wondering which ownership and control design best served the needs of all. The citizens, politicians, and company officials considered the issues within very narrow parameters and appeared satisfied with WCCR's facts-and-detail emphasis. Because he grasped a larger picture, Evans has an obligation to insist on covering the deeper dimensions, even though he was initially rebuffed by the management of his station and no one seemed particularly interested.

The overriding issue here is the concept of social justice that underlies the selection of Hawthorne's cable franchise. Evans appears to operate with some notion of fair distribution, but the principle never gets fully clarified in his mind and often becomes entangled with political realities such as city council competence and marketplace economics. The important ethical question in this case is whether one can justify allocation of this resource to all parties without discrimination. On what basis can one argue that it is morally desirable to assure comprehensive information for every person regardless of income or geographic location? Evans implies at times that there is a plausible case for equal access. Can such a rationale be constructed? If so, then the leverage exists for a publicly owned medium designed to insure equal participation by the entire resident population.

A view of social justice based on merit, to be sure, does not accede to Evans' concern.[7] There are several variants of this approach, but all of them judge on the basis of conduct or achievement and not solely on the inherent value of human beings. Thus, the argument goes, those who have expended the most energy or taken the greatest risk or suffered the most pain deserve the highest reward. Though not all differences in people result from varying amounts of effort or accomplishment, in this view, ability to pay is considered a reasonable basis for determining who obtains this service. In the same vein, it can be argued that citizens who produce more face a heavier obligation in ordinary affairs, a duty which can be facilitated by high capacity technologies. Again, there are several elements in the meritorian perspective, but a prominent canon is whether consumers are at liberty to express preferences, to fulfill their desires, and to receive a fair return on their expenditures. The cable structure would be unjust only to the degree that supply and demand or honest dealings are abrogated.

However, another notion of social justice, "to each according to his essential needs," does validate Evans' concern for equal access. The contention here is not that all felt needs or frivolous wants ought to be met, but that basic human needs must be satisfied equally. The basis for judging is not activity or achievement, but our being human. While there is legitimate argument over which needs qualify, agreement is rather uniform on most fundamental issues such as food, housing, safety, and medical care. People as persons share generic endowments which define them as human. Thus everyone is entitled—without regard for individual success—to those areas of life which permit man's existence to continue in a humane fashion. One prominent version of this need conception of justice is the Judeo-Christian ethic of love where all deserve equal consideration as God's image bearers. Thus whenever a society allocates the necessities of life, the distribution ought to be impartial.

Evans was evidently grasping toward a need conception of justice. Within this framework, prognostications generate some dispute. What really is the future of the so-called wired city? Evans assumes that an industrialized economy such as Hawthorne's will eventually be based on an information network. In his view, information technologies combining computer storage, a video screen, and efficient transmission will eventually prove as necessary to the city as do water and electricity now. He bases his predictions on technologies already in place, not on a utopian dream or imaginary figment. As a student of such other media as cinema, radio, and television, he undoubtedly realizes that a media structure once in place is incredibly difficult to revolutionize. Therefore, he feels that the system Hawthorne chooses in the early stages will not probably permit wholesale changes after the system matures and becomes more complex. Thus one could grant that cable's future course cannot be fully known, yet one ought to be morally bound to initiate the structure that best organizes cable according to the equal distribution principle. Otherwise there will be no guarantee of equitable dissemination of public services, nor equal participation in the political or educational process. Given the economics of monthly costs in urban poverty sections and in wiring rural areas, complete saturation will not be automatic in a viewdata system established on profitability.

Free competition among goods and services has been a historically in-fluential rationale for media practice, but in the case of a monopoly performing a vital function, the need-based criterion appears to be the more fitting ethical standard.

Notes

1. Charles Beard, "*St. Louis Post-Dispatch* Symposium on Freedom of the Press," 1938. Quoted in William L. Rivers, et al., *Responsibility in Mass Communication*, 3rd ed. (New York: Harper and Row, 1980), p. 47.

2. The Commission on the Freedom of the Press, *A Free and Responsible Press* (Chicago: University of Chicago Press, 1947), pp. 26–27.

3. *Overcoming World Hunger: The Challenge Ahead*. Report of the Presidential Commission on World Hunger, March 1980, p. 3.

4. Paulo Freire, *Pedagogy of the Oppressed*, trans. Myra Bergman Ramos (New York: Seabury, 1970), ch. 3, pp. 75–118.

5. Neila Petrick's account, "It's a Nice Place to Visit," appeared in *Matrix* 66 (Winter 1981): 8–11.

6. Several legal questions overlap with the moral concerns noted in this case. The reporter would, in some jurisdictions, face possible prosecution for even possessing these documents. In nearly all jurisdictions, there are penalties for enticing. This situation is based on a National News Council study of ways to avert damaging confrontations between the bar and press. See "National News Council Report: Protecting Two Vital Freedoms—Fair Trial and Free Press," *Columbia Journalism Review* 18 (March/April 1980): 75–84.

7. For a summary of various views on social justice, see Gene Outka, "Social Justice and Equal Access to Health Care," *Journal of Religious Ethics* 2 (Spring 1974): 11–32.

Chapter Five

Invasion of Privacy

The right of individuals to protect their privacy has long been cherished in Western culture. Samuel Warren and Louis D. Brandeis gave this concept legal formulation in their famous essay "The Right to Privacy" in the December 1890 *Harvard Law Review*. Thirty-eight years later, Brandeis still maintained his concern: "The makers of our Constitution undertook to secure conditions favorable to the pursuit of happiness. . . . They conferred, as against the Government, the right to be let alone—the most comprehensive of rights and the right most valued by civilized man."[1] Since that time the protection of personal privacy has received increasing legal attention and has grown in legal complexity. While the word "privacy" does not appear in the Constitution, its defenders base its credence on the first eight amendments and the Fourteenth that guarantee due process of law and protection against unreasonable intrusion. The many laws safeguarding privacy now vary considerably among states and jurisdictions. Yet the general parameters are being defined as proscriptions "against deep intrusions on human dignity by those in possession of economic or governmental power."[2] Privacy cases within this broad framework are generally classified in four separate, though not mutually exclusive, categories: (a) intruding upon seclusion or solitude; (b) public disclosure of embarrassing private affairs; (c) publicity that places individuals in a false light; and (d) appropriation of an individual's name or likeness for personal advantage.

However, for all of privacy's technical gains in case law and tort law, legal definitions are an inadequate foundation for the news business. Merely following the letter of the law—presuming that can even be reasonably determined—certainly is not sufficient. There are several reasons why establishing an ethics of privacy that goes beyond the law is important in the gathering and distribution of news.

First, the law that conscientiously seeks to protect individual privacy excludes public officials. Brandeis himself believed strongly in keeping the national business open. Sunlight for him was the great disinfectant. While condemning intrusion on personal matters, he insisted on exposure of all secrets bearing on public concern. In general, the courts have upheld that political personalities cease to be purely private persons and First Amendment values take precedence over privacy considerations. In recent years, court decisions have given the media extraordinary latitude in reporting public persons. The U.S. Supreme Court in a 1964 opinion (*New York Times v. Sullivan*) concluded that even villifying falsehoods relating to official conduct are protected unless done with actual malice or reckless disregard of the facts. The Court was profoundly concerned in its judgment not to impair what they considered the press's indispensable service to democratic life. In 1971 the Court applied its 1964 opinion to an individual caught up in a public issue—to a Mr. Rosenbloom arrested for distributing obscene books. Subsequent opinions have created some uncertainties, though continually reaffirming broad media protection against defamation suits. Thus, even while adhering to the law, the press has a nearly boundless freedom to treat elected officials unethically.

Second, the press has been given great latitude in defining newsworthiness. People who are catapulted into the public eye by events are generally classed by privacy law along with elected officials. In broadly construing the Warren and Brandeis public interest exemption to privacy, the courts have ruled material as newsworthy because a newspaper or station carries the story. In nearly all important cases, the American courts have accepted the media's definition. But is not the meaning of newsworthiness susceptible to trendy shifts in news values and very dependent upon presumed tastes and needs? Clearly, additional determinants are needed to distinguish gossip and voyeurism from information necessary to the democratic decision-making process.

Third, legal efforts assume many debatable questions about the relationship between self and society. Democratic political theory since the sixteenth century has debated that connection and shifted over time from a libertarian emphasis on the individual to a twentieth-century version much more collectivistic in tone. Within these broad patterns, several narrower arguments have prevailed also. Thomas Jefferson acquiesced in the will of the majority, while John Stuart Mill insisted that each individual must be free to pursue his own good in his own way. Two of the greatest minds ever to focus on American democracy, Alexis de Tocqueville and John Dewey, both centered their analysis on this matter of a viable public life. Walter Lippmann likewise worried about national prosperity in his *Public Opinion* and *The Public Philosophy*. Together these authors and others have identified an enduring intellectual problem that typically must be reduced and narrowed for drawing legal conclusions. Professor Emerson's summary is commonly accepted:

The concept of a right to privacy attempts to draw a line between the individual and the collective, between self and society. It seeks to assure the individual a zone in which to be an individual, not a member of the community. In that zone he can think his own thoughts, have his own secrets, live his own life, reveal only what he wants to the outside world. The right of privacy, in short, establishes an area excluded from the collective life, not governed by the rules of collective living.[3]

Shortcuts and easy answers arise from boxing off these two dimensions. Glib appeals to "the public's right to know" are a common way to cheapen the richness of the private/public relationship.

Therefore, sensitive journalists who struggle personally with these issues in terms of real people lay on themselves more demands than the technically legal. They realize that ethically sound conclusions can emerge only when various privacy situations are faced in all their complexities. The cases that follow illustrate some of those intricacies and suggest ways of dealing with them responsibly. The privacy situations selected below involve a drinking senator, uncovered spy data, small town gossip, petty thievery, and a drowning accident. These represent typical dilemmas involving both elected officials and persons made newsworthy by events beyond their own control. The information gathering and disseminating functions are both included also.

Woven through the commentary are three moral principles which undergird an ethics of privacy for newspeople. The first guideline promotes decency and fairness as nonnegotiable. Even though the law does not explicitly rule out falsehood, innuendo, recklessness, and exaggeration, human decency and basic fairness obviously do. The second moral principle proposes "redeeming social value" as a criterion for selecting which private information is worthy of disclosure. This guideline eliminates all appeals to prurient interests as devoid of newsworthiness. Third, the dignity of persons ought not be maligned in the name of press privilege. Whatever serves real people best must take priority over some cause or slogan.

As a minimum, this chapter suggests, private information regarding public persons must pass these three tests to be ethically justified, though the commentaries introduce the subtleties. Clearly, these privacy matters cannot be treated sanctimoniously by ethicists. They are among the most painful that humane reporters ever encounter. Often they surface among those journalists with a heart in a recounting of battles lost.

22. The Drinking Committee Chairman

Ellen Steenway had covered Washington for 16 years. From the beginning Washington intrigued her. Already as a journalism student she had spent her internship on the President's press secretary staff. She had accepted a position with the State Department public relations unit after graduation, until the urge for newswriting sent her to a Washington magazine and then a Washington paper before switching six years ago to her latest assignment on the Washington bureau of a New York paper.

During these professional years she had observed heavy drinking by several public officials, heard well-documented reports on extra-marital affairs by Congressmen, watched a cabinet secretary ridicule his wife, and personally knew a photographer who had followed a senator around gay bars. She had never reported any of these private episodes because she believed that these personal affairs were private business as long as they did not interfere with public duties. She also refused to pursue several of these stories for fear she might jeopardize her access to the parties and offices of various politicians.

Then one day Steenway covered the hearings of the Senate Banking Committee where its chairman was visibly drunk at 10 a.m. He asked rambling questions, interrupted the proceedings, maintained no semblance of parliamentary procedure, and had to be helped from his chair for the noon luncheon. As before, Steenway made no mention of his drinking, even though it clearly interfered with the quality of his committee work and was not merely an after-hour activity. A month later, when the Banking Committee presented a new bill on the senate floor, Chairman Williams was again visibly drunk and Steenway explicitly reported his drinking habits rather than use euphemisms such as "the Chairman did not defend the bill successfully." By any standard of fairness, Williams had now crossed over the line. A major complicated tax bill was involved and its enactment near.

However, Steenway's editor refused to include any reference to Williams' drunkenness. The paper had a policy that sex and drinking were not mentioned unless there had been arrests with documented evidence available in a public record. In the editor's view, the bill's path through the Senate certainly did not depend on how eloquently Chairman Williams defended it. He reasoned that presidential drunkenness might be reported since presidents are responsible for the nuclear trigger, but banking committees could not lead us to World War III. In addition, the editor felt that references to Williams' drinking would sensationalize the story; it was not serious news and he preferred to focus on the issues. The merit and weakness of the proposed legislation were all that really counted to him. And how did she know for sure? Maybe Williams just had a high fever that day.

Steenway reminded the editor that in 16 years she had not included personal matters nor had she reported Williams' behavior during the hearings. "Then why change your practice now," the editor demanded. "Or are you weakening just because so many cheap papers are printing that drivel." Steenway was upset, but did not feel strongly enough to resign. In fact, when the same incident occurred several days later, she did not even mention it, knowing that her editor would reject the story anyhow and might even consider her insubordinate.

Both decision makers are taking their responsibilities seriously. Neither can be faulted for outright carelessness or brazen disregard for standards. There is no evidence that the editor is merely protecting an old crony or concerned about a possible libel suit. Perhaps the editor harbors an artificial reverence for important officials, but his crusty manner makes that doubtful. Steenway does not appear to report the senator's drunkenness simply because this will move a page twelve story to page one.

In fact, Steenway could be held blameworthy for not reporting the incident. Senator Williams, in her judgment, had allowed his personal habits to affect seriously his acumen. Many readers of her newspaper were from New Jersey, the senator's home state, and they had a right to know. No sensational language had been included, though his incoherent speech, tottering, and occasional belligerence were mentioned in a matter-of-fact tone. Given Williams' long record of drinking, Steenway was convinced it could not have been a temporary physical ailment.

The editor also could be considered blameworthy if he chose to do nothing. His company policy was explicit and he upheld the same long-standing reservations, as Steenway had, about reporting on private matters. He understood the press' vast legal rights regarding public officials, but sincerely felt that the content of the bill and its potential effect were the only relevant story here. Not to overrule his reporter would mean violating his conscience and ignoring his paper's definition of newsworthiness.

In the first phase of this case, both the editor and reporter could justify their actions before reasonable people. The reporter has not wantonly invaded the senator's privacy, but limited her account to his behavior on the Senate floor. The editor, meanwhile, invokes a defensible company policy. Given the fact that the senator is not a personal friend of either the paper's owner or editor whom they were protecting, the reporter's story and the editor's rejection can be considered morally acceptable.

The issue for debate concerns phase two—Steenway's behavior after the editor's decision. The fourth step in the Potter Box process now became inescapable. Where were her ultimate loyalties? Steenway was upset, but did not resign. When Williams was subsequently drunk on the Senate floor, she made no reference to it. As an employee, she chose not to contradict company policy. Her perceived duty to the paper overrode her concern for her New Jersey readers and her own conscience.

23. Spy Data and Suicide

On Saturday night, 28 February 1976, the editors of the Dallas *Times-Herald* had a decision to make before 10 p.m. press time. The Sunday edition would feature an exposé that investigative reporter Hugh Aynesworth had been working on for three months. The article would disclose that Norman J. Rees, a former oil engineer who was retired and living in Connecticut, had been a Soviet spy from World War II until 1975. Since 1971 Rees had been a double agent working for the Federal Bureau of Investigation.

Rees had twice flown to Dallas and allowed himself to be interviewed by the *Times-Herald*. According to executive editor Ken Johnson, Rees admitted accepting money from the Russians for technical information and had been "voluntarily undergone polygraph examinations" to substantiate his account.[4] But on that Saturday afternoon before publication, Rees had called the *Times-Herald*. He asked if the story would be printed and if he would be identified. Told yes, Rees responded that such a disclosure would leave him "no choice but suicide."

On Sunday morning, the story appeared. On Sunday morning, Rees' wife found her husband's body. He had shot himself in the head.

That afternoon, an Associated Press reporter talked with Rees' son, John, a 31-year-old junior-high-school teacher. He told the reporter he had informed his mother, Ann, of the story and she was "acting like it's unreal. She didn't know the story was coming out," the son said.

After Rees' death, the *Times-Herald* issued a statement:

From time to time, newspapers receive threats about stories from people attempting to protect their identities. In our judgment, if a story is newsworthy and supported by the facts it is our policy to publish. In this instance it was decided that the story could not be suppressed, even in the face of Mr. Rees' threats.[5]

On March 13, the New York *Times* printed a letter from a reader questioning the *Times-Herald's* judgment. Wrote Nancy Boardman Eddy of Chevy Chase, Maryland:

I cannot comprehend the thinking of newsmen who, when told that Mr. Rees would kill himself if the story identified him, excuse themselves by saying "the story could not be suppressed."

I'd like to ask, Why not? To what higher moral code do newsmen adhere than we mortals do? The First Amendment may give them the freedom to print the news, but why are they somehow obligated to print knowingly a story that may lead to a man's death, and, indeed, what purpose is served? The arrogance displayed is beyond belief.[6]

On March 31, a second letter was printed, defending the press. John Pyle of Brooklyn wrote: "The threat of just such disclosure has prevented many people from committing just such infamy, knowing that possible disclosure is the price they might be asked to pay. This is possibly a greater deterrent to spying and treason than the law."[7]

Three major choices were made by people at the *Times-Herald*: (1)

someone decided the story merited investigation and publication; (2) someone decided to publish it on the Sunday morning originally scheduled; (3) someone decided to ignore Rees' suicide threat.

What considerations are relevant to each of these decisions? The *Times-Herald* policy was to publish if a story is deemed newsworthy and supported by the facts. Someone decided that both criteria were met in this case. Presumably the *Times-Herald*, because of two interviews with Rees, had the details straight and judged them newsworthy. It might have reminded readers that when Rees first began working with the Russians in World War II, Russia was an ally! It might have contained publicly useful reports on the forces Rees felt in himself and the reasons he continued to supply the Russians with secrets long after World War II was over. It might therefore have given a measure of guidance to some other public official who was contemplating disloyal conduct. Thus, judged by the criterion that it contained information which might conceivably work toward the public good, it is arguable that the story may have been newsworthy. It also is arguable that the story contained nothing that the public *needed* to know but contained only something the public might *want* to know in the form of an entertaining spy thriller.

On the second question (the decision to publish on schedule), several relevant factors enter the picture. This story is clearly one that would keep. Postponing publication would allow time for negotiation with Rees in order to see what part of the information he had given voluntarily in interviews he now would prefer to keep off the record. Further conversations with Rees might well have protected those things he wished to conceal while simultaneously serving the public's need to know. In any case, the decision to publish now a story that could have been delayed, and to do so under the threat of suicide, appears on its face to be made in indifference to Rees' well-being. The *Times-Herald's* statement about their reason for publication does not address this question.

The third matter—ignoring Rees' threat altogether—provides solid evidence of the editors' disregard of Rees' relatives or the authorities who might seek to prevent him from carrying out his threat. The failure of the *Times-Herald* to apprise someone of the threat is remarkable. Any high school sophomore should have picked up on Rees' apparent instability, and yet the paper ignored his threat even to the point of not alerting anyone that it had been made. Rees' suicide may not have been ultimately preventable if the story appeared, but it could have been obstructed through several possible actions by the *Times-Herald*. These editors demonstrated a callous disregard for the life of a human being, a life which almost certainly could have been saved simply by some editor's decision to not publish. The paper violated the basic moral principle that we should not only not cause harm, but should prevent it when doing so does not subject us to a risk of comparable harm.

It is obvious, however, that our duty to prevent harm does not mean that every threat of suicide ought to be honored automatically. One could imagine another kind of case in which Rees is a wealthy community leader respected for his charity, but he controls a blind trust owning slum property in violation of city codes. A poor family dies in a fire. Rees is unstable and distraught; he threatens suicide if his ownership is ever disclosed. If this situation were considered in terms of Rawl's veil of ignorance, publishing the story would be justified. Or, giving the issues an even harder twist, assume this Rees dies of natural causes and there had been no fire. Should his obituary indicate how this rich tenement owner amassed his wealth?

24. A Prostitute and Gossip

Candy Herbow was a model teenager. A high school student and only daughter of a prominent family in Missoula, Montana, she had won a scholarship to Radcliffe. On 17 January 1979, she was murdered in downtown Washington, D.C.[8]

The *Missoulian*, a daily of 32,000 circulation, carried a page-one story the following day—a tragedy for the community and grief to her family. But the sordid details of Candy's life in Washington were not part of that first local obituary; indeed, managing editor Ron Decker knew little until his paper was contacted by the Washington *Post* which was developing the story to its dramatic hilt: promising, talented teenager turned prostitute stabbed on the streets, presumably in the course of plying her trade.

Candy's reorientation from gifted musician to streetwalker was first manifest in an uneasy adjustment to the pressures of Ivy League competition and urban Northeastern impersonality. By Thanksgiving of 1976 she was out of college and back in Missoula, soon discontent there as well, unable to find interesting work. Six months later she met a recruiter in a Missoula bar, travelled with him to Washington, and entered the seedy world of 15th and K streets NW. The pimp was known to police, though never arrested. In December 1977, Candy was convicted of solicitation for prostitution.

All this became clear when a *Post* reporter called the *Missoulian* on

Monday, January 22, the day of Candy's funeral, to get information from the published obituary. In return for the help, the *Post* writer agreed to dictate his story over the phone on Tuesday night.

Candy's parents, Hale and Lora Herbow, first caught wind of the *Post's* intentions late Monday when they too were called by a Washington reporter. They were appalled by the encroachment on their privacy and the senselessness of publicizing their daughter's problems. Family friend and Missoula attorney John Mudd agreed to help the Herbows squelch the story. On Tuesday morning Mudd called the *Post* to request a kill. The family had suffered enough, Mudd argued. Further publicity would endanger the parents' health. At least the story should be softened, Mudd contended. The *Post* declined.

Meanwhile, Mudd learned that the *Missoulian* planned to use the story in Wednesday morning's edition. Mudd appealed to Decker, even making vague references to suicide if the story were printed locally.

Decker consulted with his publisher and editorial staff, and decided to publish the next morning. He based his decision on three criteria: (1) The story had news value; much of Candy's death was still a mystery. (2) The details might serve as a warning; apparently a pimp had first contacted Candy in a Missoula bar while she was in high school. (3) The story would certainly be distributed nationally and around the region through the Washington *Post*/Los Angeles *Times* News Service; if he printed nothing his community would question how often he suppressed other information and on what basis. Decker called Mudd at 11 p.m. Tuesday to say that the story would run. Mudd voiced a final plea to hold the story until he could prepare the family, but Wednesday's *Missoulian* did, in fact, carry a slightly edited version of the *Post* story. Deleted were certain specifics of Candy's life on the street, including the prices she commanded and her boasts of being a "pro."

The Herbows and much of Missoula were shocked at the intrusion. Businesses pulled their advertisements and the *Missoulian's* law firm dropped the paper as a client. An advertiser boycott was threatened, though it did not materialize. More than 150 letters appeared in the paper in two weeks, most of them bristling with outrage. At least 200 readers cancelled their subscriptions. The *Missoulian's* editorial page editor sided with the Herbow family and said so in a signed column, a further embarrassment to Decker and his staff.

Yet the managing editor stuck by his judgment. The publisher, after time to reflect, admitted his paper could have handled the story better by honoring Mudd's request to postpone publication for a day or two.

The clash between the outrage of the Herbow supporters and Ron Decker's news judgment arises from the disagreement whether news value for the community outweighs the invasion of privacy for those personally involved. A utilitarian framework would, in effect, argue that the benefit for the many outweighs the bite to the few. If one applied Aristotle's golden mean, however, what would be considered morally appropriate behavior?

At the one extreme, the "fallen angel" story would be eliminated as totally unwarranted intrusion. Why should victims of circumstance endure punishment through a sensational account? The pimp-in-Missoula angle received only eight words in Decker's edited version of the Washington *Post* release. All the gory details about the stab wounds were included—the number, size, and location on the body. The small town, rural-virgin-off-to-Ivy-League-and-big-city slant framed the account. And all that was an indecent, sensational, obdurate invasion of privacy.

However, the opposite extreme—reporting nothing—is ruled out as well by Aristotle's principle. The golden mean would suggest that the *Missoulian* had a social responsibility to advance citizen understanding, to investigate pimps and police in Missoula, to get that local story and take whatever additional time might be necessary to do so. A story accurately reflecting the golden mean would inspire readers to confront the community's problem with unwelcome pimps in local bars. In the process of developing the larger context, Candy could possibly be mentioned by name. But that substantive flavor contrasts sharply with the street-walking prostitute tone which actually appeared.

25. Naming a Shoplifter

The caller's request was a familiar one; in fact, the editor turned down such requests every week or two. Sometimes callers shouted at him. Sometimes they spoke in a voice that trembled. This caller was one of the latter. The editor knew from experience that the conversation would end in tears.

The woman at the other end was repeating herself: "Really, I am *not* that sort of person," she said. "All my life, I've never done anything against the law; I've never even had a traffic ticket."

"I believe you," the editor said, "and it's a shame, but we'll have to use your name. Our policy is that we print the names of people arrested for shoplifting. We have to be consistent."

"But if you publish my name I won't be able to face anybody; I just won't ever. I have children in grade school and it would be terrible for them. And I've just been through a divorce; that was bad enough. Please, isn't there something you could do? Why is it so important to print my name?"

The editor always had a hard time answering that question. "Arrests are part of the public record," the editor began. "They are public because our justice system is conducted in the open—that protects everybody from secret arrests."

"But I *want* my arrest to be secret," the caller said. "Why would it hurt to leave out my name? No one would know."

"I would know," said the editor. "I would remember when I received another call like yours. And if I said OK to you, then to be fair I'd have to say OK to the next person, and the next one after that."

"But I've paid so much already," said the caller, her voice trembling more than ever. "I've never, never done anything like that. Never. I don't know what came over me. I just saw that little bear and my son collects bears and I didn't have any money and I put it in my purse. The minute I did, I felt just terrible. And then they arrested me and I was so ashamed and embarrassed. And if you run my name, then my friends will know, and the people I work with, and the teachers at school, and my children's friends. If you run my name I swear I'll have to move away from this town. I just couldn't stand it. Oh, please!"

The tears began.

"I'm really sorry," the editor said. "I really am."

The most obvious and immediate response is to consider this newspaper's practice harmful. Naming persons charged with lesser offenses inflicts undue harm to the people involved. Publishing the final court decision—if it were reported at the time of arrest—would be a useful step in protecting reputations; but even that is not an adequate solution. Readers might see only the original story and not the final verdict. Meanwhile mere association with crime generates suspicion among acquaintances and fuels gossip. Not reporting routine charges when they are laid eliminates trivia from the newspaper and avoids an unfair presumption of guilt toward the accused. Why report minor charges such as shoplifting, petty theft (under fifty dollars), trespassing, traffic violations? On the grounds of compassion, why should coverage not be restricted to trials and convictions where sentences include a jail term?

This is a hard-luck story accompanied by an honest request to prevent further pain. The children will be hurt and teased because of undesirable notoriety to their mother. Employment may become more difficult since she now carries a social stigma. The editor justifies his action by a general appeal to newsworthiness; however, it can be reasonably assumed that he upholds the practice of publishing names because such public gossip enhances the human interest value and attracts readers.

Probing more deeply, the ethical issue may not be as simple and straightforward as inflicting unnecessary harm. The editor defends himself somewhat weakly by claiming he must be consistent and by noting that the judicial system ought to be conducted in the open. Yet the seeds of an important principle in social ethics lie underneath his comments.

Does not the public interest demand that justice be administered without favoritism? If names are suppressed, what will prevent society from concluding that this paper acts arbitrarily? Selective reporting of crimes can lead to abuses and, even if handled fairly, the public does not have an accurate picture of crime as a social phenomenon in its community.

Moreover, thorough publication safeguards the public from abuse by officials and thus protects the general liberty. Knowledge by the police that their arresting power is subject to public scrutiny provides an important boundary for them. Society has an abiding interest in knowing exactly who the police have arrested, why they have arrested them, and what has happened to them. The public rarely goes to police stations and courts; its access to such information is through the eyes of the press. While risking unwarranted abuse of personal reputations, the larger concern should be that nothing brings the administration of justice into disrepute. An open system of justice suggests that publishing names with extremely rare exceptions is superior to the general rule of not publishing names. One could argue that reporters should do a more analytical reporting of crime in a community in order to provide the public an accurate account of the problems it faces. Such aggressive reporting, however, would inevitably include names even though the stories then went beyond merely listing the bare details about the person and offense. It they are to aid in protecting the general welfare, the channels of communication ought to be open and free, and in principle report all information without arbitrary selection.

26. Photojournalism and Tragedy

The scene is a river. By the time the photographer arrives, the bodies of three boys covered with sheets lie on the bank. Firemen are still looking for the body of a fourth boy. Three of the drowning victims are from the same family. A fire policeman intercepts the photographer and tells him to leave. Family members have asked that no pictures be taken of the bodies.

The photographer ignores the policeman. He sees the parents of the three boys talking to a state trooper: To the photographer, the parents appear too numbed by shock to care whether photos are taken. He snaps a picture of them. The trooper waves the photographer away, shouting, "Get the hell out of here with that camera!"

A second fire policeman orders the photographer to stop taking pictures. The photographer explains that he is only doing his job. He shoots two shots of the sheeted bodies. Then he waits. The picture he wants most is one of the firemen bringing the fourth boy from the river.

The body is found. The photographer kneels to take the picture, but the fire policeman and a dozen onlookers surround him. His view blocked, he moves to shoot from another angle. The crowd follows him. He calls to the state trooper for police protection. "You don't deserve it!" shouts the trooper.

The mother of the three boys has been lying over the body of one of her sons. Attracted by the commotion, she looks up to see the photographer surrounded by the onlookers. She seizes her only surviving son, age two, holds him over her head, and shouts to the photographer, "Why don't you take a picture of him? He's all I have left!"

The crowd responds to her words by ripping the gadget bag from the photographer. The mother falls across the bodies of her sons. The photographer takes one more picture, then leaves.[9]

———————

Michael J. Ogden, executive editor of the Providence *Journal-Bulletin*, condemns photographs which capitalize on human grief:

I can understand the printing of an auto accident picture as an object lesson. What I can't understand is the printing of sobbing wives, mothers, children. . . . What is the value of showing a mother who has just lost her child in a fire? Is this supposed to have a restraining effect on arsonists? I am sure that those who don't hesitate to print such pictures will use the pious pretense of quoting Charles A. Dana's famous dictum that "whatever the Divine Providence permitted to occur I was not too proud to print." Which is as peachy a shibboleth to permit pandering as I can imagine.[10]

But Ogden is a rare editor. Every day in newspapers and on television, photographs and film footage emphasize grief and tragedy. In fact, professional awards are regularly given to grisly pictures regardless of whether they pander to morbid tastes.

The defense usually centers on newsworthiness. The broken-hearted man whose child was just run over; a shocked eight-year-old watching his father gunned down by police; the would-be suicide on a bridge— all pitiful scenes which communicate something of human tragedy and are therefore to be considered news. Photojournalists sum up a news event in a manner the mind can hold, capturing that portrayal which is "rich in meaning because it is a trigger image of all the emotions aroused by the subject."[11] The photographer in this case acted as an undaunted professional, fulfilling his role as reporter on everyday affairs including the unpleasantries. From the photographer's framework, to capture the newsworthy moment is an important self-discipline. He is trained not to panic but to bring forth the truth as events dictate. Photographers are schooled to be visual historians, and not to be freelance medics.

However, on what grounds can the photographer condone his behavior? All the principals at the scene condemned him: the policemen, family, and onlookers. If he were invited to justify himself morally, does any conceivable case exist? If he contends he is only doing his job—that is, providing what his editors want—that would not be an acceptable explanation. He could call on the warning bell thesis, asserting that his photos will make other parents more safety conscious; however, this utilitarian appeal to consequences has no genuine basis in fact. Perhaps in the name of reporting news, the photojournalist in this case is actually caught in those opportunistic professional values that build circulation by playing on the human penchant for morbidity.

No overarching purpose emerges which can ameliorate the direct invasion of privacy and insensitivity. Bruce Roberts presents a forthright position based on the ethical principle that all human beings are worthy of respect: "A photographer is first a human being with compassion for other human beings. If he arrives at the scene of an accident first before any aid has been summoned that is his first duty and a Pulitzer prize-winning picture possibility should make no difference."[12] By law, once individuals figure in the news, they cease to be private persons protected by applicable statutes. But it is here that the photographer should consider the moral guideline that suffering individuals are entitled to the same respect as any other human being, despite the fact that events may have made them part of the news.

Photojournalism is an extremely significant eyewitness of the humanity and inhumanity of man. In pursuing its mission, the ethical conflict typically revolves around the need for honest visual information and for respecting a person's privacy. In this case, assailed as an unfeeling voyeur, the photographer provides no evidence of wrestling with the dilemma. Perhaps he considers such judgments to be the responsibility of his editor.

Notes

1. Olmstead v. United States, 277 U.S. 438, 478 (1928). Brandeis dissenting.

2. Briscoe v. Reader's Digest Association, 4 Cal. 3d 529, 93 Cal. Reptr. 866, 869 (1971).

3. Thomas I. Emerson, *The System of Free Expression* (New York: Vintage Books, 1970), p. 545.

4. For a full account of this episode, see *Dallas Times Herald*, 29 February 1976, and *New York Times*, 1, 2, 5, 13, 31 March 1976.

5. "Spy Said He'd Kill Himself If Exposed, Then Did So," *New York Times*, 2 March 1976, p. 1.

6. Letter to the Editor, "Of News & Death," *New York Times*, 13 March 1976, p. 24.

7. Letter to the Editor, "Espionage's Price," *New York Times*, 31 March 1976, p. 40.

8. Details in Jack Hart and Janis Johnson, "Fire Storm in Missoula," *Quill* 67 (May 1979): 19–24.

9. Original source: Arthur W. Geisleman, Jr., "Take Pictures of Tragic Scenes or Flee From Irate Onlookers?" *Editor and Publisher* 92 (13 August 1959): 13.

10. John Hohenberg, *The News Media: A Journalist Looks at His Profession* (New York: Holt, Rinehart and Winston, 1968), p. 212.

11. Harold Evans, *Pictures on a Page* (Bemont, Calif.: Wadsworth, 1978), p. 5.

12. Joseph Costa, et al., "Get the Picture Or Act the Samaritan?" *Bulletin of the American Society of Newspaper Editors*, 1 June 1963, p. 7.

PART 2

Advertising

In order to begin analyzing any aspects of contemporary advertising, it is necessary to understand something of the cultural and economic context within which it functions. The following four premises serve as a useful backdrop for our subsequent description and analysis.

1. *Advertising must be considered in light of cultural expectations.* Some forget that we are, in part, a nation founded because of advertising. Daniel Boorstin observes:

Never was there a more outrageous or more unscrupulous or more ill-informed advertising campaign than that by which the promoters of the American colonies brought settlers here. Brochures published in England in the seventeenth century, some even earlier, were full of hopeful overstatements, half-truths, and downright lies along with some facts which nowadays surely would be the basis of a restraining order from the FTC. . . . It would be interesting to speculate how long it might have taken to settle this continent if there had not been such promotion by enterprising advertisers. How has American civilization been shaped by the fact that there was a kind of natural selection here of those people who were willing to believe advertising?[1]

To understand advertising, then, we must be clear about what a given culture expects of it. Some understanding is offered when we grasp the relevant rules of the game. For advertising in this country, the "rules" allow for enterprising businesspeople to pursue their self-interests through various merchandising activities, including advertising. The salesman has always been a prominent part of American culture, honored in fact and fable both for his economic functions and nimble tongue, from the drummers and patent medicine advertisers through the lionization of the often unscrupulous (but always captivating) P.T. Barnum, and the generic flim-flam man.

It is considered appropriate to attempt to persuade. This tells us something concerning our general assumptions about human nature. For why would we permit wanton persuasion to plague a helpless public? Simply because we believe that the public is not helpless, but armed with reason, guile, and a certain savvy about how to make one's way in the market.

If we are sometimes open to persuasion about frivolous products and services, it may be that we have become sufficiently jaded by affluence to let ourselves be seduced by clearly self-interested sources. And it may be, as Theodore Levitt suggests, that advertising serves not only as part of our popular culture but also as an omnipresent source of "alleviating imagery," helping us to mentally compensate for the overall drabness of our lives.[2] We understand advertising only if we understand its culture.

2. *The advertising process has varied intents and effects.* How we love to oversimplify. Psychologists say, "The human psychological tendency is toward patterning of experience." And so we say, "Advertising is ..." and "Advertisements are ..." and "Advertising does ...."

Right now, advertisers are attempting to reach and influence individuals for an enormous variety of reasons: here to sell a used power lawn mower through a classified ad; there to induce more patronage of a pizza shop through a hot-air balloon; and yonder an attempt to impart highly technical information about an automated filing system in a journal for office managers. There a detergent minidrama on daytime television. Or a message urging support for the cause of the American Indian. Here the virtues of a high alloy steel in a publication indispensable to metallurgical engineers. Or a campaign on prime time television apparently meant to influence ultimate consumers, but in fact intended to elevate morale among employees and stockholders. And a message asking support of the local police. And so it goes.

On the receiver end, Joseph Plummer, following years of intensive research, reveals four general levels of potential advertising response: unconscious, immediate perceptual, retention or learning, and behavioral.[3] Then, dealing only with the immediate perceptual level, he finds seven more common responses: entertainment, irritation, familiarity, empathy, confusion, informativeness, and brand reinforcement. The latter response in particular reminds us of the impressive evidence that suggests that the predominant effect of much advertising is not the seduction of the unwashed, but simply the reinforcement of the behavior and judgment of those who already act as some advertisers wish.

Much advertising criticism is directed to television commercials. (Not even the staunchest critic attacks the advertising function in, say, Harpers.) Much criticism and defense thus generalizes from specifics to the "All advertising is . . ." syndrome, with a corresponding loss of analytical precision. We understand advertising only if we understand its complexity.

3. *Advertising's actual effects are usually not clearly known.* Because of the number of factors involved, for most advertising, most of the time, "no one knows for sure." This explains a great deal. For example:

- The persistence of the commission system of agency remuneration in which the advertising agency receives a commission (usually 15 percent) on the space and/or time purchased on behalf of the advertiser. If we had any adequate measure of performance, advertisers would compensate their agencies on the basis of proven success. Lacking the needed measure, we rely on a system that rewards the agency not for how well its products (ads) perform, but for how the agency spends its client's money.
- The "me-too" nature of much advertising content. If the business discovers that comparison ads work, we see a rash of such advertisements. If cinema verité is thought to be moving the masses, imitators will proliferate. If fresh-faced young couples strolling in flowered fields are rumored to sell cigarettes, then witness many such pastoral sojourns. Or animation. Or humor. Or folk singers. Or nostalgia. Or candor. Or . . . .
- The lack of true professionalism in the business. Here the wife of the vice-president scuttles an advertising campaign because she doesn't like the look of the female model. There an account executive is browbeaten by an advertising manager about the failure of the agency to come up with some new, creative ideas. Or witness the pomp and circumstance of the Clio awards

amid black ties at the Lincoln Center, with giant screens for the embellish-
ment of 30-second color commercials, now transformed from persuasive
guesswork into art forms.

Servility and pageantry frequently replace performance, as many
accept proxies for the real effect of advertising. We understand advertising only if we understand its uncertainty.

4. *For all of these reasons, advertising is an ambiguous subject capable of many different interpretations.* If one wishes to see advertising
as an indispensable element of the free market, one may find what one
seeks. If one wishes to see advertising as a sworn enemy of the free
market, one may find that as well. Critics and supporters can give to
this subject whatever structure they choose. And, given the likelihood
of different biases, the inherent complexity of the process, and the lack
of certainty regarding even its narrow pecuniary effects, we can more
readily understand the existence of constant controversy.

Advertisements are bits and pieces of reality. *Advertising* is an ab-
straction from those elements, and from much more. As such, its
meaning lies with those who wish to support, to criticize . . . or to
understand. We understand advertising only if we understand its
ambiguity.

This section, Part Two, offers a reasonable crossection of case histories dealing with four major areas of ethical concern: Who are the
proper audiences for advertising messages? What are their proper subjects? What techniques should be used? How is advertising affected by
(and how does it affect) the media that carry it? Finally, in Chapter 10,
we describe and discuss four characteristics inherent to advertising
practice that call for particular attention.

The cases are drawn from two primary sources: (1) research involving questionnaires sent to practitioners in various aspects of advertising asking them if they encounter ethical decisions in their day-to-day
work, and (2) an examination of advertising practice as seen through
the eyes of critics and supporters in articles and books. Emphasis is
placed on the ordinary rather than the classic. The viewpoint is usually
that of the working practitioner rather than the star. Each case is followed by a commentary that attempts to illuminate some of the dimensions appropriate to disciplined ethical analysis. All commentaries
attempt to build on the social ethics foundation offered in the opening
section of the book.

An ancient Chinese curse charges, "May you live in interesting
times." The times for advertising will always be interesting. As Daniel
Boorstin wisely observes, "If we consider democracy as a set of insti-

tutions which aims to make everything available to anybody, it would not be an overstatement to describe advertising as the characteristic rhetoric of democracy."[4] And therein lies the ethical challenge.

Notes

1. Daniel G. Boorstin, "Advertising and American Civilization," in *Advertising and Society*, ed. Yale Brozen (New York: New York University Press, 1974), pp. 11–12.

2. Theodore Levitt, "The Morality (?) of Advertising," *Harvard Business Review* 48 (July/August 1970): 84–92.

3. Joseph T. Plummer, "A Theoretical View of Advertising Communication," *Journal of Communication* 21 (December 1971): 315–25.

4. Boorstin, "Advertising and American Civilization," p. 13.

Chapter Six

Special Audiences

To a great extent the cases in this chapter are the products of the television era. Although there has been a basic concern about special segments of the population throughout much of American history—child labor laws, women's suffrage, Medicare, for example—television's ascendency as a pervasive force in American society has heightened preoccupation with advertising's influence on particular population groups.

This is partly because television is the most indiscriminate of our mass media. It reaches the rich and the poor, the well read and the illiterate, the young and the old. In some cases advertisers have isolated particular target markets—children, for example. In other situations, the advertising intended for some (the affluent) may also reach and affect others (such as the poor).

So advertisers have been called to account. In some cases their own consciences have prompted them to raise the issues, even though they have not always resolved them. There is, for example, no clear agreement in the advertising business concerning the morality of advertising to children. In other cases, outside special interest groups have issued calls for change.

One prominent ethical matter is the question of who is morally responsible. Advertising practitioners tend to believe, rightly or wrongly, that the pursuit of their craft is socially beneficial, that for most people most of the time advertising performs a useful service. Those carrying the banner of special audiences, on the other hand, contend that the system is simply unfair to their constituencies; hence, it must change.

It is appropriate, then, that the advertising section of this book leads off with the ethical questions raised by the concept of special audiences. Today this issue remains among the top concerns of advertising's critics.

27. Fantasy for Selling

This was only one of the several groups of kids who had been gathered over the last several weeks. Perhaps it would be the last, if they could finally arrive at a winning combination. So hoped Cynthia Marx, a 35-year-old specialist in market research for one of the country's largest advertising agencies. Her most recent assignment had been taxing in a number of ways.

One of the agency's clients, a nationwide fried chicken chain, had been anxious to develop some edge in their ongoing competition with Colonel Sanders and others in the field. Impressed by the star quality of such figures as Ronald McDonald and the Magical Burger King, it was suggested that a search begin for some memorable fantasy character who might create the same competitive pull.

Not surprisingly, the agency had suggested a chicken. That's when Cynthia entered the picture. She had been asked to set up and supervise research to assess the appeal of certain chicken characters before an appropriate audience. Taking yet another leaf from McDonald's book, the audience for this part of the company's overall promotional program was to be children.

For Cynthia this was new. Her previous research work had not involved her with children as potential markets. In order to work efficiently with the agency account group responsible for the handling of the account on a day-to-day basis, and to be properly informed for directing her research, Cynthia examined the existing research in the area.

She found, amid a great deal of ambiguity about children and advertising, one indisputable conclusion: children can be influenced by television advertising, and that influence can be strongly affected by the presenter of the message. As a curb on this influence, self-regulatory practices of the television networks and the advertising business now forbid the star of a children's show to also sell products on the program. (Captain Kangaroo, for example, used to promote Schwinn bicycles.) But she found nothing to prohibit the use of imaginary personages or fanciful presentations, as long as they are not part of a clearly deceptive message. So Tony the Tiger becomes an accepted figure in the advertising environment. Fred Flintstone and Barney Rubble were liked by the children in one study, and the kids believed that Fred and Barney would like them better if they ate Cocoa Pebbles.

The company and the agency seemed on the right marketing track. And nothing in the message itself, or in the use of the chicken figure, would violate any business, media, or government stipulations.

Another group of kids had just arrived to be tested. The research design was sound, the audience appropriate. Over the last several weeks Cynthia had tested different actors in different costumes, different theme songs, and chicken voices from high tenor to basso profundo. She had shown the chicken in a typical restaurant, in kids' homes, in a special chicken coop. The approaches had been varied from clownish to dramatic, including the chicken as an adventure hero. Through it all the researchers kept asking the kids, "Which do you like best? Do you like this chicken? Would you like to see him on TV?"

Cynthia had no doubt that she would ultimately discover the most effective character. The device had worked for others. It would work for their client. But *should* it? This potentially seductive approach? With *this* audience? Well, the kids certainly seemed to like *that* chicken. . . .

Cynthia is a researcher. She has been trained to gather information in a systematic way in order to help answer some question. In this case the assignment is to get chidren to develop a preference for the client's product. The heart of Cynthia's undeveloped ethical problem is a feeling that she is using empirical tools for morally troubling ends.

How undeveloped? First, she recognizes the legality of her actions and of the intent of her client. Nothing in the formal stipulations of the advertising business, the television networks, the NAB code, or the Federal Trade Commission prevents the advertiser from using this particular approach on this particular audience as long as the message is not deceptive.

Cynthia might also have reasoned that the results of a successful promotion using the chicken figure would be generally positive: (a) parents will ultimately make the purchase decision in any event, and

(b) the food is wholesome, not the crinkly snacks and sugar-laden products that have so irritated groups such as Action for Children's Television.

Cynthia also apparently believes that the market system is just. Thus far at least, she seems willing to accept the idea of children as markets, and to think in terms of the need for competitive pull. She observes that fantasy approaches have worked for others, with the implicit understanding that advertisers can legitimately pursue their self-interest in this way.

But now her reasoning begins to muddle. Does the system also work for the parents? The children? Does it turn kids into little nags on behalf of the advertiser's product, replete with unreal expectations due to their belief in the fantasy figure? Is it proper to use the best tools of market research to get at children, some of whom are still too young for school?

To whom is moral duty owed in this case? As the Potter Box emphasizes, choosing our loyalties stands at the heart of the real issues. But Cynthia has not yet thought it through clearly enough to address the question. Is she troubled by advertising to children per se, merely the use of fantasy figures, or only her involvement at the moment?

If Cynthia concludes that advertising to children is wrong under any circumstances, then she could be assuming that moral duty is owed to the society at large. To be consistent, she should not only refuse to continue with the project, but actively protest the agency's involvement with clients promoting products to children.

If her trouble is merely the device of the fantasy figure, then she could still refuse further participation, or at least attempt to persuade agency strategists to take another approach. Here moral duty is seen to be owed to society in some cases, but Cynthia could presumably operate comfortably with other approaches to the same audience.

If she simply wishes to abandon the project for the moment and thereby postpone her ethical confrontation, then Cynthia would be asserting that moral duty is owed to herself, based solely on the quandaries of this particular situation. (All of these choices do, of course, pose questions concerning the reactions of her employer to her request for withdrawal.)

Cynthia follows none of these alternatives. Rather, she continues with the project, somewhat troubled as she moves ahead. The ethical issue is left undefined, with an unfocused allegiance to her job and, indirectly, to her firm and client.

Thinking through the ethical dimensions of complex situations requires reflection. Lacking that, the routine of standard professional expectation frequently prevails as the alternative of least difficulty, in the short run at least.

28. Some Families Hear "No" Too Often

Stan Clark had expected a routine evening. As the program director of a network outlet in a middle-sized midwestern city, he always had his ear to the ground for any rumbles of discontent that might become serious during the FCC license renewal cycle. So the invitation to speak to a local Parents Teachers Association (PTA) on the subject "Children and Television" hardly seemed threatening. He anticipated the usual complaints about kids logging more time watching television than studying. He would agree, and suggest, lightly, that this was a problem we all faced.

Teachers, and some activists who always seem to show up at these things, would suggest that the quality of most programming available for children is quite low. This Stan could not dismiss so lightly. There was a dearth of children's programming that approached the capability of the medium and of the talented people associated with it. The so-called kid-vid of Saturday and Sunday mornings was populated by recycled comic book heroes or their clones moving through unimaginative plots by means of production-line animation. Virtually nothing original was shown during after-school hours; Stan's own station offered a daily diet of "Batman," "Gilligan's Island," and "The Brady Bunch."

But Stan would argue there are bright spots too. His network was now carrying occasional prime-time specials for children. And, of course, there is Disney. If all else failed, Stan could wring another drop of juice from the economics of television—expensive time, subsidized by advertisers at no direct cost to the viewers, and so on. No one except the lunatic fringe seriously wanted to cut back on the total hours of television available. Given that, there was always room for negotiation. All things considered, perhaps the innocuous kiddie comedies, for all their lightheadedness, filled the time frame as well as anyone could hope at the present time.

Stan's speech went according to pattern until he opened the floor to questions. What happened then was something his administrative position and socio-economic background had not prepared him for—a cry of anguish from the inner city.

Perhaps it was the time of the year—early December—but a large part of the audience came alive with the question: "Can't you do anything about the stuff our kids see advertised? The ads drive me nuts!"

Before he could give the usual response about parent-child interaction and the like, another parent sounded off: "That's right. My kids watch TV as much as anybody else's, and they see all these wonderful toys and expensive snacks and they bug us." "Yeah," came another protest, "and when they get to school, they hear their friends talking about the same things. But there's one big difference. Their friends will probably get those toys; our kids won't."

"You know how much some of that stuff costs? Those electronic games and cars and Star Wars dolls? Sorry, friend, but we're on welfare and there's no way I can buy that stuff. But that's what the kids want because they saw it all on TV. Do you know how that makes me feel?"

"Damn right!" yelled another frustrated parent. "I work, and when my little ones get home I want them to stay in the house. So they watch TV. And they get a *big* dose of what the kids on the tube are playing with and eating. Hell, my kids are human. Why shouldn't they want it all? And I'll tell you, brother, I get damned tired playing the heavy."

Stan was getting uncomfortable. Finally he responded. "You folks are really asking for a way to prevent some advertisers from reaching into your homes. Obviously that's not possible, unless advertisers totally withdraw from children's programming. And if that's what you want, you'll also get a drastic cutback in the time devoted to children's programming and less production quality of what little might still be offered."

The audience obviously did not like that alternative. With television viewing in low-income households consistently higher than in the affluent, the frustration was deep seated. Stan tried to end on an up note: "I hear what you're saying. The system isn't perfect, but given the way it's paid for, it seems to work out reasonably well most of the time."

"That may be," a woman said as Stan sat down, "but it wears you down saying 'no' so often. And some of us have to say it a lot more than others."

When this case was shown to a senior advertising executive, he commented, "Is there an answer to this question?" His point is well taken.

Most observers see something harmful here, but what can be done about it? What is the source of the wrong?

Is it Stan Clark's station? Probably not. His is a network affiliate and carries a high percentage of network programming and network advertising. The children's programming provided by the network is at least slick and professional. Judged by the ratings, the kids seem to like it. As for "Batman," "Gilligan's Island" and the like, kids watch them. If Stan's station dropped those shows in favor of more elevated fare, one of his competitors would probably snatch them up and win over the viewers for his advertisers.

Is it the advertisers? Most companies operate on the assumptions of the free market system: I take actions in my own economic self-interest and, by the very nature of the system, end up satisfying the needs of others. The system prompts the advertiser to seek programs that attract the largest audience, the largest market. By advertising on that program, he is also supporting entertainment demonstrably valued by the children.

Are the parents to blame? Certainly they could forbid children to watch certain kinds of programming, and most parents do. But the problem here is not directly the programming, but the advertising. Short of saying, "Watch the show but not the commercials," parents are left with allowing exposure to the public television channel (if the community has one) or the Draconian measure of throwing out the baby with the bath water by ruling out television altogether. Given the importance of television in American life, particularly as a baby sitter in a home with working parent(s), the latter hardly seems a palatable solution.

Where are the villains, the guys in the black hats? The parents are crying out at one result of the television system—the continuing stimulation of their children with messages for products beyond the parents' financial capacity. Yet at the same time they register support for the programming underwritten by the advertising. They do not want to let the salesman into the house to tantalize their children, yet this salesman also entertains, occasionally enlightens, and quite often provides a needed babysitting service.

Stan Clark acknowledges that the complaints are legitimate, but he is a card-carrying member of the system. His response ("It seems to work out reasonably well for anyone most of the time") is pure utilitarianism (the greatest good for the greatest number) which largely underlies capitalist economics and the system of commercial television in this country.

Can an equitable solution be found within this system? One remote possibility—following the perspective of John Rawls—is to reconceive the greatest number to better account for minority rights through the public airwaves. The elderly, for example, should not be ignored simply because they represent a less viable market than younger, more affluent viewers. (It is no coincidence that perhaps the only regularly scheduled national television program for the elderly is on public television—"Over Easy.") In relation to children, this could mean conceiving of her or him as something more than a potential consumer. Non-sponsored programming could be tried and some measure of consumer education could be implemented as an act of social responsibility. Thus, if kids were exposed to the tantalizing promises of advertising, they could learn to be more wary of the intent of advertising per se as well as more informed about the costs involved.

A more radical approach was suggested by Action for Children's Television. The networks, they suggested, ought to conceive of children's programming as part of their public service requirements, part of the reasonable price to pay for access to the people's airwaves. Children's programming would carry *no* commercials.

As Stan Clark drove home that night he admitted that the commercial system basically presumes a duty to advertisers. To change that—to alter the priorities so that preeminent obligation is to an extremely variegated public—would severely wrench the rules that currently govern the game. And it is, Stan reminded himself, a game that most enjoy now. Perhaps another system (say, cable television) will provide a solution.

In the meantime, he saw the utilitarian rationale as workable, enduring. Or is it, perhaps, inevitably flawed, as Mill warned, by the "tyranny of the majority"?

29. You May Be Getting Better, but You're Also Getting Older

Clairol certainly had not been trying to put down the elderly with their eminently successful hair coloring theme ("You're not getting older; you're getting better"), but now they found it being used as a classic example of the advertising business's presumed insensitivity to the postPepsi generation. Is it not possible, the representatives of yet another abused minority protested, that one could get older *and* better, not to mention the asinine denial of the aging process per se. You're not getting older? Ha! Ten out of ten do.

And now the pressure had come to Keith Benson's office in the presence of two representatives from the Gray Panthers, the most visible and effective of the growing number of pressure groups for the elderly. Keith's agency handled some products directed to older demographic segments—a dental cleanser and an insurance company that offered a "Golden 50" plan—but his visitors' concerns were more pervasive.

In the first area there was little room for disagreement. The Panthers wanted more recognition of the elderly, roughly those 55 and above, as a sizable, affluent, and important consumer market. No argument there. Keith assured them the population's demographic profile made the older segment's market potential crystal clear. Indeed, it will become even more pronounced in years to come as the children of the baby boom move into the upper age segments. Keith's agency simply found it good business to recommend ways that their clients could make money. And one obvious strategy was marketing existing products to older Americans, as well as urging companies to consider natural extensions of their lines, as the more far-sighted cosmetic companies were starting to do, following the leads of successful ventures from firms such as Gerber and Wrigley.

But the second area of concern was on considerably softer ground. The Panthers were urging a full-blown crusade on the part of the advertising business to arrest the predominently unfavorable depiction of the elderly in both the print and broadcast advertising of national advertisers, and to replace that depiction with one more clearly representing the true vitality and varied life styles of today's senior citizens.

"Today's marketers," they argued, "*must* abandon the stereotype of the elderly as poor, feeble, occasionally quaint rejects in wigs and orthopedic shoes. It not only distorts others' views of older people, it troubles many of the elderly themselves. Good lord, our society worships at the shrine of youth so slavishly that it's hard to find positive images for an older person. How many know that Franklin was 70 when he helped draft the Declaration of Independence? Or that Verdi composed 'Falstaff' at 80? Titian did his finest painting shortly before he died at 100."[1]

Advertising was only one target of their concerns. They also voiced strong objection to a great deal of television programming, films, popular music, comic strips, and popular fiction. But advertising is pervasive, they reasoned, and influential, and reachable (the number of advertising agencies accounting for a substantial percentage of television advertising is less than a hundred). Advertising must, they contended, stop flaunting youth as the be-all and end-all of life. Ads pledging youth, youthful appearance, and the energy to act youthfully are an insult to the diversity of human experience in general and an affront to a sizable population segment in particular. Older people should be shown on television as a normal part of the population in rough proportion to their real numbers.

The Panthers also pointed out that older people used in television ads are overwhelmingly men. Yet there are substantially more older women. Advertising must begin, wherever and however possible, to erode the terrible burden society has placed on the older woman to be more accountable than men for the physical aging process. And, whenever possible, ads must stop depicting the elderly as meddlesome, out of touch, or obsessed with ailments.

There were other musts, but this was the thrust. It is hard to be old in this society, and advertising seems to be hurting rather than helping. What actions would Keith's agency take: A pledge? A press conference announcing support? A memo to its clients?

Keith's response was artful. He would strongly advocate that the agency contact the National Advertising Review Board, the business's most successful self-regulatory body, and suggest that they convene a renewed consulting panel on advertising and the elderly in the pattern of the "Advertising and Women" effort of 1975. Further, he would insist that the panel's report include a compilation of evidence to determine the extent of misrepresentation, and conclude with a set of recommendations for remedy.

His visitors would emerge with a promise of action that they could, in turn, report with some pride back to the movement's directors. Keith would not, however, have committed the agency or its clients to any specific sets of action other than a communication to an institutionalized regulatory unit.

It was not that Keith disagreed with what he had heard. It was simply that any unilateral concessions would be too confining. Advertising was, after all, a form of persuasive communication. Persuasion was far more an art than a science, and those who prepared the messages should be given the widest possible latitude to express a message in the client's best interest. If his agency did not, others would. Advertising simply cannot be produced by a formula. Besides, what of the other special interests: blacks, women, Hispanics, and homosexuals? They had their gripes and would like their expectations met too.

In general, he felt, the market would take care of any serious abuses. The offended simply would not buy. And, as women and the elderly and blacks as a whole really change, advertising will change too. It has to, to serve the best interests of all involved. In the meantime, Keith reasoned, let the regulatory apparatus handle the guidelines. We can deal with their rules as they come across our desks.

Advertising and its relationship to stereotyping has been given prominence with the rise of vocal special interest groups in the 1960s. Concerns have focused on women and minorities, more recently on the elderly. Basically, the contention is that advertising has negative effects on both social and self-images by either creating unfavorable stereotypes (the cleanliness-obsessed housewife) or by reinforcing existing stereotypes (the quaint oldster).

Keith Benson found little trouble dealing with his visitors' first concern, that of recognizing the elderly as a market. In reply he was able to fall back on the comfortable utilitarian premise that the greatest good for the greatest number was in fact being served when his agency and its clients actively pursued older citizens as special consuming targets. In this case what made good economic sense happened, in the bargain, to be defensible by a standard ethical principle.

The second issue was less easily solved. By arguing that the agency become active in helping older citizens achieve positive self-images, the Grey Panthers were going well beyond expediency. On the one hand, they would alter one of marketing's most precious underpinnings: that "youth" sells, not only to the young, but to the majority of people who wish to identify with the young. Should the agency recommend to its clients a course of action that, given contemporary societal values, seems destined to be economically unproductive? Keith had pointed out that advertising tends to follow markets, and as the so-called baby boomers continue to age, marketers will cater to them simply because of their numbers. But such a reply had not appeased Keith's visitors, who were concerned with existing marketing and advertising priorities.

Then there was the matter of how the elderly are depicted in advertisements. Here the spokesmen called for more positive images. Their emphasis was on positive images, even though they claimed to want to see the elderly depicted as they really are. This latter point could not have been their true desire. For to give an accurate description of the elderly would involve some negative images simply because of the varieties of human physiological and psychological forms. Some elderly persons do suffer illness and are feeble. Keith's visitors should have been more precise and less simplistic.

Yet the base of the Panthers' concern is touching and real. "It's hard to be old in this society, and advertising is hurting rather than helping," they claimed. Rather than arguing a well reasoned set of particulars with clearly defined solutions, the two representatives were voicing a heartfelt cry for help.

Keith was no more precise than they. He seemed unconvinced that there really was a problem, and chose to lean on the market structure as an early warning system. If there was a problem, he presumed the market would signal it through consumer indifference at the cash register. The market responds to economic stimuli. Thus, if the elderly were not being properly addressed as consumers, they would protest through purchase decisions. But this solution avoids the more pressing problems of stereotyping. A great deal of stereotyping of the aged takes place in advertisements aimed at younger population segments. For example, past concern has been the depiction of "Gramps" in the Country Time Lemonade commercials. Clearly this product was not targeted to the elderly, hence they could not express disapproval through traditional market mechanisms.

Keith's overt solution was to pass the ethical question to an institution one level above his agency. By turning to the National Advertising Review Board (NARB), he was postponing the issue while supposedly resolving the immediate confrontation. Even if the NARB did issue corrective guidelines, Keith assumed that advertising is enough of an art to provide room for tactics that would still be in the best interests of the client, given the highly competitive nature of the business.

The Panthers offered the agency no reward for honoring their advice other than the good conscience that comes from doing right. Keith, committed to his agency's current message performance, and desirous of maintaining creative flexibility, relocated responsibility away from his agency and its clients, a move inspired more by expediency than principle.

Could more have been done? If Keith were to find himself behind Rawl's veil of ignorance, not knowing whether he would emerge an advertising executive or an elderly citizen, what would he choose? Where would the buck stop then?

30. The Market Illiterate

Hostile speakers have regularly appeared on the program of the American Association of Advertising Agencies (AAAA). Throughout the years, the advertising business has been remarkably open to the views of those critical of its activities. During the 1970s, various public-interest and government speakers had their hour at the forum, not to mention critics from within such as the late Howard Gossage, an iconoclast of the first order. The business's principal trade paper, *Advertising Age*, has consistently editorialized with candor and opened its pages to dissenting positions.

This address, by a Congressman from Michigan, however, was unusually sweeping and poignant, getting to the very heart of advertising as a communication form.

Advertising owes a special obligation to tens of thousands of Americans who are unrepresented by any special interest group. Call them the "market illiterate," if you will. They are generally low in income, low in education, and extraordinarily naive about the ways of the market. As a result they are far more trustful than others in the most accessible form of market communication—advertising. Yet they have a lower tolerance for shopping error because of marginal or sub-marginal incomes.

Consider this:
- Those with lower incomes are more likely to buy national brands—almost always more expensive.
- Alternative forms of information, such as *Consumer Reports*, are overwhelmingly used by those who least need it—the market sophisticates.
- Working market knowledge, such as the parity of many soaps, beers, detergents, shampoos, paper products and the like, is extremely limited among low-income shoppers.
- The potential for abuse is rampant in the 'medicine show' of off-the-shelf drugs and other health-related products, due to this population's tendency toward self medication.
- The nutritional habits of this segment are generally poor and the potential for abuse in advertising is high. Lacking even elementary nutritional knowledge in many cases, these consumers, even if motivated, have no dependable way of learning the sugar and salt content of heavily advertised products.

You are all well aware of this. Yet, some of you react like the employee of an agency known to all of you: "I can appeal to uneducated consumers with possible unnecessary product appeals. Uneducated, lower-income consumers, for example, are 'easy sales' for laxatives and the like."

The advertising business is not wholly insensitive. It has opened its meetings to voices such as mine, and individuals in the business have donated their talents as well as media space and time to countless meritorious causes. Yet who would deny that the dominant ethic of the business is not one of social responsibility, but rather a pecuniary philosophy? What praise is there in alerting Americans to the dangers of high blood pressure when all but the most market wise will be unable to learn the sodium content of the foods portrayed in alluring ads? What are the consequences to these market illiterates of the normal practice of excluding potentially negative (but arguably relevant) information?

Minutes later the speech concluded. The audience of account executives, copy writers, art directors, television producers, media buyers, and researchers was left to ponder the parting challenge:

What is *your* obligation to the 'market illiterate'? What decisions, what actions, can *you* take *every day* to assure the elevation of this significant group from exploited markets to meaningful participants in the system you cherish? The need is real. The obligation—at least in part—is yours.

Since the first organized outcries against abuse early in this century, the advertising business has attempted, with great or little success, to consider social responsibility as part of its milieu. On the more formalistic level, the result has been a host of codes, advisory papers, and the like. On the work-a-day level there may simply be a pulling of the punches, particularly in the creation of advertising messages. Whether or not this loose patchwork of formal and informal safeguards has been adequate depends on where you look, who you ask, and what is defined as the central problem.

In this case the problem is a fundamental one indeed. Fundamental in the sense that the speaker is, however disarmingly, striking at the very heart of the advertising process—the nature of biased communication. Consider his charge that some out there, lacking formal and functional education, are ill equipped to participate intelligently in the market. When lack of knowledge is coupled with low buying power, the possibility of painful purchasing mistakes becomes quite high. And advertising can be the seducer.

What is advertising's responsibility compared with that of other relevant institutions such as the schools or community organizations, both of which could also provide some form of market education?

What action is the speaker recommending? Does he want the AAAA to take a stand on the matter? If so, what? Or is the problem a matter of individual responsibility? If so, are conscientious individuals adequate for the dimensions of the problem?

The speaker failed to deal with these and other relevant issues, and may have done his cause a disservice. The audience, left with an uneasy and unfocused sense of guilt, and lacking a structured call to the barricades, could shrug off the issue as something somebody ought to deal with—that is, it is simply too pervasive for one individual's actions to make a difference.

Advertising, in keeping with the ethos of the market system, is self-interested communication. Given the assumptions of self-interest, the presumed rationality of man, and a sufficient number of buyers and sellers so that market power is diffused, it is philosophically consistent for sellers to offer persuasive communications in their own behalf. Thus, puffery, the use of fanciful themes, and selective presentation of factual material, are considered justifiable.

All of the cases in this chapter have challenged that set of assumptions in relation to particular market segments: children, the poor, the elderly, and, now, the market illiterate. In relation to the latter, what could advertising practitioners do to "assure the elevation of this significant group from exploited markets to meaningful participants"?

If we assume that one-sided communications will collide in a marketplace of ideas and that deliberate and calculating humans will make the wisest decision among alternatives, well and good. Lacking that, it must be assumed that individuals are not getting enough information to make intelligent choices, or simply are not capable of sorting through the conflicting claims, no matter how completely presented, to make a wise decision.

The latter case builds an argument for government intervention. If it were found that no matter what advertisers do, individuals still buy high priced over-the-counter drugs that are really nothing but aspirin, then perhaps the government should forbid their sale. This is a hotly contested question among consumerists, various special interest groups, government, and the business community. The approach is fraught with uncertainties, due in part to the difficulty of gathering conclusive evidence, not to mention the over-riding theoretical issue of individual freedom of choice.

In the former area of proper information, advertising comes most directly into play. To alleviate the problems outlined by the speaker, advertisers would need to supply more information *in their own advertising* than they are now doing. Would it be proper for Anacin to reveal that its extra ingredient is caffein? Should the producers of compact cars note in the advertising the danger of injury in the event of crash? Should Jello inform that it is more than 80 percent sugar?[2] If this information is not now coming out through the natural flow of market forces, and if it is relevant to wise purchasing decisions, then it presumably should be made available in some manner. But is it asking too much of an advertiser's working ethics to disclose potentially negative information about his or her product or service for some hazy ideal of serving some undefined segment of a generally complacent consuming public?

Most advertisers assume that it is right to attempt to persuade. Furthermore, they assume that successful persuasion will be financially rewarding, and take it as a vote of confidence by the consumer as well. In short, successful persuasion is seen as socially beneficial.

But what of those whom the speaker claims are victimized by this presumably symbiotic relationship? Lacking a clear call for action from the congressman, the practitioners in the audience could be excused for assuming that the problem is best handled by institutions—churches or schools or community groups—whose ethical concerns identify specifically with the disenfranchised.

Advertising by its nature is biased communication. To alter its form to serve the minority better would likely dilute its effectiveness to both the self-seeking seller as well as to the materialistic majority who are willingly seduced by the promises and perils of consumer abundance. So speaks the utilitarian. But what of those who find themselves between the cracks of the greatest good for the greatest number? Whose constituency are they?

Notes

1. Borrowed from *Grey Matter*, Grey Advertising, Inc., 1978, No. 1.
2. As discussed in "Too Much Sugar?" *Consumer Reports*, March 1978, p. 139.

Chapter Seven

What to Advertise

As a way to approach the cases in the area of advertising content, consider three premises:

1. Because of an operating world view that casts doubt on the deliberate and calculating nature of individual decision making, advertising content emerges as an area of concern. That is, if we all believed that people can, in fact, best make up their own minds about the products and services they want, we would not be concerned about their being objects of advertising's persuasive appeals.
2. Given the nature of advertising as a potentially powerful form of mass persuasion, individuals, groups, and organizations will desire to use it on behalf of their products, services, and ideas.
3. The real dilemmas in this area arise because of the alleged effect of advertising content on the thinking and/or behavior of individuals. But, due to the complex stimulus field in which advertising operates, there is often no clearcut proof of either the presence or the absence of these effects.

Our approach to case studies here also requires that we recognize certain regulatory structures already in place. The following serve to a greater or lesser degree as gatekeepers:

Government. Federal, state, and local governments regulate the advertising of some types of products and services. For example, certain federal regulations deal with the advertising of liquor, particular types of drugs and firearms, in addition to the well-known ban on cigarette advertising in the broadcast media. Until recently some states prohibited the advertising of prescription drug prices and optometric services.

Media. Regulation occurs on two levels here. The first is represented by media-wide codes such as that of the National Association of Broadcasters, which prohibits the advertising of such items as liquor and birth control devices. The second level consists of the standards of particular media vehicles: the acceptance criteria of CBS, NBC, *The New Yorker, The Los Angeles Times*, and so forth. It can be contended that this is the key pressure area concerning what is advertised. Simply stated, if a media vehicle assents or demurs, advertising opportunities are affected accordingly.

Individual enterprises. Particular advertisers and agencies take stands about what should be advertised. For example, Kraft, Procter and Gamble, and several other large advertisers have adopted guidelines concerning the types of television programming in which their advertising will appear, generally "family fare" rather than excessively violent or sexually-oriented programs. (Pressure groups such as Coalition for Better Television have been very active in this area.) Also, some advertising agencies refuse to accept certain types of accounts, most commonly politicians and cigarettes, although the majority are not so discriminating.

Against this backdrop, there is ample opportunity for complex ethical confrontation. In some cases the issue concerns the advertising of a subject per se, in others whether a particular medium or vehicle provides an appropriate forum. In the absence of clear cause-and-effect facts, heat is often generated by the fires of passionate conviction, colliding with equally intense economic interest, and, as we shall see, different assumptions about nothing less fundamental than human nature.

31. A Magazine and Its Audience

Sue Chord had recently accepted the position of assistant advertising manager with one of the country's leading magazines for the liberated woman. She was justifiably proud. Her new employer was several cuts above the *Cosmopolitan* vision of the modern woman as a sexually obsessed, narcissistic, clothes and recreation zealot. *Woman*, in contrast, prided itself on sensitivity to the triumphs and tragedies of American women through thoughtful editorial reporting ranging from case histories to provocative interviews, complex features, and a smattering of well-balanced self-help articles. It was, in short, a magazine worthy of the name, and Sue was happy to be on board.

Woman, she knew, was also extremely popular with a wide range of advertisers interested in reaching the magazine's generally well-educated audience—the people called opinion leaders by media buyers. She had not, however, realized quite how much advertising was carried in a particular product category, cigarettes.

The pages were festooned with colorful ads extolling the virtures of brands aimed directly at the modern woman. All were screened by the magazine's standing ban against sexist ads, but there were plenty nonetheless—many using women models, all extolling their taste, tar and nicotine content (low, of course), and/or a provocative lifestyle.

Now beginning to feel a part of the publication's editorial mission, Sue found their presence troubling. She was a nonsmoker, but recognized the rights of others to choose for themselves. What troubled her was the seeming incongruity between the careful and respectful treatment of women in the editorial pages and the seeming disregard for their well-being in the advertising material. Of course there are differences in tastes, and the kinds of products and services individuals prefer. She recognized that. However, in her judgment there was no longer any reasonable doubt about the hazards of smoking in general, and particularly for women. Consider:

- Per capita cigarette smoking of women has been rising.
- Advertisers are increasingly singling out women as a market.
- Women have now achieved virtual equality in a formerly male dominated area—lung cancer.
- In addition to its linkage with gastric ulcers, chronic bronchitis, emphysema, and heart disease, it is now known that smoking may cause hazards for unborn children.

Cigarettes, Sue felt, should perhaps not be advertised at all, but certainly not in *Woman*. To do so was simply inconsistent. If the magazine staff chooses editorial material with the goal of helping modern women live more fulfilling lives, should they advertise products—particularly in this product category of clear-cut danger—that work contrary to the best interests of these same women?

It was not a matter of not trusting the readers—as if they might be

lured into smoking by the ads—but rather of bringing the caring attitude from the editorial pages over to the advertising. Sue's approach
was, if readers want to smoke, okay, but this magazine should not
promote habits that have been *proven* harmful. Such a policy seemed
reasonable enough to her. Was she the only one who thought so?

Sue approached the advertising manager with her observations. She
was told that cigarette advertising constituted a significant part of
Woman's advertising revenue that in turn helped finance the vigorous
editorial side she found so attractive; that cigarettes are still legally
sold in this country and can be legally advertised in the print media;
and that *Woman*'s readers are wise enough to make their own
decisions.

During the next six months Sue's dilemma became more and more
discomforting. Cigarette advertising directed solely at women was increasingly plentiful, and *Woman* was a marvelously efficient, even
prestigious, vehicle. Meanwhile the press—though not necessarily
Woman—carried new studies on the health-threatening effects of
cigarettes. Eventually, she resigned.

On the surface, Sue's ethical dilemma may seem relatively straightforward—an act of personal defiance against what she perceived as an unconscionable practice. But the issues here may be more subtle.

What is her basic objection? She apparently is not against the advertising of cigarettes per se. Rather, she claims that it is the apparent incongruity between the editorial dimensions of the magazine, which
seem to demonstrate a care and responsibility for its readers, and what
she sees as the callous indifference to that responsibility when potentially harmful products are advertised. Sue presumably recognizes the
rights of intelligent individuals to decide about smoking. But if she
really has faith in the readers to make their own choices, why is she upset about the potential effect of the advertising material?

There is no disagreement between Sue and the advertising manager
about the facts of the case. First, the presence of large amounts of
cigarette advertising is acknowledged, as is its profitability. Second, the
manager does not debate the potential dangers of smoking. Here is a
genuine ethical conflict, not merely a disagreement about the interpretation of facts.

One way of sharpening the issue is to see it as a disagreement about
consequences. Sue, despite her disclaimer, does seem concerned about
the types of choices the readers will make as a result of exposure to the

cigarette advertising. She assumes they will be harmful. The magazine staff, by contrast, seems indifferent to the effects of the cigarette advertising directly, but rather sees it as instrumental to other beneficial consequences, such as funding significant material.

To Sue, the greatest good to the greatest number is served by eliminating cigarette advertising from the magazine. Implicit in this assumption seems to be a lack of faith in the decision-making power of the readers. For the magazine staff, the greatest good for the greatest number is achieved through accepting the advertising of legal products and using the revenue to produce a high quality editorial product. Implicit in this assumption seems to be a belief that individual decision making should not be guided—at least in relation to advertising content.

Sue may find it difficult to justify her position on the grounds of the greatest good for the greatest number, given (a) the indifference of the magazine staff to her concern, and (b) the apparent lack of protest from the readers. Ultimately her resignation can be seen as an act of personal relativism; that is, I am protesting a practice that is wrong because I say it is wrong.

The magazine, on the other hand, is apparently operating in a split-level ethical house. On the editorial level there is concern for what is best for its readers, with certain normative values implicit. Yet, on the advertising level, guidance is left entirely to the individual readers.

Sue forced an ethical dilemma for herself by noting that the concept of what was right in her area of concern, advertising, was incongruous with the concept of "right" on the editorial side. Confronted, however, the rationale that if advertising abuses existed they would be brought to the fore by troubled readers, she could find little ethical support other than her personal belief in the wrongness of the system. And, given the apparent strength of that belief, she acted consistently.

Meanwhile, the publication continues to function with coexisting credos of (a) responsibility (editorial), and (b) laissez faire (advertising). The magazine presumes this to be sufficient justification for the promotion of a controversial product. This split-level ethic is not uncommon in the media. Neither, then, are the ethical questions that ensue.

32. A Question of Responsibility

The citizen's group was angry, aroused from dormancy by one sudden event and the continuance of others. The first was the abduction and subsequent sexual abuse of an elementary school child. The second was the recurring incidents of rape in the community, especially on the college campus. Now the group was here at the town's only evening newspaper to demand an end to the advertising of X-rated films.

Their position was clear. The frequency of sex-related crimes against women and children had risen appallingly in recent years, and the increased permissiveness of our society provided the climate for that malignant growth. The group was here zeroing in on one very visible part of the larger morass—the advertising of X-rated films for the town's two porn theatres. From recent issues of the newspaper the group produced ads for such films as: *Randy the Electric Lady, Little Me and Miss Maria, Little More Than Love,* and *Sexteen.* Even the recent R-rated *Humanoids From the Deep* was promoted with the line, "They Came With Only One Mission—To Mate With Human Women."

These films and their ilk, the group contended, promote a climate in which women are objectified, regarded as objects to be used and abused. They portray antifemale behavior, and by offering the films as legitimate entertainment choices, the paper was sanctioning them and their potential results. Freedom of speech, the group noted, does not give a person the right to yell "Fire" in a crowded theatre. Neither does freedom of the press give a paper the right to throw gasoline on an already open social flame.

The newspaper staff responded. Where does one draw the line? What about theatrical plays? (*Oh! Calcutta!* was recently in town with a road company.) Books? Many best sellers that are advertised and publicized rely on openly sexual themes. How about news stories, or television programs such as the raunchy "Dynasty"? Are they not suggestive as well?

Would not the banning of X-rated film ads give readers a narrower view of what's going on in their community—warts and all? Then of course there is the simple fact that porn houses and porn shops stay in business because citizens of this town support them. Are all these citizens—and there are a goodly number from all social strata—to be deprived of an information source about a legal business?

The newspaper already refuses to publish sexually explicit photos or copy. These ads go back to the distributors for alterations. And the financial loss, should the paper ban this type of advertising, is, for once, not a key factor. A recent edition contained seven column inches of X-rated theatre ads out of a total of 3,200. The loss would be minimal, especially for a financially secure paper such as this. (The New York *Times,* on the other hand, dropped ads for porn houses in 1977 at an estimated annual loss of $750,000.)

The meeting ended with the newspaper reaffirming its advertising screening policy, and vowing to continue to cooperate in any way they could with community groups such as this and the more institutionalized Women Against Rape. They would also continue to publicize the number of the Rape Hot Line and pursue their consistent editorializing in support of preventive and punitive measures. The paper would not, however, eliminate the problematic ads.

Should pornographic films be advertised? Obviously the citizens' group felt they should not—at least not in this town and in this paper. The newspaper representatives, however, supported the practice.

Both are concerned about consequences. The citizens' group deplores the acts of sexual violence in their community. The newspaper is also socially concerned, both in its editorial voice as well as in cooperating with various police and community efforts to deal with the problem. Where, then, does the dispute arise?

At one level it could be seen as a simple disagreement about facts. The citizen's group contends that the advertising of pornographic films is linked with sexual violence and the newspaper does not. But the facts here are extremely vague. Acts of violence have been committed. Advertising of pornographic films has occurred. These are facts. The citizens' group is quite willing to move from this correlation to causation; the newspaper is not. Even at the highest levels of scientific inquiry there is honest disagreement about the effects of pornography on individuals. Small wonder, then, that these two local combatants seem locked in confrontation on essentially ethical, rather than factual, grounds. And what do they contend?

The citizens' group feels that the newspaper is ethically bound to eliminate the stimulation caused by the advertising of pornographic movies. It apparently operates from the assumption that the presence of these materials will lead to acts that would not be committed in their absence. Indeed, the very presence of this type of advertising in the town's only newspaper may be seen as sanctioning the sexually provocative content of the ads, and, subsequently, the films. Again, there is apparently no evidence here beyond common sense observation and strong conviction.

Are the citizens acting in an ethically consistent manner? Why are they concerned with the advertising of the films rather than the films themselves?[1] Presumably, if the advertising were stopped, the films would still be shown. Are they assuming that individuals who would attend pornographic films and be stimulated to sexual violence by them need the incentive offered by the advertising? It would seem that their consequential reasoning is, at this level, not well focused.

What of the newspaper's charge that there is an abundance of sexually provocative material in our society? Are the citizens equally concerned, and active, with television, books, and plays? If not, why concentrate on the advertising of films? In fairness, if the newspaper is held to be committing a wrong act, should it not be made clear why this act is presumed wrong, either in terms of consequences to the readers or in relation to some formal statement of belief? Should not all impersonal sexual stimulation be considered wrong, regardless of the consequences? The citizens' group, however well meaning, apparently cannot operate on a factual level and yet does not have its ethical arguments particularly well ordered either.

The newspaper is, however, far from uncorrupted. For all its professed concern about responsibility, its cooperation and editorial trumpeting is more in a supportive than a leadership role. There is no mention made of investigative enterprise, creative proposals, or other innovative steps. The paper merely views with alarm and opens its arms of cooperation. Again, we see the emergence of the assumptions of laissez-faire liberalism; that is, if the service is legal, information should be supplied about it so that individuals can exercise their own judgments and send messages back through the system by their actions. Therefore, if it works, it must be okay.

But can the presumed self-adjusting system be as readily defended if it works for a criminal element as well as the more general population? Also, if the paper wishes to stand on the need for market information, would not a mere listing of the films, rather than display advertising with provocative graphics and illustrations (no matter how altered prior to publication), suffice? Would this not seem a reasonable compromise with the concern of the citizens' group, especially in a factually ambiguous arena? (In fact several major urban papers follow exactly this policy.)

Then there is the matter of the burden of proof. The newspaper is saying, "Prove that these ads are linked to the problem." But could not the citizens' group respond, "As the town's only newspaper you prove they're not. Our common sense suggests they are."

Given the enormous difficulties of establishing causal linkages under these circumstances, the situation seemed to become a contest of imprecise ethical assuptions concerning responsibility. The Citizens' Group felt the newspaper was being irresponsible by publishing the ads; the newspaper felt they were performing a responsible act within their already imposed limits.

But, as alluded to earlier, was there not a compromise that both overlooked in their desire for confrontation? A simple listing of the film offerings would seem to satisfy the newspaper's defense of the practice in terms of market information and reader decision making, while eliminating probably the most provocative elements for the citizens' group. Lacking better articulated ethical positions on both parts, this could represent a shaky golden mean in this situation. At least until another interested party's voice is raised—that of the theatre owners.

33. The Best of Good Taste and Discretion

- The first commercial showed a group of wholesome young men spurred on to heroic athletic achievement by the promise of a particular light beer for the winners.
- The next depicted several individuals known to the audience as former professional athletes. They extolled the virtues of a beer while enjoying an apparently boisterous dose of male camaraderie.
- Another follows a group of lifeguards undergoing rigorous lifeboat drills. Their strained faces are shown in closeup and their triumph over the stopwatch is duly celebrated at the local bar.
- Idyllic mountain streams and snow-capped peaks provide the prominent visuals to this celebration of the great outdoors. The beer is associated with all of this. (Another is attested to have been brewed in "God's Country.")
- The scene is a party of young couples, all having the very best of times. The presence of the sponsor's beer, and their obvious association with it, seems at least correlative, if not causal.

Finally, after a dozen more of this ilk, there is the inevitable American cowboy—independent, stalwart, face lined by weather, and rugged in body and spirit. He, too, ends his working day with a round or two at the nearest tavern.

The members of the Television Code Review Board of the National Association of Broadcasters knew what would follow. And it did. The speaker from the National Association Against Alcohol Abuse minced no words.

I'm sorry we don't have more time, ladies and gentlemen, but that's a fair sample taken from the airways during prime time and highly popular sports broadcasts. Now, I submit to you that *all* of these fall within the stipulations of the Television Code you administer. To review: "Advertising of beer and wine is acceptable only when presented in the best of good taste and discretion." Further, your "Interpretation No. 4" states that "This requires that commercials involving beer and wine avoid any representation of on-camera drinking."

Now, I submit to you that these guidelines are simply not adequate given the magnitude of the problem of alcoholism in the United States in general and among teenagers in particular. Who are we trying to kid? Who among the viewing public would not have *some* desire to emulate those attractive social situations, the savoir-faire, the exuberance for life, the virile and beautiful people? Is it good taste to associate such people, places and promises with the intake of alcoholic beverages? Is it the better part of discretion to know that teenagers and even younger children form a major part of the audience during the times these messages are shown? And, as for your Interpretation No. 4 against on-camera drinking, this is hypocrisy of the highest order. The characters in many regular television programs seem to find alcohol an essential part of their daily existence. Are actors in the commercials not actually drinking beer going to suggest that viewers use caution? Nonsense!

I will spare you the recitation of the statistics on alcoholism in this country. Suffice it to say the cost in human and material terms is appalling. And it's getting worse, particularly among young people. Surely the advertising of beer on television is not the only factor involved. But it is *a* factor! Can you deny the appeal of these commercials so skillfully conceived and artfully executed? Can you deny that the dominant impression given in these ads is that the good life is associated with alcohol?

The time is *now*, ladies and gentlemen, to join many other civilized countries of the world in banning the advertising of all alcoholic beverages on the country's most pervasive and indiscriminate medium—television. Do it *now*, this afternoon. Surely your consciences cannot allow any other choice.

Is this an ethical issue or merely a disagreement about facts? Clearly, the facts of alcohol abuse in this country are beyond dispute. As with many of the other cases in this chapter, however, there is no indisputable evidence linking mass media content directly with social acts. The causative web is simply too complex to allow for clear "The media cause..." statements, except in the rare instances of direct emulation—for example, a particularly graphic act of television violence shortly afterwards executed in the real world in an identical manner.

No action has yet been taken. What, then, are the possible options and their ethical dimensions? The existing policy could be continued. The rationale for this course could involve the following:

- The existing policy is reasonably prudent for a legally available product. There is already a self-imposed ban by the liquor industry on the advertising of liquor and other beverages of high alcoholic content in the broadcast media.
- No models are allowed who appear too young.
- Basically, it is up to individuals to make their own decisions about drinking alcoholic beverages.

This could be interpreted as representing a utilitarian position; that is, the greatest good for the greatest number. By putting heavy reliance upon individual decision making about beer consumption, the code board has, in essence, shifted the burden of concern to the system. Thus, if the existing policy is causing problems we will become aware of it. This necessarily requires a softening of the problem as outlined by the representative of the special interest group, and an implicit reliance on grass roots protest, or the lack of it.

The television advertising of all alcoholic beverages could be banned. The ban would not have the force of law since not all television stations in the country subscribe to the NAB Code. The rationale here could be:

- The present advertising clearly encourages drinking—implicity if not explicity—and given the clear evidence of alcohol abuse, it is important to remove this powerful stimulus.
- The responsibility to the society as a whole, and television's unique place in it, transcends individual decision making, at least as associated with this particular medium, which is, after all, using the public's airwaves.

Here we see a formalist position in the Kantian legacy: regardless of any clear linkage (consequence), it is simply wrong to perpetuate this seductive call to potentially anti-social behavior. Moral responsibility is owed to the society as a whole.

Some sort of a compromise could be adopted. Is this possible? The issue needs sharpening. Is the objection to the potential effect of beer advertising on everyone, or is the real agitation centered around the potential effect on teenagers? If it could be construed to be the latter, perhaps a compromise could be struck whereby beer advertising would be banned in all programs whose audience contains more than a given percentage under 18 years of age. Advertisers would undoubtedly protest, but there are other more selective media available to them. The ethical position in this option could then be seen as an endorsement of both a concern for individual decision making (of those 18 and older) as well as a paternalistic concern for a particular segment of society (those under 18).

By delineating the available options and examining their ethical underpinnings, we can presumably aid our own decision making, either by matching a position with our own existing stand or making a judgment about the best of the options in a particular situation. In the process we not only sharpen the ethical issues, but, perhaps of greatest importance, force an examination of our own ethical stance in the ongoing rules/situation debate.

34. The 30-Second Candidate?

The selling of political candidates via some type of advertising has been around for the better part of this country's political life. But it was really with the successful use of television spots by Dwight Eisenhower in the 1952 campaign that the modern dimensions of the political sell began to take form. (It is said that during the filming of these short and simplistic messages Eisenhower was overheard to murmur, "To think an old soldier should come to this.") Now the use of television and radio spots (usually 30 or 60 seconds in length) is a commonplace in today's political campaigns at the federal, state, and local level.

That bothered Jason Bradley. At 32, a successful copywriter with a large East Coast advertising agency, Jason had been asked if he wished to join the ad hoc agency team that would play a major role in the advertising efforts of a presidential aspirant. The primaries were only a few months away and it seemed likely that the candidate could make it at least to the party convention. Indeed, there was a possibility he could become the party's candidate in the fall elections.

The candidate was well qualified, personable, and with the kind of liberal voting record and inclinations that Jason found personally attractive. Perhaps of greatest importance, he was well heeled financially. The combination seemed to make him close to the ideal type to make effective use of advertising—particularly broadcast advertising—as a political vehicle. Finally, the candidate's past and present media exposure had been solid. He was thus reasonably well known and exquisitely marketable on the national level.

So why not join the group and get on with it? There were certainly no company constraints on Jason. The agency had always been careful to avoid pressuring any of its employees to participate in the promotion of causes (and, to a lesser extent, products and services) in which they personally did not believe. It would, of course, result in a more frantic work schedule than he would normally experience in the already high-charged realms of big-time advertising. Time pressures would be severe; changes in the copy approaches would be frequent due to the thrust and counterthrust of opponents; worse, there would be a multi-layer approval process involving various strategists, technicians, advisors, and hangers-on. Still, it was heady stuff. He would be participating in a major way in the quest for political power, and for a candidate he honestly believed would serve the country well.

The bottom line for him, though, was still what he felt to be the unholy alliance between broadcast advertising and the quest for political office. During his career he had helped scores of clients promote hundreds of products and services on television. Many had succeeded. Some, for a variety of reasons, had not.

Yet the very nature of the advertising dimensions of the medium imposed the same discipline upon all. In 30 or 60 seconds the message had to be simple rather than complex. It needed to strive for high memorability with the aid of striking visual images and/or musical themes. Basically, it had to leave an impression favorable to the advertiser.

People watching television are usually in a passive state. They are not actively seeking information, and, as a result, are not likely to put forth the mental effort to acquire a great deal unless the subject is particularly meaningful to them personally.[2] And, even here, the discipline of time imposes itself. (Stations will not usually sell television time in segments over one minute in length. Longer segments interfere with other programming.)

Now, all of these characteristics of the medium may not seriously interfere with the successful promotion of a beer, cosmetic, soft drink, soap, automobile tire, or bra. But a serious candidate for political office? At the very best the message could concentrate on some aspects of his record—either in the candidate's own words or those spoken by an appropriate high-credibility announcer. And what then of all that is *not* said? The nuances? The complexities of real-world issues, programs, events, compromises?

Many of the accepted forms are beneath contempt. Consider the man in the street. Or the candidate as a man of the people. Or carefully edited campaign appearances with lots of crowd reaction. Or, God forbid, the candidate and his family. The impressions may linger. The substance of intelligent evaluation is almost inevitably eliminated by the form itself.

Of course the candidate would go on without Jason. Of course his opponents would use television, and their use might be more skillful and contribute in some way to his candidate's voice being stilled in the national arena, at least for that year. Jason knew these things, and he regretted them.

But someone somewhere must put his reservations into some form of action, ineffectual though it may seem at the time. Television advertising time, Jason asserted, is simply not a proper forum for political discourse. The stakes are too high, the medium too restricted, and the influence on an often passive public too potentially compelling.

Let it be, he concluded, one small act of protest; not against the candidates, but against the promotional system upon which so much of their political success has come to rely.

The decision not to join the agency team is based on a generalization about the relationship of broadcast advertising to politics. Jason could have resolved the question by checking the specific candidate involved. He might have proceeded without reservation if this candidate proved to be totally honest and sincerely wished to communicate the issues to the public. Undoubtedly several others in the task force may also have worried about the increasing trends toward political ads of 60 seconds or less, but reasoned that each situation must be evaluated on its own terms. The question for them may not have been the selling of politics as a broad problem, but whether a campaign could be designed with integrity for a particular politician.

Jason, however, decided on the basis of principle. This candidate, in fact, pleased him. The issue centered on his complicity in weakening the democratic process, and he therefore declined to participate. But does he now have a responsibility to do more? Jason's complaints were serious and he believed them deeply. In that light the simple act of not joining the team seems incongruous and even meaningless. A vital aspect of social life is being threatened, he declares, and yet he reacts in a way that costs him little.

At a minimum, should he not protest his own agency's involvement? Several advertising firms in the United Stated refuse all political accounts. For some, this is a policy of self-protection arising from the poor credit risk that most campaign accounts actually represent. But a few object on grounds similar to Jason's. The question he ought to face is whether he has a responsibility to pursue every means until his agency adopts such a policy, or, at least, more enlightened voluntary guidelines. Some television stations have chosen to refuse to allow anything less than five minutes for paid political broadcasts. Jason's company could enact a similar policy for the political campaigns it designs. Perhaps one can even argue that he should resign if all attempts fail to influence his firm.

The public policy arena is an important one also. Laws regarding campaign expenditures are constantly discussed and frequently rewritten. The 1974 Campaign Reform Act placed a ceiling on the total amount ($21 million) presidential candidates could spend on their campaigns. This did not include any specific provisions regarding political ads, but by cutting total expenditure over 1972 by 50 percent, the amount for television advertising has been reduced also. Legislation, however weak, has helped curb the trend toward political commercials somewhat. But stronger alternatives are possible. Great Britain has had a longstanding policy preventing anyone from buying commercial time for election campaigns. The major parties are allocated an equal amount, and television stations are required to broadcast the programs free. All other exposure occurs in news situations, coverage over which politicians have no control. Regardless of the options proposed, should not such possibilities of reform be on the forefront of Jason's agenda?

In the absence of any effort to take his own conclusion seriously, an observer could be suspicious that Jason is only using rhetoric to make himself appear righteous. Underneath the expression of concern, his real calculations could involve all the extra work hours and the possibility of failure. In other words, he may not be sure this project will prove useful to his own career as an adman and therefore chooses not to join. He does not excuse his own responsibility for making a decision; he does not argue that political commercials are only a fraction of the material available to voters and they must seek out more details before voting. But, in deciding, it is not obvious he has done so except for highly personal reasons.

There is a possibility that the moral dimension needs sharpening before more radical action becomes compelling. Precisely what is Jason's ethical objection to political advertising? In thinking through the problem he speaks largely in sociopolitical terms about the needs for enlightened citizens. He warns against slick and simplistic ads in a complex world. Clearly these concerns represent strong political values, but the ethical issue could be focused better. What if he would conclude specifically that political commercials of 30 to 60 seconds are inherently deceptive? Even if no outright lies are permitted, he could contend that short spots inevitably and fundamentally distort both the candidate's style and content.

A form of deception seems to be the moral issue here, and if Jason defined the question in those terms he might be motivated not simply to decline participation in the task force, but to demand changes in his company and in public policy as well.

Notes

1. At the time of this writing a group of women protested in front of Champaign/Urbana's two porn theatres. Some property damage ensued.

2. One of the most influential arguments about the television mode is to be found in Herbert Krugman, "The Impact of TV Advertising: Learning Without Involvement." *Public Opinion Quarterly* 29 (Fall 1965): 349–56.

Chapter Eight

How to Say It

In some of the research conducted for this book, advertising practitioners were asked to cite the ethical confrontations most common to their
day-to-day activities. The nature of the advertising message led the
pack.

Advertising is, by its nature, communication with a purpose. It seeks
to alter the thinking and/or behavior of those receiving the message in
a manner beneficial to the advertiser. In the process of attempting to
achieve that end, advertisers have at their disposal a host of verbal and
nonverbal symbols that can be arranged in virtually infinite combinations.

Whether this potential is considered a problem or not depends to a
great extent on what assumptions are made about human nature
(about whether or not a man is deliberate and calculating, for example) as
well as the ultimate fairness of the market system within which advertising flourishes.

The cases in this chapter were chosen to represent some of the more
persistent and bedeviling situations confronting practitioners in the
practice of their craft:

- Exaggerated differences
- Sins of omission
- Matters of effectiveness versus taste
- Puffery

Keep in mind that advertising's actual effects are often quite difficult to determine, even when there is agreement on the nature of effect meant. What results is often a scarcity of fact and an abundance of opinion. The source and nature of that opinion is crucial to an understanding of ethical decision making in this complex and fascinating arena.

35. A Miniscule (and Tasteless) Difference

The soft drink market in the United States is big and competitive. Cynthia Brace was the advertising manager for a large regional soft drink company. The line leader for the company was their strawberry soda, and that was the current bone of contention.

The advertising agency had recently finished a comprehensive study of the company, its competitors, and the soft drink market in general. Their basic conclusion was complimentary—Brandco offered a product of consistent quality. Indeed, production control was such that their product could be properly identified as high quality.

The problem was that this particular selling point had little impact on potential consumers. Quality was, at best, an elusive concept, perhaps better associated with cars or television sets than an essentially taste-dominated product such as a soft drink. So the agency had been searching for another way of asserting a competitive edge. In essence, they sought a proxy for high quality.

They thought they had found it with a "natural" theme, expressed in the slogan, "A little bit of natural flavor in every drop." An initial screening by the television networks resulted in the routine inquiry, "Can you prove it?" The agency turned to Cynthia and asked for the anticipated verification that Brandco's strawberry soda did indeed contain natural flavoring.

It did not, she told them. "You mean there isn't any?" they responded. None, as it turned out, for the simple reason that natural strawberry juice simply tastes terrible. All of their other flavors do contain varying degrees of natural flavoring, but not strawberry, their best seller.

The agency was adamant. The natural theme would not only denote

Brandco's justifiable high quality, but also nicely catch the country's move toward more basic life styles. "Natural" had certain highly positive symbolic connotations at the present time, and a competitive edge could be gained through using it.

Cynthia was subsequently asked if Brandco could not add some natural strawberry flavoring to verify the claim. She pointed out that any amount that could be tasted would result in a negative change for the popular soda. What then, they asked, of a miniscule amount, just enough to support the slogan "A Little Bit of Natural Flavor in Every Drop" but not enough to affect the taste?

The president would have to decide that, Cynthia knew. After all, it would represent the first change in the formula in the 70-year history of the brand. But should she support it?

Ultimately, she did, based on the attraction of the promised competitive edge, as well as her assessment that no real harm would be done to anyone. The networks can honestly clear the commercial. The agency can stand behind the slogan. The customer can continue to enjoy the taste of a soft drink that has become a best seller based on its flavor. And, finally, the company can continue to offer high quality soft drinks in an extremely competitive market.

As standards in the soft drink industry go, Brandco apparently has a good quality product. The initial problem here is to discover some way to get across the idea of quality without stating that theme explicitly, as it has apparently little motivating power for consumers. So "natural" is seen as the best compromise. It was only necessary to add enough natural strawberry juice to verify the claim, but not enough to change the taste.

Cynthia's decision to support the addition seems based on her feeling that no real harm would be done to anyone. That assumption needs close examination. Often businesses rely on basically utilitarian assumptions interwoven with a belief in the basic fairness of the market mechanism. But where is the greatest good for the greatest number here? Presumably Cynthia's company will benefit from increased sales. But there is apparently no enhanced good to existing customers and possibly negative effects for potential customers to the extent that their reasons for brand attraction are based on misleading impressions. In short, Cynthia's action, under closer scrutiny, seems narrowly self-interested in the corporate sense, although there seems no direct benefit to her personally.

She could have relied upon the categorical imperative of truthtelling.

Operating from this premise she could have concluded that it is simply wrong to misinform, whether by what is included in the message or what is omitted. Even utilitarianism, carried through to such conclusions as those discussed, could have altered her decision.

Basically it would seem Cynthia acted without any overriding sense of what is right short of what is best for the company. Certainly this is expedient for an employee in terms of her or his business career. In a larger context, however, it assumes that the company good is to be equated with the public good. In this case at least, that seems a dubious assumption.

Lacking any apparent set of working premises that does not begin with the company, Cynthia seems destined to confront each issue anew with increasingly predictable conclusions. As her longevity with the company grows, past decisions may well solidify into an operative set of company-serving rules that shortcut thoughtful decision making in all future situations.

Making an ethical decision involves reflection. Based on this case, and her apparent decision-making criteria, Cynthia seems destined to avoid its trials as well as its triumphs.

36. Sins of Omission: Sugar

The meeting in the offices of the Federal Trade Commission included members of the commission's investigatory staff as well as volunteers from relevant advertisers and their advertising agencies. The specific subject was sugar, but, in a more fundamental sense, the question concerned nothing less than the proper role of advertising as a source of market information.

The staff presented their report. It began with the assertion that every American eats, on the average, 128 pounds of sugar each year, and that a great deal of that consumption occurs unknowingly. Does a typical American shopper realize:

- That Heinz Tomato Ketchup has a higher percentage of sugar than Sealtest Chocolate Ice Cream?
- That Wishbone Russian Dressing has more than three times the sugar concentration of Coke?
- That Coffee-mate Non-Dairy Creamer (a substitute for cream) has a higher percentage of sugar than a bar of Hershey's Milk Chocolate?
- That many chocolate drink mixes for children are over 90 percent sugar?
- That Jello, which is often promoted in recipes as a salad staple, contains 82.6 percent sugar?[1]

Of course, many more examples could be added. Now, they continued, given the reasonably well documented linkages between sugar and tooth decay, and the health-related dangers of obesity (there seems little evidence so far to support sugar's alleged association with heart disease, diabetes, and hyper-tension), how is the consumer to be most properly alerted about sugar content?

The most obvious solution would seem to lie with package information. At the moment, however, there is no way that even a diligent consumer can determine the percentage of sugars in a product. Ingredients are, of course, required to be listed in order of presence, but no figures are required, and even a well-informed guess can be misleading. For example, Post Raisin Bran lists sucrose as its number three ingredient, corn syrup as number five, and honey as seven.[2] Together, these sugars would undoubtedly represent the primary ingredient in the product. Obviously, the report continued, if we are trying for informed customers, this is an unacceptable situation, and the Commission should be working with the Food and Drug Administration to seek a remedy.

But what about the more immediate matter of concern to the staff—disclosure of relevant consumer information in the advertising of products or services? They could attempt to require that advertisers disclose the percentage of sugar in their products. They would, however, like to avoid that avenue at the moment for two reasons—one pragmatic, one philosophical. First, the conservative political climate in the country simply did not bode well for more charges of intervention in the marketplace. (Indeed this staff report itself was a holdover from the days of a more activist FTC.) Second, and more satisfying in terms of its future fruits, the staff would prefer to explore cooperation on a matter they still considered of some importance.

There is, they concluded, no reasonable doubt that Americans would be much better off consuming less sugar. And it seemed simply unfair that those wishing to regulate their sugar intake lack information in their two most common sources of market information: advertising and packaging. Through bitter experience, the staff report continued, the Commission has learned that consumers simply do not read packages carefully. However, they do see, do remember, and are influenced by a great deal of advertising—witness the success of the products mentioned in the report.

Did not, then, the advertising practitioners feel it their ethical responsibility to disclose to potential customers information that might help them make a satisfactory purchase, even when that information might not work to the advantage of the advertiser? Clearly, it was felt,

Jello's sales could be adversely affected if potential and existing customers knew it was 82.6 percent sugar. But does that give them the right *not* to include that information in perhaps the most prevalent source of market information for most people?

The problem was present. How could it be resolved? The staff was hopeful they might stimulate some form of cooperative effort among producers. Or was that simply asking too much of the system?

Would cooperation be possible with a rear guard staff of a federal regulatory agency? In this case no decision had yet been reached. Indeed, given the ad hoc nature of the group representing the advertising business it was uncertain there could be a decision at any level above personal commitment. Apparently these are volunteers from some advertisers and their agencies. No business-wide rule-making groups such as the American Association of Advertising Agencies, the Association of National Advertisers, the American Advertising Federation, the National Advertising Review Board, or the National Association of Broadcasters were represented. Perhaps they would be contacted later. In any event, these representatives could not even decide for their own firms. They could carry the message back and initiate relevant discussion. But, again, there was no business-wide effort apparent.

As the FTC staffers admitted, this was not a particularly good time to be proposing more legislation, even within their own agency. The conservative (free market) political winds were dominant in the Reagan administration. So the staff group hoped for cooperation. The problem must be dealt with, they contended. It was simply a matter of how.

How would the firms react? At one level they could simply disagree with the FTC staff that this represented a relevant problem. There was, first of all, controversy about the exact effects of artificial sugars on human beings. So there could be honest disagreement about the facts that allegedly classified this as a problem to begin with. In addition, even if the problem was acknowledged, there was by no means uniform agreement on who the culprits were. The cereal companies, for example, have claimed that their sugar-coated cereals are not likely to promote tooth decay, whereas candy is.

Second, the firms could simply ignore the problem, secure in the expectation that the FTC and FDA would not mount a legislative effort.

There is, of course, the more fundamental question that places the issue squarely on an ethical plane: Do firms have a responsibility to provide information in their advertising and/or packaging that could prove helpful to their customers but detrimental to themselves?

Two premises seem reasonable: (1) Given the choice, firms would prefer to have percentage-of-sugar information appear in the packaging rather than the advertising. The packaging is simply not likely to be read carefully, and the symbolic freedom of the advertising form would certainly be curtailed with the inclusion of such factual information. (2) Given the possible negative effects that the disclosure could have on sales, it is extremely unlikely that individual firms will undertake such a practice unless all firms do likewise.

Companies may thus seem to be operating under their own assumptions of what constitutes fairness. Is it fair, they might argue, to require a producer of a successful product to present information about that product in the most negative form? Types of sugar are now listed on many packages for those interested. Is it not fair to assume that the consumer carries part of the responsibility? They can explore other sources of relevant information (for example, *Consumer Reports*). Is it fair to place the entire burden of market information on the profit-seeking firm when other sources such as the schools are more institutionally suited to the task?

The other side of the fairness curtain is equally apparent. Is it fair to those desiring to control their sugar intake not to make information on sugar content available in the most accessible form? In a more general sense, is it fair to withhold information about a product or service that, if disclosed, could cause consumers to reappraise their choice of the product?

Perhaps a compromise on the order of Aristotle's golden mean is one avenue out of this particular standoff. Business-wide groups could propose that all firms in specific industries (such as cereals) agree to more detailed content listing of sugars on their packaging. Thus the information would be available in some uniform manner for those who choose to use it. At least the alert consumer would benefit. The companies would be relegating the information to the least spectacular format, have the cooperation of their competitors, and, potentially, gain an explicit competitive edge.

However, it seems unlikely that even such a relatively modest step would be taken unless legislation is pending. The belief in the essential fairness of the market system is a strong ethical touchstone for many businesses. Thus, given the lack of public outcry through falling sales, or more powerful special interest pressure on the regulatory agencies, it is quite likely the firms will do nothing, relatively secure in the belief that they have satisfied their ethical responsibilities by producing good products apparently well accepted by the American people.

When and if the outside pressures change, the firms may be moved to something resembling the compromise noted above. Even then it seems likely they will feel unfairly treated.

37. Sins of Omission: Parity Products

Harry Feldner was a 46-year-old creative supervisor with more than 23 years experience in the agency business. He paused over the question on the form before him. A group of faculty were trying to find out something about the ethics of the advertising business. Talk about old wine in new bottles! The question read, "Do you feel that you encounter ethical decisions in the practice of your job?" Harry immediately wrote, "Not really. All our work is carefully scrutinized by lawyers internally—as well as at the client and networks." He stopped, thought a bit, and then asked, "I have not yet decided whether 'puffery' is unethical. Yet I do feel that if an advertiser has to tell the whole truth he may as well not advertise—there'd be no competitive advantage since most products are parity—with only minor shades of difference."

Parity products, Harry reflected. Advertising's bane and triumph.[3] Face it, a very large number of the mass-advertised mass-consumption brands are substitutable for one another without any noticeable difference in performance. They are all over the cold remedy shelf in the drug store, not to mention deodorants, margarines, household cleaning aids, as well as a great number of that little army of laundry products. And what of the beers and cigarettes? Test after test had demonstrated that even the most brand loyal could not consistently pick out their brand from other unidentified samples. What was it *Consumer Reports* wrote recently? "Every one of the tested [19" color television] sets can deliver a pleasing picture; the differences we noted from model to model were minimal."[4] In some cases the products are exactly identical, due to government requirements (for example, with some drugs), or, commonly, the producers simply sell some of their output to retailers for marketing under their brand name(s). Simply, parity products are a fact of the contemporary marketplace. And, to think, he reflected, a shaker and roller like Marion Harper could have predicted that "by the 1980s few parity products . . . will be advertised extensively . . . ."[5] Tell that to Kellogg's Corn Flakes and Post Toasties, or many detergents, or canned vegetables, or . . . .

The intriguing thing about parity products, he thought, is their curse and challenge. The curse is best summed up by that memorable quotation from the old master of the hard sell Rosser Reeves: "Our problem is—a client comes into my office and throws two newly minted half-dollars onto my desk and says, 'Mine is the one on the left. You prove it's better.'"[6] The challenge, of course, comes precisely from the lack of physical or functional difference. It enables the copywriter and art director to move with considerable comfort into the realm of the consumer's emotions—to attempt to create moods, distinctive product identities and the like.

- A green giant? A doughboy? A talking rabbit? A rugged cowboy? A modern woman? Attach them successfully to chemical or paper or plastic things, and to real or artificial substances and, behold, there is more here than the physical and functional item.
- Or have recognizable personalities speak for the product and let their charisma wash over.
- Or sing. Yes indeed, sing about that thing made of bubbles and syrups and water. Call the people who drink it "Peppers" and, again, there is more here than form and substance.[7]

A challenge then: to suggest a difference where none, in fact, exists in any real sense. A former colleague, the late Howard Gossage, used to make much of the distinction between image and identity. "An image," he often said, "is how you want others to see you. An identity, on the other hand, is what you really are."[8]

Obviously, Gossage felt one is on much firmer ethical ground dealing with identities. But, Harry added, therein lies the essence of a great deal of advertising. And, until the government tells us we cannot sell differences where none exists, I will lend my talents to the cause.

Harry was responding to the first question on a form the authors sent to advertising practitioners. His initial response tended to equate right with what is considered legal. In other words, if the lawyers at the agency, the client, and the network consider it acceptable, then it is. But Harry knew there was more. His response about puffery seems to address the more fundamental question in this case: regardless of specific consequences, is it wrong to imply differences where, functionally, there are none?

This strikes at the heart of parity products, as Harry knew. But his wanderings in difficult ethical territory were short lived. He was soon reflecting on the curse and challenge of parity products, but note this was focused on the *advertising practitioner*, not on the public. Parity products, Harry seems to be saying, are a curse in the sense that it is hard to provide a successful difference where none exists, but they are also a challenge to create a difference that establishes brand loyalty.

Harry seems to shrug aside concern over effects of this type of advertising with "We all do it, don't we?" We are, he seems to be suggesting, all creatures of symbolic meaning and are therefore not ill served by communications of high symbolic content. Indeed, we may feel more comfortable with Corn Flakes than with Post Toasties, with Marlboros than with Winstons, because of the symbolic content that makes the difference for us. Thus, Harry seems to imply that the greatest good for the greatest number is served by making parity products different because people want them different, either consciously or unconsciously. After all, he might reason, look at all those people who pay a staggering premium to buy Bayer aspirin over their drug store's brand.

But is this, in fact, so? Would it make a difference if people knew that certain brands were identical in terms of their performance? Would they say, "I don't care if my brand *is* the same as another, I want to buy it anyway"? Perhaps, but if knowledge of the parity nature of some brands *would* make a difference in individual purchasing decisions, then the greatest good for the greatest number is not being served by concealing it, and the utilitarian justification is weakened if not eliminated. But Harry does not even address the question.

What ethical justification would he have left if he had? Basically the conviction that moral duty is owed specifically to the advertiser ("I need to establish a difference for his product; it is my job"), or, more generally, to advertising as a communication form ("That's the essence of a great deal of advertising," or "That's the way the game is played"). If utilitarianism fails, his loyalty to his client or business would, it seems, be the only ground left.

Harry's experiences as a practitioner could have led him to confront two troubling premises: (1) What is good is what is legal. (2) But what is legal is not necessarily what is good for the public. Wishing to believe his work ethical, Harry has refused to address the second. Venturing into that area beyond his currently uncritical thinking could force him to ask questions that he would apparently not wish to have answered.

38. Sins of Omission: Negative Material

Kevin Rothschild had never satisfactorily resolved his personal dilemma about the material. Although he had now been teaching advertising at the university level for more than five years, he still confronted the issue anew before every semester. ·

It centered on the Survey of Advertising course that Kevin taught twice a year at a large midwestern university. Over the academic year the course attracted between 500 and 1,000 students, a healthy percentage of whom later declared themselves to be advertising majors. More majors meant more student credit hours, more inter-departmental budget clout, more faculty, healthier salaries, and more research funds.

It was a fascinating area for many students. They enjoyed hearing about the strategies behind familiar advertising campaigns, jousting— albeit briefly—with issues such as the morality of advertising to children, and generally left with most of their stereotypes of the glamorous world of advertising relatively secure. Here, Kevin knew, was the crux of the dilemma. There was another side to advertising to which he could expose them far more readily than he did now, a side that cast doubt on whether advertising was, in fact, a desirable institution.

Should he give more class and reading time to a significant body of information and opinion that included:

National advertising serves primarily to artificially differentiate parity products and to inhibit existing and potential competition, making possible pricing discretion and discrimination and manufacturer domination of markets, with consequent misallocation of resources and monopoly transfers. All these functions are incompatible with both classical- and neo-liberal values; and we have said nothing of advertising's harmful effects on the mass media and its questionable (at best) effects on other aspects of our lives.[9]

Sure, Kevin touched upon some of this material in passing, but it was generally in the let's-see-what-the-critics-are-saying-about-advertising mode favored by most introductory texts. Under the best of circumstances, the issues were superficially presented and quickly dismissed. As, for example, "Advertising encourages—not discourages —competition." But there was much more to it than that, and Kevin knew it.

And, perhaps of even greater complexity, how far should he go toward explaining that there are those with quite credible credentials who feel that advertising does not provide a working environment conducive to positive individual growth? Should he expose them to insiders' views such as these:

- David Lyon, agency principal: "As I see it, the only legitimate reason for going into the advertising business is that you enjoy the work and the money. Service to humanity just isn't in the picture."[10]
- Sociologist Joe Bensman, who spent eight years in an agency: If one "has genuine talent or creative ability in any field, advertising is the last place for him to be." If one is "kind, gentle, ethical or religious and believes in spontaneous social relationships, advertising would be an incompatible profession. Advertising requires strong defenses, toughness, nerve, and the willingness to exploit oneself and others."[11]
- Paul Stevens, a copywriter who was fired when his book was published, warned his readers that "it was not a collection of marvelously witty anecdotes about all the swell guys in the ad game, mostly because there are no swell guys in the ad game. They are a group of cold, hard-nosed businessmen who happen to have your number."[12]
- Jerry Della Femina, agency principal: "When you think of advertising, don't think of Rock Hudson manipulating Doris Day. Think of H.R. Haldeman trying to screw up some tapes, because that's closest to what large-agency advertising men are like."[13]
- Jack O'Dwyer, former advertising columnist for the New York *Journal-American* and the Chicago *Tribune*: "On the outside, the advertising business is a beautiful tinseled world of smiling, good-looking men and beautiful girls. But on the inside it is boiling hostility, hate, jealousy, fear, insecurity, lies, cheating and rottenness."[14]
- Howard Gossage, agency principal: "I don't know a first-class brain in the business who has any respect for it."[15]
- Nicholas Samstag, late director of promotion for *Time*, said, "The half-truth is the essence of advertising." And he asked,

But what impact has this on the advertising man? The need to deal only with truths which further his purpose cannot help carrying over into his life outside his work. As he proceeds along the path of his career, he is likely to become less and less real, more and more lop-sided ("half-assed" is a good word for it).

What he is *really* paid for is a quality that we might term "eclectic amnesia," the ability to select the weaknesses in his product and bury them in his forgettery, so that he can concentrate on what's left for his advertising campaign. The better he does this the more he prospers. If he cannot do it, he is fired. He alone . . . must, in a sense, blind himself to earn a livelihood.[16]

- Anthropologist Jules Henry came to the same conclusion: "Advertising men do not contradict themselves or lie to one another *in terms of their own culture*. The central issue is that they have lived so long where double-talk is the *only* talk, and where *contradiction* is *affirmation*, that they do not perceive in what they say what we of the more traditional culture perceive."[17]

Kevin could, of course, include all of this bad news of the business's alleged effects on society and on the individuals in advertising, but offset it with strongly supportive information and opinion: a fair balance, in other words. He could. But if he did, the amount of time consumed would require that a lot of other material—some of the most popular stuff—be eliminated. The tone of the course would become considerably more somber. Kevin could predict the results: a decline in class enrollment and substantial drop in the percent of students from the course who elected to pursue advertising as a major.

But did Kevin not owe the students as penetrating a look at the business as he was capable of offering? After all, many of them would be making decisions about the direction of their future careers. Would he serve them well if they decided to commit themselves to future employment based on clearly incomplete information? Indeed, could it not be argued that the greater the potential hazards in a business—to the society and its employees—the greater the ethical necessity to examine them?

And yet, there was the enrollment, and the subsequent well-being of his colleagues. Of course, his department head would surely view declining enrollments with alarm, and he might be shifted to a teaching assignment of a less critical nature. In any event, advertising majors are required to take a number of professionally-oriented courses before their graduation. They would, he reasoned, certainly get enough of a balanced picture there to determine whether they had made a wise choice.

So, better not fool with a successful course, at least this time around. He would, however, try to include a bit more of the more controversial material in his lectures. If only he can find time to fit it in.

Here is a clear conflict between belief and behavior. But before focusing on that, it is useful to examine the various ethical rationales Kevin might have employed in deciding to endorse his class's status quo. He could have decided on the basis of personal relativism. My act (or rather lack of it) is right because I say it is right. Using utilitarian thinking he could have argued that the greatest short-run good to the greatest number (his students) was served by keeping the course light, enthusiasim high, and by soft-peddling the negative material. Certainly his teaching colleagues and members of the business would be served by his decision as well. But what of the long-run good? Here his decision can be questioned. Is it serving the greatest good for the greatest number to leave students with an incomplete understanding of the business they may seek to enter? And what of the commitment of their academic career to an advertising major? What, in a broader sense, of those who already work in the business? Is it serving their best interests to encourage young people to become part of their enterprise when they may be subsequently disillusioned? Will they be productive employees?

The same type of thinking pervades questions of where moral duty is owed. Student short run? Student long run? Colleagues? Himself? Apart from the long-run interests of the students, Kevin's decision would seem to be supported.

If only short-run consequences are considered, the ethical answer is a resounding "Don't change!" Consideration of long-run consequences is much more difficult because of the degree of conjecture involved. How will his decision now affect students in their advertising careers several years in the future? Obviously that is more difficult to answer than the question of how the department head would respond to declining enrollment.

And now we return to the matter of principle. Kevin would appear to be ethically inconsistent. He knows that the negative material is there and is legitimate. He also knows that advertising is a complicated business, with neither angels nor demons, and that credible positive material could also be presented. In short, he appears to believe in the ideal of the rational mind and the concept of the clash of ideas as representing a desirable educational plane. Yet he has chosen to act in a manner that makes that process impossible.

Thus considered, Kevin's decision is unconscionable. From a Kantian perspective there is only one right course, and it is not affected by perceived consequences. Kevin did not choose it; rather, he compromised the key element in the dilemma—his moral integrity.

39. Gun for Hire?

The 27-year-old copywriter had been in the business long enough to be involved in the evolution of a great deal of broadcast advertising. And once again she was ready to make a judgment. Before her was a blank sheet of paper in a typewriter. Shortly (and it better *be* shortly!) the paper would be full of words and suggested visual elements dealing with a well-known package good—a cold capsule, in this case. The commercial would eventually be aired in the heart of what she had come to know as the flu and cold season—the high water mark for the client's annual sales.

She had written dozens of commercials for the client before. Perhaps that was one of the problems, she thought. You get locked into certain formulas, certain predictable ways of dealing with the problem of promoting the client's product, and you crank out the next entry. It would not be all that hard—that was one advantage of using a message format. The problem was more fundamental than that. She hated a lot of advertisements, sometimes including her own.

She was reminded of the words of another copywriter from the early years of television.

My children know I'm in advertising, but it doesn't interest them much. They don't ask me about it. The other day, though, we were all sitting watching television, and one of these cartoon commercials came on. It showed two big wrestlers coming into a ring, one with the label PAIN on his robe, and the other with the label ORDINARY PAINKILLER. Something like that. Anyway, PAIN threw ORDINARY PAINKILLER right out of the ring, and stomped around afterward. Then another wrestler came on, with the brand name stenciled on his robe, and he threw PAIN out of the ring, knocked him out completely, you see.

I didn't think much of it, one way or the other, but my younger boy called me aside, out of the room. He said, "Dad, am I to understand that a bunch of grown men sat around and thought up that thing? And another bunch of grown men sat around and said it was a good idea? And another bunch of men went to all the work to make a movie of it?"

What could I say? I told him that was just what had happened. He walked away, shaking his head.[18]

Well, my advertising does not include cartoons, unless you can regard the characters I create as cartoons. But what of the simplistic and repetitive dialogue I put in their mouths, on their relentless concern with suffering, and their shining gratitude at the relief provided by the client's nostrum?

All advertising is not pap, she mused. A great deal of magazine advertising reflects the interests and tastes of those in the audience. A lot of newspaper advertising is a good friend—informative, helpful. Industrial and business advertising has to be straight forward most of the time. It's just the combination of television and certain products that seems to provide the most fertile climate for this tripe.

The bottom line is that it seems to work. Look at "Ring Around the Collar," and "R-O-L-A-I-D-S" and Mr. Whipple, and Robert Young, and those lovely deodorant and women's hygiene products. Her own agency's research had indicated that brand name recognition and recall of major sales points was higher with the approach they had been using than a more civilized (she thought) technique she had been allowed to test in rough cut form. So what does that say about the television audience, she wondered. Break through their passivity with mind-dulling repetition and cardboard characters? So it would seem. After all, whose money is being spent anyway? The client produces an honest product and deserves the most productive advertising we can give him.

And if it happens that I am reluctant to claim authorship? If I am ashamed to admit a grown woman created that? Maybe it's enough to know that the client can laugh all the way to the bank.

Rather than a matter of the information content of the advertisement, or the lack of it, this case focuses on personal taste. The copywriter has apparently dealt with this problem sufficiently to indulge in at least some preliminary reflection. She has concluded that the problem was not one of advertising per se. She recognized that there are other combinations of media and product classes that could result in advertising messages that reflect the interests and tastes of those in the audience.

Yet this thought suggests that she has not pushed her thinking as far as it could productively go. Her concept of audience, in particular, seems muddled. Basically, she is involved in producing advertising that she personally finds offensive. It is mind dulling, repetitious, simplistic, and the characters are cartoon characters.

The unasked question seems to be whether the audience itself shares this assessment. She has apparently not followed this through very carefully. She could make the following conjectures to the question, "Does my advertising do harm to the public?" Yes, in the sense that it is vapid, superficial, and ultimately downright irritiating. It fails to treat them as intelligent human beings, and, in the process, demeans them. No, in the sense that this type of advertising seems to work. The "work," of course, refers to the best interests of the advertiser. But, as she is promoting an honest product, and people seem to be buying it due at least in part to the advertising, is not this apparently a mutually satisfactory arrangement?

If she accepts the first argument, she seems to be saying that the audience's tastes agree with her own and something should be done. But what of the fact that the advertising seems to work? Perhaps the product succeeds in spite of the advertising. Either that or the audience members do not find the advertising as offensive as she does.

If she accepts the second argument, then she is admitting that her tastes are different from those of the audience and that she, not the advertising, is not synchronized with the system. Does not advertising, as she asserts, reflect the audience? If so, she would seem to be disillusioned with the people to whom she is attempting to sell.

A quandary of personal standards then. It is not easy to know the depth of her concern. This could be a relatively insignificant thought at a random moment or it could represent a recurring theme that is increasingly important to her self-concept. In either event, some steps could sharpen the issue.

She should reflect more about her concept of the audience of her messages. Does she really believe they are being harmed? If so, then she must test her commitment to their well-being over her own.

She states that her more civilized approach did not test well, based on recall criteria. However, it is possible that it would test well at the behavior (sales) level, which is the ultimate criterion for most advertising success. Since recall is sometimes a poor proxy for sales, she could encourage more testing (albeit expensive and complex) at a level closer to actual sales behavior. If those tests proved reassuring, her approach might yet win the day.

She could ask for a transfer to an account where the message and medium combination would allow her to produce advertising that is closer to her own taste, and still "works." This option assumes a considerable depth of commitment on her part. She would, after all, be leaving a relatively easy job for one less certain, and, in the process, rock the boat by requesting a transfer.

Given the need for advertising communicators to develop symbol packages that are first arresting and then persuasive in fixed space and time and with a relatively disinterested audience, conflicts between communicator tastes and effectiveness seem inevitable.

Perhaps the key factors in resolving these questions are some reflection on the communicator's concept of audience as well as her or his depth of personal commitment to the issue. What works, be it in advertising, painting, films, novels, or plays, may not be always what the communicator likes. Thus, inevitable conflicts between creator and audience will present themselves. The ethical options are suitably complex, and, as always, require sometimes painful reflection, and, perhaps, even more painful action.

40. Larger Than Life

Among its accounts, a large New York agency represents a major regional potato chip company. The agency is preparing to launch a new campaign for the chips, and has sent commercial scripts to the production department.

Mike Skillings, television production coordinator, reviewed the scripts and made preparations for taping. The script called for a party scene where an attractive woman opens a bag of chips and pours them into a bowl. Mike made the necessary arrangements for the needed properties and talent, setting the taping for one week later.

Two days before the taping, Mike received a phone call from Marsha Young, the chip account executive, who wanted to know how the commercial was coming along. Mike assured her that all was arranged, and that she would have the commercial on time. Marsha was pleased, and explained that the new campaign was critical to the continued success of the chips in an increasingly competitive snack food market.

At the taping the actors and actresses were briefed and rehearsed the scene. When the actress opened and poured the bag of chips, some were broken and discolored. At the end of the scene, Marsha called Mike aside and suggested that they open several bags of chips, combining the light, unbroken chips to make one perfect bag. Mike explained that it was now standard practice that food products be visualized exactly as a consumer will see them after purchase. Marsha argued that consumers expected some chips to be dark or broken, so that no harm would be done by this sample exaggeration. After all, she noted, puffery is an acceptable element of advertising expression, even today.

She is right there, Mike thought. A certain amount of puffing is regarded as part of the advertising process, even by the standards of a recently activist FTC. Leaf through any magazine:

- "Incredible Art Value!"
- "The Answer to Your Foot Care Needs"
- "The Ultimate Weapon in the War on Grass and Weeds"
- "Nothing Performs Like a Saab"
- "Sophisticated"
- "No Rum Reflects Puerto Rico Like Ronrico"
- "The Symbol of Imported Luxury"
- "A New Standard of Value in Sports Sedans"

It's true in a visual sense as well, he knew. No, not much attention had been paid to puffery through *nonverbal* symbols, but it was all around: exaggeration, a normal boast, a bit of presumably acceptable wishful thinking on the part of the advertiser. Consider:

- The models chosen. Memorable. Frequently handsome, beautiful, articulate.

- The settings. Awful or splendid as the selling argument called for. Quite often simply fanciful. Consider the hang glider perched on the rim of a stunning canyon at dawn. And just to dramatize a stick of chewing gum!
- The colors. Show the girl with drab hair in somber colors, the one with revitalized no-fuss in brights.
- The mood. Upbeat/exciting or dull/flat—at least until an application of the sponsor's product.
- Graphics. Absolutely brilliant photography or cinematography. Crisp editing. Deft retouching. Careful matching of type of music with the mood desired.

These are common and acceptable practices. Sure they exaggerate. Advertising is almost always larger than life, is it not? Perhaps because people want it to be. What was it that Pierre Martineau, the researcher, had said?

The consumer doesn't feel that he is being victimized or cheated by the retailer and the producer. On the contrary, he loves his stores and the mechanical triumphs of his age—the colorful automobiles, the pink washing machines, the garage doors with electric eyes. He is far, far more interested in the people who make Polaroid cameras and power tools, color TV sets and low-cost air conditioners than he is in what the intellectuals and politicians have to offer. This is what he works for; this is what he wants from life—not the frustrated pouting of some university hermit.[19]

Okay, Mike reflected, puffery may not be real life, but it doesn't seem to victimize either. So, let the commercial's potato chips be a little better than they would normally be. The consumer's previous experience with chips and their general expectations about advertising should provide enough safeguards.

———————

Scholar Ivan Preston has noted that puffery in advertising receives forgiving legal treatment because it is assumed to have no effect, but it is used by advertisers because it does.[20] A puffing of claims about a product or service is generally to be expected in advertising, the courts have decided. It is presumably unlikely to have any detrimental effect on even a relatively naive consumer. In short, when an advertiser says his product is the greatest, no one really believes him.

This stand has been arrived at largely through assumptions rather than evidence. As research evidence has become relatively common in legal proceedings concerning advertising content, the limits to puffery have generally been drawn in.[21] But, as this case suggests, there is still ample room for interpretation.

It is doubtful that this advertisement would result in any legal challenge, unless a competitor raised objections. Potato chips are not, after all, a product closely linked with health or safety concerns and therefore not likely to be high on any special interest watchdog's priority list. No, most likely Mike will be able to offer the public a commercial with perfect chips, without any legal ripples.

The ethics of the situation are another matter. In deciding in essence that everybody does it, Mike is embracing the exaggeration as part of the nature of that self-interested form of communication called advertising. In the process he is apparently making certain comfortable assumptions about the audience, their capabilities and priorities. Specifically: (1) People *are* deliberate and calculating. They have had previous experience with potato chips and will carry that experience over to this commercial. They realize that advertising is paid propaganda and will weigh their own experience against the advertising in favor of experience and devalue at least that part of the advertisement. (2) People are *not* deliberate and calculating. They live in worlds of symbols where colors, moods, design, and psychological and sociological suggestions are very real parts of their lives. Hence, they frequently confront exaggeration in many facets of their lives and may, in fact, like it. Scholar Theodore Levitt has suggested that advertising serves the function of "alleviating imagery" for many consumers, and thus should not be relegated to transmitting mere product information.[22]

Buttressed with these assumptions, it is not surprising that Mike could conclude that puffery is not likely to victimize. The first envisions a consumer constantly on guard against advertising's exaggerations. This defense posture is usually adequate.

In the second set of assumptions, the individual apparently welcomes the blandishments of the advertisements. This is a willing seduction. Here the encounter is not between adversaries, but friends.

From an ethical perspective it could be contended that in the first case Mike is shifting the burden of what is right to potential consumers. Let him or her be on guard. Let them filter advertisements through their own experiences and make an appropriate judgment. This is very close to the idea of deliberate and calculating man envisioned under classical liberal philosophy, finding its market manifestation in the concept of *caveat emptor*, let the buyer beware.

But should he endorse the second set of assumptions, the responsibility would seem to shift back to the advertiser. For here he is presumably dealing with a vulnerable public, one quite open to the spinning of symbolic meanings and the manipulation of priorities.

It would seem, under closer examination, that Mike might find somewhat more difficulty in justifying his decision with the set of assumptions involving open man rather than those positing guarded man.

In any case he has refused to verify his assumptions as fact. He could ask that a rough cut of the commercial be tested with both a perfect and a normal bag. If individuals are left with impression that these chips are more likely to be lighter and unbroken than competitors, then the action would seem clear if the public is to be served. The normal chips must be used.

If there is no difference reported in the test, then no practical harm (or good) would seem to have occurred. There is then the more fundamental question of whether, regardless of the consequences, it is right to misrepresent the experience that an ordinary consumer is likely to have with this or any other product.

From the perspective of Preston's observation, it would be contended that Mike made his decision about puffery in an extremely casual manner. Further thought might have led to conclusions that: (1) If it *does* make a difference then it is at least wrong on ethical grounds and probably on legal as well. (2) If it does *not* make a difference, why indulge in the exaggeration anyway, particularly when its effect in the long run may be a continuing devaluation of advertising as a credible medium of market information.

Simply, the chips do *not* look perfect under normal circumstances. Mike concluded it was permissible to suggest they do. In the process he apparently assumed both a guarded and an open model of potential consumers, yet also assumed the responsibility should rest with the consumer in both cases. Pushing the situation beyond assumptions to fact would likely have made his decision difficult to justify, regardless of the outcome. However supported, expediency triumphed over reflection.

Notes

1. See "Too Much Sugar?" *Consumer Reports*, March 1978, pp. 136–42.
2. Ibid.
3. See E. John Kottman, "The Parity Product-Advertising's Achilles Heel," *Journal of Advertising* 6 (Winter 1977): 34–39.
4. *Consumer Reports*, January 1981.

5. Marion Harper, "The Agency Business in 1980," *Advertising Age* 44 (19 November 1973): 15.

6. Martin Mayer, *Madison Avenue U.S.A.* (New York: Harper & Brothers, 1958), p. 3.

7. See Harry Wayne McMahan, "How to Sell a Product Without an 'Advantage'," *Advertising Age* 44 (31 December 1973): 15.

8. See Kim Rotzoll, "Gossage Revisited," *Journal of Advertising* 9 (Fall, 1980): 6–14.

9. Vincent Norris, "An Ethical Problem for Advertising Teachers." Unpublished manuscript, School of Journalism, Pennsylvania State University, 1980.

10. David Lyon, *Off Madison Avenue* (New York: G.P. Putnam's Sons, 1966), p. 11.

11. Joe Bensman, *Dollars and Sense* (New York: Macmillan, 1967), pp. 66–67.

12. Paul Stevens, *I Can Sell You Anything* (New York: P.H. Wyden, 1972). Reissued in paper under the pseudonym Carl P. Wrighter [Stevens] (New York: Ballantine Books, 1975), p. 3.

13. Speaking on Public Television, January 1975. Further discussion appears in Della Femina's *From Those Wonderful Folks Who Gave You Pearl Harbor* (New York: Simon & Schuster, 1970).

14. Regrettably we can no longer locate the date of this quotation, which appeared in Jack O'Dwyer's column and in *The Gallagher Report* in the mid-1960's.

15. Howard Gossage, "Advertising Has Tremendous (Unwanted) Economic Power and Here Are Things It Should Do About It," *Advertising Age*, 5 May 1969.

16. Nicholas Samstag, *How Business is Bamboozled by the Ad Boys* (New York: James Heineman, 1969), pp. 98–100. Italics in the original.

17. Jules Henry, *Culture Against Man* (New York: Random House, 1963), pp. 92–93. Italics in the original.

18. Martin Mayer, *Madison Avenue, U.S.A.* (New York: Harper & Brothers, 1958), pp. 119–20.

19. Pierre Martineau, *Motivation in Advertising* (New York: McGraw-Hill, 1957), p. 192.

20. Ivan Preston, *The Great American Blow Up* (Madison: University of Wisconsin Press, 1975).

21. See Herbert Rotfeld and Ivan Preston, "The Potential Impact of Research on Advertising Law: The Case of Puffery," *Journal of Advertising Research* 21 (April 1981): 9–17.

22. Theodore Levitt, "The Morality (?) of Advertising," *Harvard Business Review* 48 (July–August 1970): 84–92.

Chapter Nine

Media Considerations

For most of this century the newspapers and magazines of the United States have relied heavily on advertising revenue as a major source of income. Virtually from their inception radio and television networks and stations sought their funds for operation and profit from advertising subsidy as well. In this arrangement, the media exist in part as conduits of advertising messages to particular audiences. The larger consequences of this accommodation will be discussed in the following chapter. Here we concern ourselves with the ethical confrontations faced by some who work for the media in their unique and sensitive positions between advertiser and audience.

The very nature of this positioning is central to many of the problems raised in this chapter.

- What advertisers will be granted access to the pages and/or time in order to expose their message to a particular audience?
- What are the ethical considerations when the interest of the media channel and that of the advertiser conflict?
- How should media personnel use confidential information gleaned from

their normal exposure to advertisers who are often competing for the same business?

The situations described in these cases are scarcely of cosmic consequence. Yet they are very real and very frequent for individuals involved in this intriguing dimension of the advertising process.

41. The Limits of Controversy

Paul Blair was vice-president of a major television network. He faced a decision: should three commercials of a giant aluminum company be allowed on the network's advertising time?

On the surface it was a relatively simple matter. The commercials were unabashedly controversial. One dealt with government curtailments of free enterprise. Another with a perspective on a national energy policy. The third with the cost to the economy of government red tape. All reflected the self-interested view of the corporation; all called for viewers to write to the company or the government because "your voice can make a difference."

They could be rejected because of the network's policy of refusing any advertising deemed controversial. In recent years, Paul's network had rejected ads from:

- The Stern Law Firm, a consumer advocate group urging drivers of particular model Chevrolets to take their cars to dealers for the installation of a safety device.
- Allstate Insurance, praising the effectiveness of air bags as safety devices.
- A consumer group warning of the dangers of snowmobiling.
- Phillips Petroleum, advocating offshore drilling.
- The Energy Action Committee, in favor of legislation to break up the eighteen largest oil companies.

All these were considered too controversial, not to mention the dozens of special interest groups that had in the past claimed that they should be given (or in some cases be allowed to buy) time to challenge buying brand-name aspirin, using permanent life insurance as an investment, and so on.

The network's position was clear. On the high road it had been argued that the short time segments normally available to advertisers did not provide an appropriate forum for the debate of issues of national controversy. Also that the Fairness Doctrine of the Federal

Communications Commission would require the network to offer time for opposing positions.

Here the network's motives began to tarnish. In at least some cases the equal time would have to be offered free in order to guarantee balance. This prospect delighted the networks not at all. Nor did the idea of adding tension to the otherwise benign selling climate that the networks provide for their advertisers. In many ways this may be the key, Paul thought, for his network had already rejected the offer of a major oil company to buy two minutes of television time: One for themselves and one to be offered to the strongest advocate of the opposing view. So it was not just short-term money, was it?

The Supreme Court, at the moment anyway, was on the network's side. The Court had interpreted freedom of the press in the broadest sense to mean freedom to publish (broadcast), thus putting control over the entire content of the magazine, newspaper, television or radio station solely in the hands of the owners. This, the rejected advertisers felt, ran afoul of *their* rights to free speech.

The aluminum company could make an eloquent philosophical case of the need for debate on issues of national controversy and of the alleged bias and/or inadequacy of the coverage of these issues on the network's newscasts. Perhaps of greatest importance to their argument was the unquestioned uniqueness of network television as an avenue to the American people and the consequently enormous gatekeeper power of the three major networks. It was not enough that some 89 percent of the nation's television stations will accept issue advertising under certain conditions, or that ABC was involved in a year-long experiment to allow this type of advertising in the late evening. They wanted access to the mass audiences that only the three major networks could provide, and at times *they* would choose.

The problem, Paul thought, is that nobody is wearing white hats. Certainly the network's motives were suspect due to their economic self-interest. And, those clamoring for air time were commonly not earnest citizens, but self-interested multinational corporations, along with special-interest consumer groups with particular axes to grind, and nothing approaching grass roots support.

Still, Paul was frequently reminded of Walter Lippmann's characterization of the networks: "It's as if there were only three great printing presses." And, Paul wondered, all they can use their advertising time for is toothpaste?

Well, one thing was certain. Given the agonizing decisions to be faced by this society in the next several decades, there would be no lack of controversy. Nor, he was sure, would those attempting to alter the networks' policies abandon the battle. Television was simply too important a medium and the networks too vital a funnel.

The battle, then, could be fought another day. For now, he rejected the advertising.

Why is Paul Blair troubled? His decision, at least on nonethical grounds, is not a complex one. The advertising in question is plainly controversial, and, hence, to be rejected by the network rule against controversial advertising.

On the surface the issue is fairness. The networks, because their affiliated stations use the public airwaves, are overseen by the Federal Communications Commission, whose Fairness Doctrine requires an opportunity for conflicting points of view to be represented fairly. Operationally, should Paul's network accept one of the commercials in question, it would presumably be obliged to offer equal time for response from a group espousing a different view—in this case probably an anti-big-business activist organization.

The reasoning behind this is quite consistent with belief in the marketplace of ideas so important to the American political and economic system. If you could imagine yourself behind Rawl's veil of ignorance, not knowing whether you would emerge as a broadcaster or an advocate of a special cause, fairness would seem to dictate that you would endorse the idea that provided you access to such a vital media conduit as the major networks.

But apparently the waters are muddy here. Paul might well argue: fairness to whom? There are more parties involved than simply networks and advocates. What of the public, for example? Would it be fair to fill their television time with esoteric squabbles among special pleaders? And what of the other advertisers whose reliable revenue makes possible network programming (including news)? Is it fair to have their commercial messages surrounded by warring parties?

The network decision tries to assure fairness by avoiding the issue entirely. No consequentialists, they. *All* controversial messages are rejected. To be fair by avoiding "fairness"? This can be examined more closely.

Fairness to whom? The public? There is apparently no evidence that the viewing public would be disturbed by advertising dealing with controversial issues, and considerable philosophical support that they would benefit by being better informed. The existing advertisers? Reasonably, they would be happier without contentious competition. What of the advertisers excluded? Be they multinational conglomerates or earnest but underfinanced special-interest groups, they long for access to the massive audiences of the networks.

So ultimately the matter seems to clarify itself in terms of consequences rather that principles. Paul's network has set a rule based on apparently lofty ethical planes that would seem, on closer examination, to have been shaped primarily by concern for the network's regular advertisers and, consequently, the financial well-being of the network itself.

The facts in this case are simply not clear. No one knows for certain how the other advertisers would react; nor the public—whether or not public enlightenment, confusion, or irritation would be the outcome. It comes down to a value judgment. The rule under which Paul operates is championed on elevated formalistic ground, yet, as we have seen, a case can certainly be made that it is, instead, narrowly consequentialist in its concerns. (There has been no apparent attempt to seek a moral middle ground. Perhaps particular time segments could be set aside solely for advertising dealing with controversial themes; thus those who wish to watch could.)

Rules, Paul may have reflected, can be either ethically liberating or confining. What may have seemed particularly troublesome was the underlying answer when, following the Potter Box to step four, he asked to whom moral duty was owed. Paul answered that question in favor of his employer, but he also recognized an alternative response. And that is what caused him concern.

42. Advice from a Biased Source?

The advertising manager for retail accounts had just issued the marching orders. Given the tight economic times, increasing pressure from the cheap free-subscription shopper, and the new aggressiveness of television salespeople, the newspaper was beginning to see a decline in its retail linage. The message was clear: we need to be more aggressive in promoting the use of our newspaper's advertising space by the community's retailers. Sell them on the idea of:

- The newspaper as a preferred advertising medium
- This newspaper as the best of that breed
- Frequent advertising versus infrequent
- Big space versus small space

And that, Dick Lutz thought, is the nature of the business, at least in his ten years in retail sales. Newspapers are convinced they need substantial advertising subsidies in order to function. As economic times grow uncertain and competition becomes tighter, that income source is threatened. And then comes the call to the barricades. Sell harder. Be more creative. Become indispensible to your accounts.

There, Dick reflected, may be the heart of the dilemma that virtually all media salespeople face. Advertising, by it very nature, is an uncertain process. Most people, most of the time, cannot determine with any accuracy just what they are getting for their advertising dollars. And although retailers are closer to the actual sales transaction than a manufacturer like Procter and Gamble, the problem is no less real. The ad could have been fine but the timing was lousy. The timing may have been fine but the ad was not. Both may have been swell but competitors were more active. In addition, few retailers are able to use the expertise of advertising agencies. As a result they often handle advertising in their free moments, or delegate it to some idle employee. Sometimes this works out to their great advantage. Frequently, it does not.

And there, Dick knew, is where people such as himself enter the picture. He can offer at least the appearance of expertise to retailers struggling with the question of advertising, and at no cost. For the actual preparation of a newspaper ad—the writing of copy and the physical layout—is provided by the paper's staff, without charge. Within this set of expectations—a desirable service offered in an ambiguous area—it was hardly surprising that Dick and his colleagues would be consulted for answers to more fundamental questions: When should I advertise? How big should my ad be?

The answer to these questions from the paper's point of view was simple. Advertise as much as you possibly can. (Dick also knew that it would be desirable to encourage advertising in the paper's light editions, Monday and Saturday, rather than the very popular Wednesday and Friday.)

Of course his own financial future was linked directly (commissions) and indirectly (the paper's overall financial health) to the paper's prosperity. Ideally, as retailers prosper through increased advertising, so will the paper.

But those reasons rarely allow Dick the opportunity to suggest:

- "You don't need to advertise as much as you're doing now."
- "You can get by with smaller space than you're using."
- "Honestly, I think you'd be better off in radio."
- Or (horror of horrors), "Jack, I really think you'd be better off not advertising at all and putting the money into hiring better salespeople."

In the land of the blind, Dick mused, the one-eyed man is king. He may not have all the answers about advertising's effectiveness, but his experience can certainly be helpful to uncertain retailers. But should his advice be followed when his motives are so clearly directed by self-interest? What kind of person can rise above self-interest when it conflicts with the well-being of another? Perhaps a salesman who is thereafter unemployed?

The ethical dilemma Dick Lutz faces is common for media personnel dealing with unsophisticated advertisers. Under the best of circumstances and intentions, advertising is an uncertain process. Because of the host of other variables that can confound a simple cause-and-effect assumption, even giant advertisers with state-of-the-art research are often unsure exactly what they should be saying, to whom, and with what size and frequency. And for every advertising colossus there are thousands of small producers and retailers whose advertising savvy is extremely limited. They represent a potentially vulnerable population.

It is often difficult to get some retailers to advertise at all ("I tried it once and nothing happened") or to switch from one medium to another ("I've had good luck with radio, why should I use television?"). But once an account has been established and a salesperson becomes a regular partner in the advertising efforts of the store, the door is open to become something more than simply an order taker.

Dick can satisfy himself with the knowledge that the services he and his paper provide—particularly the actual preparation of the ads—are valuable to many retailers and may well increase their advertising efficiency. Indeed, the advice and services that he offers often approach the ideal of enlightened self-interest for all parties. That is, "We help you because you're advertising with us, and if you succeed you'll advertise more with us, and . . . ."

But Dick knows full well that the formula—big ads + high frequency = success—does not work for all retailers all the time. What are his choices then? His first choice is to seek the self-interest of the newspaper in all situations. Quite often that will result in sound advice for the advertiser as well. If not, the decision to advertise still belongs to the retailer, who is certainly aware that an ad salesperson is a biased adviser. Even if the newspaper should sacrifice some of its self-interest for the retailer, the results of specific advertising are often too obscure to make a difference. Moral duty is owed first to the paper, and secondarily to the retailer, assuming the harmony of self-interests.

Dick's second alternative is to serve the best interest of the retailer in all situations. As the retailer perceives Dick operating against the newspaper's short-term interests, respect may grow. More business in the long run—either from that retailer or from others who respect Dick's advice—could be the result. Then when Dick does recommend a major campaign, it may be taken more seriously. Here Dick honors his notions of fairness to the retailer. The market payoff can be seen to be long-term rather than short.

Dick's dilemma is intensified by the reality of the marketplace. His competitors—the salespeople for the shoppers, radio and television stations, and others—are quite likely attempting to persuade the same retailers from their own narrowly defined self-interests. Thus, if Dick pursues the retailer-sensitive option, the newspaper may suffer losses, at least in the short run. Since the advertising manager's call to the barricades was stimulated by short-run losses, how receptive will he be to Dick's argument that unbiased advice will benefit the paper in the long run? "If they want unbiased advice, let them hire a consultant," may well be the manager's reply.

Depending on the depth of his moral convictions, there may be another option Dick could pursue. By quitting his job and becoming a hired consultant to retailers, he could use his knowledge of the local advertising scene to benefit all of his clients, and in a far more objective manner. But that is a difficult and uncertain way to earn a living.

43. Normal Expectations

Charles Arnett had been on the job only a few months. He was pleased to be on the sales staff of a network affiliate in one of the country's largest television markets. After college he had worked for two years writing catalog copy for Sears; the face-to-face challenge of selling was a welcome change.

Now the sales manager had given him an additional responsibility. A major soft drink company, one of their largest advertisers, had asked the sales staff of his station to analyze expenditures of other soft drink advertisers in the station's "ADI" (Area of Dominant Influence.) In short, they wanted to know how much their rivals were spending on television advertising in the market. The company could have secured this information from specialized research services, but they knew they could get it cheaper by using station staffers.

The job was not difficult, just tedious. Some of the information was available in standardized forms while the rest could be gleaned from a series of discrete inquiries, making use of friends, and friends of friends.

Charles was pleased with the final report, and set up an appointment to present it to the sales manager. At the meeting his boss listened attentively and expressed appreciation for Charles' thoroughness. Only one change was needed before the final report was presented to the advertiser, he said: inflate all the figures by 15 percent.

"Why?" Charles asked. "The figures are accurate now."

"Yes," the manager countered, "but overall they suggest that the company's competitors are getting by with *less* television advertising. Those Fizzy-Pop people are so profit oriented, the first thing they'll see is that they can get by with less as well. Presto! We lose hard-won advertising dollars in a *very* competitive business. Besides, everybody exaggerates a bit. That's the nature of the game."

"If Fizzy-Pop wanted purer data, they could have paid for them through an outside research firm," the manager concluded. "Push up the figures," he demanded, "and take my thanks for a job well done."

Well, why not, Charles decided. His boss would be pleased, the station could hang on to Fizzy's generous advertising support—perhaps even increase it—and Fizzy could certainly afford it. After all, advertising is a very competitive business.

The outcome of this encounter is clear. Charles assented to the lies. For what good? This bears closer examination.

His boss informs him that the system tolerates, even encourages, exaggeration, due to its highly competitive nature. Since his station is part of the system, it is appropriate that it abide by the rules of the game in its own self-interest. And since Charles is a part of the station, which is in turn part of the system. . .

As noted in previous discussions, a common ethical touchstone for many in the advertising business is an implicit belief in the basic fairness of the market system. This assumes that people act in their self-interest through a deliberate and calculating path with enough competing parties to assure that no one's pursuit of self-interest exploits others. The long-range outcome is the good of all through the natural harmony of self-interests.

This situation, however, has no such well-meaning rationale. The system here is a narrow one indeed. Examine the pieces. Charles benefits by playing along and giving his boss what he wants. His boss benefits by doing a favor for a valued advertiser, however tainted the market analysis may be. By maintaining the appearance of commitment to his advertiser, the manager enhances his position with his own boss, the station owner.

From here on, however, the good-for-all thesis becomes increasingly unsupportable. It is conceivable that Fizzy-Pop's advertising manager could benefit from Charles' exaggeration simply because he is constantly engaged in a battle with Fizzy executives for a share of the overall company budget, and budget share equals power. Thus, illogical as it may at first seem, it is unlikely he would say to his boss, "We don't need as much money for advertising as we thought! Use it someplace else in the company." Certainly the company at large fails to benefit because it is required to commit financial resources to a problem that has been deliberately exaggerated.

But, perhaps of ultimate importance here, the public is never considered. As we have seen, some other areas of advertising practice are rationalized precisely because of public action (or inaction). For example: "We advertise cigarettes because people buy them. If they didn't want them they wouldn't buy them, and our advertising wouldn't work." Yet, there is not even a whisper of acknowledgment of the public in this case. Will the public benefit from more soft drink advertising than they need to make a consumer decision? It would be difficult to so argue, but in any event the question is never raised.

What emerged ultimately, then, was a decision to lie based on an extremely convoluted utilitarian rationale. The good for the many in this case is defined only as Charles, his boss, and possibly a self-interested executive in the client company.

"Everybody does it" can be a compelling rationale, as all of us know from experience with our peer groups. For those concerned with thinking ethically, however, it should not be sufficient. Who is everybody? Who will benefit from the lie?

To justify his behavior, Charles must accept extremely narrow interpretations of these essential questions. Of even greater importance, he begins to accept this altered approach to the system as a rule to be applied in all future situations. The next time Charles faces such a dilemma, its resolution will seem considerably less complex.

44. Inside Information—I

As a food advertising specialist for a midwestern city's dominant newspaper, Kristine Larrimore called on the supermarkets and specialized food stores of the area. Depending on their needs, she would simply take their prepared advertising and arrange for scheduling, or get information for an ad to be turned over to the paper's copy department for layout and production. Given the monopoly position of her paper, little hard selling was necessary. Rather, she simply pointed out opportunities in upcoming food supplements and the like, and downplayed the growing number of free shopper papers that some advertisers were beginning to find attractive.

In the course of her job, Kristine acquired a great deal of inside information concerning upcoming promotional plans and general advertising philosophies of her regular advertisers. Then one morning a few weeks before Thanksgiving, a manager in one of the city's largest supermarket chain stores told her just how much that information was worth.

First, Joe Gibbons reminded her of the cut-throat nature of food retailing, particularly during uncertain economic times. Second, he pointed out that the ultimate beneficiary of all this competition was the consumer, and if the customer does enough business with a store offering low prices, everybody benefits. Then came the clincher. Joe offered Kristine $500 cash for one small piece of information: what will Saveco's Thanksgiving turkey prices be. "Frankly," Joe pointed out, "we don't want to go any lower than necessary. But if we knew Saveco's price, we could at least match it, if not undercut it. The customer wins, and you'll be $500 richer for helping the transaction."

In the awkward moment, Kris refused. (She wondered later if she would have done the same thing if her paper had not been in a near monopoly position and Joe had someplace else to go.) First, she told Joe that the paper explicitly forbids the leaking of confidential information to interested parties. (She knew, of course that there were breaches of that ideal.) But, perhaps of greater importance, she contended, if she shared such information with Joe there was no guarantee she would not share his prices when it was in her interest to do so. To work efficiently for both of us, she said, we have to trust one another.

Joe was embarrassed and angry. Without the information he wanted so badly, he set his turkey prices, and found them two cents a pound higher than those of Saveco. Joe's chain suffered heavy sales losses in the holiday rush.

Kristine's subsequent dealings with Joe could be best characterized as strained. But, over time, they regained much of their prebribe rapport.

This case provides an opportunity to use relatively structured ethical criteria for examining four fundamental questions for ethical analysis:[2]

1. *What makes a right act right?* In this situation, Joe Gibbons relies on the standards of personal relativism. It is right to offer a bribe to Kristine because it is in his best interest to do so. His allusions to a public benefit are a point to be examined later.

   Kristine initially equates right with her paper's policy. Her employer explicitly forbids it, therefore she cannot. Her second argument, however, transcends that limited standard. The criterion that violating the trust of other advertisers is simply wrong, regardless of the consequences, or the guidelines imposed by others, depends on such universal principles as justice and fairness. Does it say anything about her own standards to note the order of argument?

2. *To whom is moral duty owned?* Joe feels that moral duty is owed to himself. By serving himself, he argues, he will ultimately be serving others, namely his customers.

   Kristine first suggests that her duty is to her employer. Secondarily, she asserts that an obligation is owed to her clients—those advertisers she contacts on behalf of the paper.

3. *What kinds of acts are right?* The contrast here is particularly instructive. Joe is concerned with the consequences of the situation. His self-interest is evident, but he also contends that the public will benefit; in other words, the greatest good for the greatest number. The strength of this conviction weakens, however, with his admission that he has no desire to price his turkeys any lower than necessary. His profit margin is still the important factor. There is the unspoken concern that, lacking Kristine's information, he might price his turkeys too low—for him, not the public.

   Kristine, by contrast, is arguing on a relatively more formal level. Regardless of the consequences, the bribe is wrong, specifically because her paper forbids it, and generally because it would represent a breach of faith. Obviously, the second rationale is more fundamental than the first.

4. *How do rules apply to specific situations?* Joe is stressing the importance of this particular set of circumstances. Kristine, in the first instance, is equally concerned with this particular situation since it is covered in her employer's rules. Her fairness argument, however, touches on basic standards of human conduct that transcend specific conditions.

Both parties felt guilty—Joe because he recognized that his action transgressed accepted norms and was held to account on their behalf; Kristine because her client had been compromised and, perhaps, because she was uncertain how much of her decision was due to leverage created by her paper's monopoly position.

Kristine's initial reliance on situation-specific criteria for right suggests that her ethical standards could be compromised in the future.

How will she decide when the company's rules do not cover a particular situation? Are her more universal standards of fairness and justice strong enough to stand the pressure of a moment without the support of her employer's rule book?

Ethical thinking requires reflection and analysis. Lacking that, an individual may assume a mantle of righteousness when one is, in fact, a prisoner of events.

45. Inside Information – II

The classified advertising section of any reputable daily newspaper comes as close to the ideal of pure market information as any advertising is likely to provide. Sellers and buyers find it a constantly renewing forum of exchange, generally free from the verbal and graphic hyperbole of the more pervasive display advertising. As such, its information is frequently prized.

Martha Louwens, a 28-year-old mother of two, had recently re-entered the work force as a classified advertising salesperson for the town's only paper. Actually "salesperson" was misleading. Basically she was an order taker. Individuals would call when they had decided to place a classified ad. Martha and her colleagues would then tell them the rates, take down the exact wording for the ad or, rarely, help the customer compose the ad over the phone.

In this role Martha acquired a great deal of timely information. She learned of the pending sale of items prized by herself and her friends: "Big Wheels" for the kids, room air conditioning units, used children's clothing, home furnishings in good condition, and so on. Then there were the job openings. Frequently employers listed a telephone number and placed priority on a first-come first-served basis for qualified applicants.

Since Martha had this information a day, or at least several hours, before the paper's next edition, she got into the habit of sharing the news with friends who she felt might be interested. (On some occasions she would follow up herself.) As a general rule she asked her friends to wait until just about the time the paper hit the streets. That way no suspicion could be cast on her or her department. Such caution had caused her friends to lose a few good opportunities to sharp-eyed early readers, but usually not. When someone can plan their action in advance, he can usually operate with considerable advantage.

Martha's caution indicated the presence of an ethical, if not administrative, question, though there were no specific prohibitions. She knew that the information in the classifieds was intended for the newspaper readership in toto, not for a select few and their friends. Indeed, some people out there could possibly use the items or jobs a great deal more than Martha or her friends. The classifieds as an open forum are less open under these conditions. She knew that.

Still, Martha was not troubled enough to stop. First, it happened on only a small fraction of all the material she handled. Also, was not the purpose of a classified to sell the item, fill the job, or whatever? She was certainly facilitating that. Finally, she had to admit, there was the special feeling of being an insider who could offer her friends favored treatment. She might not be able to give them hot tips on Wall Street, or tickets for the ball game, but at least this was something.

_____

Martha is scarcely a shaker and mover in the advertising business. Yet even in an ordinary job dealing with matters of little economic significance, she confronts ethical decisions.

Apparently, she feels vaguely guilty. Why? It is not clear whether her coworkers offer similar favors to their friends, but the basic cause for her unease may be that she knows full well she is violating the spirit if not the letter of the newspaper's policies. Would she have acted in the same way if the ethical dimensions had been made explicit? Perhaps, for her desire to feel important in her first venture into the workplace since her children were born may have proven too strong even then. In any case, the absence of a specific rule has allowed her the latitude to act on her own.

Who is served by her actions? Without doubt the seller, who is usually not concerned with who buys, merely that someone does and as rapidly as possible. Her friends benefit, of course. Given the bite of inflation, an inside track on bargains or a desirable job is an extremely valuable commodity. And, at the heart of the matter, Martha benefits by being important to others in a job whose objective dimensions are not likely to impress.

Martha has apparently constructed her rationale so that her decision making has become routine. She will provide information to friends unless it is of no use to them. Her rule of serving the relatively small universe of self, friends, and seller supersedes the spirit of fairness.

Suppose Martha encountered Rawl's veil of ignorance, and was unsure whether she would emerge as the ad taker with inside information or a member of the public at large, very interested in good buys and good jobs. Would she choose the course she now follows, or assure access to the marketplace by *all* the newspaper's readers?

Others handle this type of information too—her coworkers in classifieds, those in the composing room, and the printers. Each kind of worker is in a position to short circuit the normal function of classified ads.

Given that the purpose of the ad is to sell, never mind to whom, and the relatively elusive notion of fairness, it may be that responsibility lies with the newspaper's administration to develop an ethical code that explicitly protects the interests of the readers.

In the meantime, Martha will probably remain a functionary at her newspaper. Yet her custom-made ethical code raises questions, not only about her own moral integrity, but about the effects of her actions on others. Jules Feiffer called his book about the day-to-day tribulations of living in New York City, *Little Murders*. In like spirit, it is the little compromises of people such as Martha that establish and maintain a working environment where short-run advantage triumphs over long-term integrity, personal gain over fairness.

Notes

1. For a recent assessment see S. Prakash Sethi, "Battling Antibusiness Bias: Is There a Chance of Overkill?" *Public Relations Journal* 37 (November 1981): 22–24, 64.

2. Summarized from Robert Veatch, *Case Studies in Medical Ethics* (Cambridge, Mass.: Harvard University Press, 1977).

Chapter Ten

Macro Issues: Inherent Ethical Milieus

In this final chapter of our inquiry into the ethical dimensions of advertising, we offer not case histories, but issues. These issues, it can be contended, are inherent in the practices of advertising. That is, all advertising must face questions of setting priorities; all advertising must face questions of privacy; all advertising in utilizing the mass media must encounter questions of the effects of that usage; and all advertising is related to resource allocation.

So merely by entering the field the individual becomes a part of the rules by which the institution performs and is perpetuated. There is a great deal to grapple with here. As we shall see, whether advertising is considered saint or sinner is strongly affected by the assumptions made by individuals about such fundamental concepts as human nature, the proper role of the individual and the state, and so on.

They are not issues with starkly clear resolutions. It is hoped that the analysis will illuminate some of the dimensions of ethical decision making that are evident for all those wishing to see.

46. The Alteration of Priorities

Advertising, by its nature, is self-interested communication. The advertiser is paying for this form because he hopes that its use will provide a financial return in excess of his investment. With sums of money available and the task undertaken of profit potential, the advertiser seeks to reduce the risk of financial loss or sustain existing financial gain by attempting to rivet the consciousness of the intended or existing patrons of the product or service.

This is endemic to virtually all forms of advertising. Thus advertisements attempt to elevate the choice of one brand of beer over another to significant social proportions. They assign personalities to inanimate objects (witness the Marlboro man, the Chanel woman and their ilk). They attempt to associate the good life with the acquisition of relevant products and services rather than spiritual qualities that may be associated with character. In general ads say, *"Pay attention to this! This is important!"*

Obviously all advertisers do not succeed. Some are simply inept. Others offer little of perceived worth. Many cannot achieve their wishes because of lack of funds. Virtually all, however, would like dearly to try, and therein lies a systemic element of advertising, fraught with ethical dimensions. Consider:

- The film "Superman" was introduced with some 6.5 *billion* messages through radio, television, magazines, and newspapers, in addition to the separate promotions of more than 1,000 Superman-related products.
- Procter and Gamble, one of the country's largest advertisers, has successfully promoted brands such as Duncan Hines, Crisco, Ivory, Crest, Gleem, White Cloud, Charmin, Pampers, Tide, and Cheer into the consumer consciousness. After acquiring a regional coffee company called J.A. Folger, it promoted the Folgers brand city by city with enormous promotion. In Philadelphia P & G mailed free samples to 1.5 million homes, and twenty-five cent discount coupons to a million more. The formerly obscure brand is now a market power.
- The Federal Trade Commission has stated that in 1979 cigarette companies for the first time spent over *$1 billion* on advertising.
- The promoters of the movie *Jaws* bought 30-second spot announcements on 95 percent of all the prime-time television network programs for three full days before the opening day.
- Virtually all advertising, as historian David Potter noted some 30 years ago, is training us to be consumers, with all that implies.

Individually and collectively, then, advertisers are basically attempting to alter priorities; to get their brand, their idea, and their suggested life style to the top of our mental shopping lists. To get us to think: "I *must* see that movie. I *must* try that brand. *That* is a great way to live. I never thought of *that* before."

None, of course, have the power to compel, no matter how vast their promotional efforts. They do, however, have the power to prevail —prevail in our magazines, newspapers; prevail in our radio and television programs; prevail on the shelves, and in the store windows; ultimately, prevail in our priorities.

Virtually all advertisers wish to do this. It is, again, part of the system. And so, then, are the ensuing ethical consequences.

As we have noted several times, advertising tends to thrive in a market system of resource allocation. It is hardly surprising that advertising practitioners frequently use the ideology of the market to defend and promote their craft. Thus, advertising is defended because it promotes competition among self-seeking advertisers who are always held in check by the inherent rationality of consumers and the relentless forces of competition. The mechanism of this constant interchange of self-interest is thought to be the "invisible hand," leading self-interests in directions that will ultimately serve the best interests of all.

To the charge that advertising by its nature attempts to direct consciousness to serve the advertiser's self-interest, the practitioners respond "Guilty." But, it would be added quickly, what works well for the successful advertiser also works well for customers. We rely upon the basic assumptions of the classical liberal market with its strong utilitarian rationale (greatest good for the greatest number).

Why then the ethical concern? Because two of the key assumptions underlying the harmony of interests of the classical liberal market can be strongly contested, and, with them, the inherent fairness of the system.

There is the matter of man's rationality. Most people, most of the time, are not careful shoppers, and they do not have extensive knowledge about alternatives. The continued success of Bayer aspirin in the face of countless lower-priced and functionally comparable competitors serves as a case in point. Heavily advertised movies often are rewarded (but not always) by strong initial patronage, regardless of the quality of the film. If consumers are not always driven by the internal drummer of a deliberate and calculating nature, the argument for man's inherent good sense weakens, and the contention of manipulation is strengthened.

And what of the safeguard of competition? The ideologues of the classical liberal market assumed a large number of competitors offering virtually identical products, all competing on the basis of price, with no one big enough to influence the outcome. Contrast that with the pre-pared cereal industry, where three dominate, the automobile industry with three and a half domestic firms, and so on. At the producer, and, increasingly, the retail level, concentration, rather than diffusion of market power, continues to be the fact of the marketplace. Enjoying market power, the firms commonly choose to avoid price competition and compete on the level of brand, with a rich supporting cast of sym-bolic dimensions contributed through packaging, advertising, and merchandising.[1]

If one takes the erosion of these two assumptions of the market's supporting ideology seriously, then advertising emerges with the poten-tial for exploitation. The biggest advertiser, rather than the producer of the most efficient or satisfying gadget or service, is able to attract pat-ronage due in large part to pervasiveness of the symbol packages we call advertising.

Defenders renounce this thinking. Advertising, they assert, cannot compel. The self-interest of the advertiser requires that he interpret the product or service in terms of the self-interest of potential consum-ers. So constituted, advertisements serve busy individuals as handy guides for efficient buying. If the buyer is not interested, the effort fails, and the producer is left to ponder new advertising or, perhaps, a new product.

Frame the issue in terms of moral responsibility. By asserting belief in the rationality of consumers (consumer sovereignty), and the basic fairness of the market, the advertisers are in essence pressing responsi-bility on to the consumers themselves. They are the final judges. They can best make the decisions between competing stimuli. They know what they can afford, what satisfies them.

Those who raise the ethical dimensions, on the other hand, are arguing that moral responsibility is not served by simple reliance on the impersonal forces of the market. The advertisers, government, or some combination, need to assume the task of assuring that the best interests of individuals are served. The system, they contend, is *not* working for the good of all concerned. People are paying more than they need to, eating less healthfully than they should be, spending their money less wisely than they could be. It is unethical to assume that responsibility rests with individuals alone.[2]

47. The Invasion of Privacy

Simply, regardless of the content of the messages, advertisers are trying to get at us. It is inherent to the system, and the advantages are strongly on the side of the advertiser. As critic Jerry Mander noted, *all advertising is an attempt by one party to dominate another*.[3] The first party is the advertiser, and the second, the potential consumer.

With the exception of predictable market information forums like the phone directories, classifieds, and weekly supermarket ads, advertising seeks us out; we do not seek it. Against the backdrop of that relentless seeking, ethical dimensions must necessarily emerge.

As Mander sees it, the essence of the advertising process is that the advertiser talks and we listen. We have very little opportunity to alter the monologue or even avoid it. If a friend constantly talked at us, we could tell him to change the subject, request his silence so we could respond, or walk away.

Advertisers, however, monopolize the subject in whatever manner and frequency and volume they choose, seek us out in virtually every facet of our lives, make it extremely difficult for us to avoid them, and provide us with no opportunity to respond except at the point of purchase. The result is a system destined to intrude.

The term "behavioral interdiction' in advertising circles means putting an advertisement in front of someone as they go about their daily affairs—to interdict their behavior. Thus:

- As we watch the college football game, hot-air balloons with advertisements painted on their skins rise above us.
- As we listen to the radio, the announcer moves from a news story to a commercial announcement with only the slightest pause.
- As we travel the highways, signs compete for our attention.
- In our favorite magazine the editorial matter can be found amid a growing forest of ads.
- As we walk down the streets friends pass wearing faddish shirts bearing advertising messages.
- As we struggle home with the Sunday New York *Times* we know full well that a great deal of that bulk is not editorial sinew.
- At our favorite baseball stadium the walls and scoreboard bristle with advertising messages.
- Relaxing on a beach, the sky is bisected by a plane pulling a banner reminding us where to spend the evening eating and drinking hours.

The result of this, Mander feels, is that we develop a defensive posture; we shut ourselves off in order to retain our privacy. But at what cost? And why should we have to? "Why do we tolerate this? What right do advertisers have to treat us this way? When did I sell the rights for them to run pictures in my mind? Why is it possible for people who are selling things to feel perfectly free to speak to me . . . without my permission, all day long?"[4]

From the perspective of our system of business, these complaints are crackpot: the right to persuade is assumed. From the perspective of ethical reasoning, the question of privacy is harder to dismiss.

———————

Privacy has been an essential element of civil liberty from the founding of this republic. Chapter 5 deals with some of the ethical issues faced by journalists when considering where the individual's privacy ends and the public's right to know begins.

At this point, the issue is raised in relation to a form of communication that is both pervasive and generally tolerated: advertising. Why is privacy an ethical issue here? Simply because of the advertising process itself, where the advertiser talks and we either listen, try to ignore it, or hide.

The best defense of advertising practice is found in the classical liberal ideology of self-interest ultimately serving the public good. In practice, however, that ideology faces staunch challenges. To begin with, the mass media that carry advertising messages in this country are terribly indiscriminate for advertising purposes. Those watching a given television program are likely to span virtually every demographic category. Thus, it is quite likely that a sizable part of any television audience will not be interested in the advertising carried on that program. The messages themselves must inevitably tend toward the common denominator in order to make the appeal as wide as possible. As a result, even those interested in a toilet bowl cleaner may not be attracted by the particular appeal in a specific message. Finally, there is the simple reality that advertisers control both the content and frequency of the messages. That is, rather than having the messages appear at our convenience with a message content that reflects our needs, the advertiser decides what is in his best interest to say (and not to say) and how often and where to say it. Sometimes (as the classical liberal ideology would suggest) this works well for all parties. Sometimes it does not, leading to frustrations from inappropriate timing and irritating repetition, or exasperation from mindless content.

The ethics of civilized communication require a polite and attentive interchange of ideas between two consenting parties. An individual has a perfect right to attempt to persuade another as long as (1) the party accepts the attempt to persuade initially, and (2) after making the best possible attempt at persuasion the initiating party accepts the judgment of the other and ceases his efforts.[5]

Can advertising meet either or both of these criteria? Perhaps the first in the sense that any astute individual in this culture who picks up a magazine or newspaper or tunes in a radio or television station is aware that a sizable portion of the content will be persuasive appeals. It is easier to avoid this element in print than in the broadcast media, but, in any case, forewarned is forearmed.

In the second instance it is difficult to see how the current state of the art offers much hope. No advertiser, no matter how zealous, wishes to waste money attempting to persuade someone who will not be budged. Rather the problems here rest with the indiscriminate reach of the media and the complexity of consumer behavior. If advertisers could neatly reach only those interested in their offerings, they would surely do so. Regrettably, the media do not gather audiences along these lines. Even with highly specialized publications, for example *Jogger's World*, some readers will not be interested in the content of a given message. A lot of advertising reaches people who are simply not attentive, and it reaches them over and over.

Then, there is the fickleness of the consumer. People change. An old advertising axiom is, "Your customers are a parade, not a mass meeting." Thus advertisers feel reasonably justified attempting to reach the unpersuadable with the expectation that, perhaps, one day soon. . . .

In spite of its obvious successes, advertising can be seen as a wasteful form of communication for both advertiser and receiver. The advertiser frequently pays to reach disinterested individuals, and is unsure how often he should advertise to achieve his ends. The consumer does not always find advertising when he is interested, and, when he does, it is not usually in a form that facilitates efficient and rational shopping.

To the extent that we still believe in the ideology of self-interest, we fail to recognize privacy as an advertising problem. Perhaps, as Mander suggests, advertisers should ask themselves a simple question inherent in ethical discourse: Am I welcome here?[6]

48. The Media Subsidy

If one were asked to select apt adjectives to describe the mass media of the United States, one of the first offered would be "privately owned." Close behind would be "advertiser supported."

The two have not always been so closely linked. For the better part of the eighteenth and nineteenth centuries in this country, publishers were essentially producing a low-cost convenience good. Their efforts were supported largely by simple reader subsidy; that is, the reader paid the entire cost (plus whatever profit was possible) of the newspaper or magazine.

But, by the early decades of the twentieth century the pattern had been altered. Rather than continue to raise the price of their commodity to their readers to reflect increases in production costs, most publishers chose to keep the cost to the reader low and use the contented readership to attract more advertisers. Thus, the advertising subsidy increased as that of the reader diminished. The consequence was inevitable: publishers became "brokers in blocs of consumers" as advertiser support became proportionally greater than that from the readers.

Thus today the vast majority of the media vehicles in this country owe their financial livelihood to advertisers first and readers/viewers/listeners second. Now, presumably one constituency could not be satisfied without the other, for if the readers/viewers/listeners are not attracted, advertisers will not be attracted.

Yet, it is uncontestably clear that the needs of the three central parties—publishers/broadcasters, advertisers, and listeners/viewers/readers—do not always harmonize.

Publishers/Broadcasters

How far does the publisher/broadcaster go to accommodate the advertiser? Is it, for example, ethical to:

- Attempt to accommodate more advertisers by either adding more advertising pages, or (as in broadcast) reducing the length of a standard commercial so that more may be aired?
- Create new units (for example, home buying sections, network news breaks) largely for the purpose of selling more advertising?
- Arrange the magazines, newspaper, radio or television programming largely for the benefit of the advertiser—for example, spread editorial material throughout the magazine so overall advertising readership may be higher; break into televised movies at points of advertiser rather than viewer convenience; stop televised football games at predetermined times, and so forth?
- Attempt publishing and/or broadcasting ventures only in terms of market-dominated criteria? "Are there enough advertisers willing to pay to have me gather these people into an audience?" It could be argued that there is a need for a mass media vehicle dealing with the concerns of the urban poor. But can you imagine an advertiser-supported magazine called *Ghetto Life*?
- Stop publication of a newspaper or magazine entirely due to weakened advertising without even questioning the readers as to whether or not they would be willing to shoulder more of the fare to keep their publication in business?[7]

Advertisers

What are the ethical dimensions of:

- Withholding support from magazines or newspapers whose editorial treatment of company-sensitive issues is not supportive?
- Regarding the audience as individuals who were gathered to read/view/listen to nonadvertising material and are, therefore, due no particular respect? Thus the advertisers feel free to repeat, shout, badger, seduce, or frighten as their needs dictate.
- Selecting media vehicles predominantly on the basis of impersonal readership/viewership/listenership criteria rather than making an attempt to determine the degree of commitment that exists between the vehicle and its audience?
- Knowing that withdrawal of advertising support for a particular vehicle may be partially responsible for depriving thousands or millions of individuals of that vehicle?

Listeners/Viewers/Readers

Audiences are consigned to a passive role if advertisers seek them out rather than the other way around. The audience must realize that their patronage of particular media vehicles sends messages back through the system. If they respond positively (or at least passively) to particular television/radio/newspaper/magazine content, they are quite likely to get more of the same. If they watch "whatever is on," they are clearly responsible for perpetuating the television forms so favored. If they find it less demanding to read *People* than *Harper's*, the ultimate consequences are predictable. If they silently tolerate advertising abuses of volume, content, taste, or sheer leverage, they encourage continuance of the same.

Other ethical dimensions for all of these actors should readily suggest themselves to the perceptive reader. We are talking here of ethical quandaries inherent in our system of media. Merely by participating in advertiser-subsidized mass media, the individual confronts potentially troubling issues. Given the nature of these elements so related, there is no way around it. The issues are there.

If one assumes that the sole purpose of media vehicles in this country is to make money, then the ethical issues are simplified considerably. The publisher or broadcaster simply produces an editorial or entertainment package that attracts the largest possible audience of interest to advertisers. Advertisers and their agencies, in turn, select those vehicles with the lowest cost per thousand or those that yield the most efficient demographic segments. Both can rationalize their single-mindedness by assuming they are supporting media vehicles that offer the public what they want. And the attraction of listeners, viewers, and readers completes the circle.

If, however, one raises questions of whether reliance on advertising revenue leads to a vigorous and satisfying mass media for the society, then other questions emerge. For example, how might advertising support be related to the quantity of media vehicles in this country as well as the quality of their content?

Quantity. The media landscape in the United States is abundantly populated. Daily and weekly suburban papers have flourished even as the number of urban dailies declines. Magazines appeal to every vocation and avocation, frequently supported by advertisers grateful to reach a homogeneous audience of hang glider addicts, antique buffs, or science fiction enthusiasts. Specialized radio programming abounds on both AM and FM, and even television, still the massiest of the mass media, continues to fragment through ad hoc networks, cable, pay television, and other accommodations to the laws of competition for advertiser money and viewer tastes.

As media vehicles serve advertisers, their missions change accordingly. They become brokers in blocs of consumers; they seek out not simply interest blocs, but markets. Since markets are associated with the kind of disposable income needed to buy the baubles of our consumer society, it follows that the media will follow markets. Thus the young, affluent, and well educated will likely be overindulged with media attention, while the impoverished will be ignored.

Quality. Regardless of the quantity, is the content of these media vehicles strongly affected by advertising? If so, for good or ill? Here the critic and supporter fail to reach even tentative agreement.

- Critic—Mass media in the United States are regrettably in the business of gathering audiences for advertisers. As a result they try to attract as many from a desirable market as they possibly can. This is typically accomplished with lowest common denominator content that emphasizes the titillating and sensational rather than the substantive and thoughtful. In short, the media "attract the eye without engaging the mind" while offering a degrading diet of truncated news, violence, sex, and simplistic comedy and drama.
- Supporter—The media in the United States are diverse and vigorous, their content ranging from the profound to the profane. The variation in content is a reflection of the interests and tastes of the American people. The media, after all, are surviving in a market. If they do not serve the needs of

an audience, they will falter and disappear. The reader, listener, or viewer has the ultimate veto authority. Finally, support from a variety of advertisers is far more likely to produce a press free to criticize the government than would be the case if government supported the media, as it does in many other countries.

Only an extremely narrow, profit-only conception of the media would free advertising professionals from ethical questions regarding the interplay of commercial messages and media programming. Given the stakes, the issues must be raised and confronted.

49. Resource Allocation

Any planet, any continent, any society, any city, home, or individual, faces the problems of resource allocation. There is only so much time, so many raw materials, so much money. Decisions must be made and resources allocated appropriately. Advertising has been criticized and championed as playing a significant role in this allocation process, either to reinforce existing values, or, far more ominously, to alter the old and shape the new. It is a matter inherent with advertising and laden with ethical questions.

A favorite classroom gambit is to suggest to students that the instructor will be visiting them in their hometowns and wishes to be taken for a ride around the city. The only stipulation is that "somewhere along the line we travel past the homes of the most successful people in town." Asked about where their tour would go, students inevitably offer descriptions of well manicured lawns, large and impressive houses, ample driveways, and so on. And then the sting—"I didn't tell you to include the homes of the *richest* people in town, only the most successful." What, they are asked, of the school janitor in his inconspicuous home? He has worked hard all his life to support a family and make their life better than his. He gives of his time and money (such as it is) to others, and is, after 35 years of thick and thin, still devoted to the same woman. Why is he not successful?

Because those are not the values that our market system has come to honor. Advertising, critics assert, is very much the handmaiden in this market enterprise, as its overall effect is to equate achievement with things, and fulfillment with the consumption of goods and services. If the market has no goal except to meet market demand, advertising can be said to help direct that demand toward a warped system of values that sees more spent on the advertising of pet foods than on many social programs.

Assume for a moment that advertising is merely a *reflection* of consumer sovereignty. If we have too many cars and not enough beautiful drives, it is the consumers' will that it be so, and advertising is only following the market directives. But if advertising *leads*, if it shapes and directs demand, then the tens of billions spent for it may well lead us to equate cars with social status, cigarettes with assertion of gender, and pills with relief from the strains of everyday living.

At the time of this writing, many secondary and elementary schools are in deep financial crisis. Library acquisitions are being cut, educational programs curtailed. Suppose, that for a period of one year, the amount now spent for cigarette advertising (over $1 billion) were spent (with similar expertise) advertising school bond issues. Would we have better schools?

The matter becomes more troubling when one's perspective is widened. A recent church publication offered this picture.

If the world were a global village of 100 people, 70 of them would be unable to read, 1 would have a college education, over 50 would be suffering from malnutrition, and over 80 would live in what we call sub-standard housing.

If the world were a global village of 100 residents, 6 of them would be Americans. These six would have half of the village's entire income, and the other 94 would exist on the other half.

An authoritative scenario for the year 2000 depicts a widening gap between the haves and have-nots. Does advertising accelerate the situation? Can advertising improve it? Or is it merely a passive element totally dependent upon other motivating forces such as political systems? Should those who work in advertising be concerned with these matters? By way of extreme example, should ethical questions be raised about the promotion of a cheese-flavored dog food when thousands of people are dying of malnutrition? The questions, and the difficulties inherent in any answers, are not likely to disappear.

In the spirit of these concerns, Carl Ally, one of advertising's more outspoken figures, proposed that advertising should take upon itself the task of helping to solve the world's economic ills. He noted that the condition of 20 percent of the world's population consuming more than 80 percent of the world's products cannot long endure, particularly with the rising aspirations of many Third World countries. Advertising, Ally suggested, can help by leading the more affluent countries to accept a

new ethos featuring curtailed consumption, assuming that the resources thus conserved could be more equitably distributed.[8]

Many of us may remember, as youngsters, parents admonishing us to
finish the food on our plates because of the starving children somewhere else on earth. It was never made clear how eating our remaining
food, which was to be thrown in the garbage if we did not oblige,
would fill the stomachs of children half a world away. Yet the idea was
right: waste less and have more to share.

Many would nod in agreement with the sentiments suggested in
Ally's farsighted message. Yet to implement it would involve enormous
change. As we have seen throughout this book, if one endorses the
motivating force of self-interest inherent in the market system and also
assumes that the safeguards of rational man and atomistic competition
are in place, then good will be the ultimate result. To return to the extreme example mentioned earlier, the producer of cheese-flavored dog
food can believe he is behaving ethically by seeking his self-interest
that will in turn affect the well-being of his employees, contribute to
the viability of the domestic economy, and keep the country's economic
sinew better able to respond to the less fortunate of the world.

Basically, the market follows the currents of demand from the multitude below, rather than the edicts of planning from above. If advertising merely reflects that demand it is a relatively passive force and, at
best, may reinforce values already held. On the other hand, if advertising, fueled by self-interest, helps shape that demand and direct the
market, then two conclusions follow: (1) To the extent that advertising
encourages private consumption, particularly of products and services
high in energy consumption, it can be held to account for a shameful
misallocation of resources to the few at the cost of depriving the many.
(2) But if advertising is, in fact, powerful enough to direct this allocation of resources, it could also be used to redirect it to more socially beneficial ends. (Refer back to the idea of the ad budget of cigarette
companies being used instead to advertise the needs of schools.) And,
indeed, there are examples both large and small of such efforts. A
brief sampling:

- The efforts of the Advertising Council on behalf of such noteworthy efforts
  as aid to black colleges.
- The advertising of the foster children programs, and the various relief
  organizations.
- The numerous charitable promotions for hospitals and research on crippling
  diseases.

To the argument that these and other efforts are woefully under-financed, two answers: (1) Yes. But even a little of the right advertising can make a difference. For example, a single ad in each case was responsible for:

- The reintroduction and subsequent passage of a rat extermination bill for the city of New York.
- The killing of a bill that would have led to the damming of the Grand Canyon in order to provide hydroelectric power for the peak-hour needs of Phoenix.
- Asserting the independence of the tiny Caribbean island of Anguilla in the face of a pending landing by the Royal Marines to establish British sovereignty. After a single ad, opposition grew to such an extent that a member of the British press observed that the government "wouldn't dare land a canoe."

(2) Yes. It is a drop in the bucket and the only real solution is to introduce a more authoritarian political and economic system than we now have. In essence, government should then take control of the market to direct it in ways deemed desirable by those in power.

For advertising practitioners there may be three courses of action: (1) To endorse the values of the market system and assume that the good for all will ultimately prevail due to the motivating force of private interest and the basically fair allocations produced by the "invisible hand." (2) To find work in companies, agencies, or special interest groups that promote socially helpful causes. (3) To agitate for change in the political and economic system to replace the market as a resource allocation device with a more authoritarian system, expecting that the subsequent direction of resources will be more just.

Innocent bystander or dynamic agent of change? Channel of charity or selfishness? Advertising and resource allocation is an appropriate cosmic issue with which to signal the end of this section of our book, and, we hope, the commencement of ongoing study into the ethics of this complex, pervasive, controversial element of our culture.

Notes

1. For a far reaching discussion of this milieu, see Vincent Norris, "Advertising History According to the Textbooks," *Journal of Advertising* 9 (Summer, 1980): 3–11.
2. For a provocative statement of many of the issues in this chapter see, Jerry Mander, "Four Arguments for the Elimination of Advertising," in

Advertising and the Public, ed. Kim Rotzoll (Urbana: University of Illinois Department of Advertising), pp. 17–28.

3. Ibid., p. 19.

4. Ibid., p. 21.

5. Paul Keller and Charles T. Brown, "An Interpersonal Ethic of Communication," in *Messages*, ed. Jean Civikly (New York: Random House, 1974), pp. 41–50.

6. For a discussion of the advertiser's concept of "audience," see Kim Rotzoll, "Gossage Revisited," *Journal of Advertising* 9 (Fall, 1980): 6–14.

7. Ibid.

8. "Advertising Must Help Solve World Economic Ills: Ally," *Advertising Age* 45 (29 July 1974): 1, 54.

PART 3

Entertainment

When the question whether to worry about motion pictures came up before the Hutchins Commission on Freedom of the Press, the first reaction of several of those august scholars was "rubbish." The movies are diversionary, escapist, and silly. What claim can they make to be counted part of the modern press?

Fortunately, a more farsighted view prevailed: However unsophisticated, movies were part of the culture and needed a careful look. The commission invited Will Hays (chief of the Motion Picture Producers and Distributors of America) to present the case for industrial self-regulation, and eventually the Hollywood model of codes and intra-industry regulations was adopted by the commission as the best way of expressing social responsibility in a democratic society.

On both counts the commission displayed wisdom. While news and consumer information are the vital stuffs of media programming, clearly entertainment occupies most of the broadcast spectrum, the cinema screen, and a healthy share of the printed page as well. From these media we receive symbols of who we are, what we should believe, and how we should act. Entertainment, for all its recreative value, does much to educate and socialize its patrons, who are all of us.

Should entertainment programs be subject to ethical reasoning? Robert Redfield, distinguished anthropologist and one of the Hutchins' commissioners, urged that the direction of all our social productivity be toward a "new integrity" of idea and institution, a creative order wherein symbols and practices make "coherent sense when we state them and when we comply with them," leading to a "model society that will command the confidence of other free peoples everywhere."[1] Redfield, no dreamy chauvinist, was arguing the interdependency of social institutions (like the media) and social beliefs (like the sanctity of life). Yes, he would argue, the entertainment media must be put to the test of ethical reasoning.

The following chapters raise only a few of the questions and suggest some ways of approaching answers. Violence is a pressing concern; its threat to social order is immediate and dramatic. But what of the distrust bred of high financial stakes, or the indignities born of stereotypes and outright bias? When does the need for restraint become censorious, and when is moral exploration a better scheme than caution? It becomes clearer, as we proceed, that every level of the entertainment industry—producer, actor, writer, and viewer—is involved in close encounters with decisions of an ethical kind.

Notes

1. Robert Redfield, "Race and Human Nature," *Half a Century— Onward* (New York: Foreign Missions Conference of North America, 1944), p. 186.

Chapter Eleven

Violence

Few issues have commanded as much attention from media reformers as violence on television and in film. Some violence, of course, is inevitable in any drama, or even in comedy, as when Barney Flintstone bangs his nose into a door jamb. But the irrepressible climb in real violent crime, much of it perpetrated by juveniles, has been often linked to the rough and tumble lives of Theo Kojak, Dirty Harry, and Kung Fu. What a juvenile sees, it is argued, too easily becomes what a juvenile does. Since society cannot endure the anarchy of crime rule, it must move to eliminate the causes.

Against the censors of violence are combat-hardened libertarians who want all speech protected. Violent programming may or may not breed violent behavior, but curtailment of speech, they contend, surely heralds a retreat from democracy into feudalism. Or even worse, they view restrictions here as a return to the monastery where utterances are controlled and political choices programmed. Such a fate, they claim, is worse than all others, and avoiding it is worth the risk of giving too much latitude.

The problem of violence in entertainment media is our peculiar target in the cases that follow. "Born Innocent" brings up the effects argument: show a violent program, reap a violent crime. One of the standard industry replies to the effects argument is the rating system, which alerts responsible adults to potentially harmful programs. Who is responsible when ratings seem to fail? That is the problem in "Papillon."

If violence is tragic, a lot of violence is tragic for a long time. Such is our feeling about the Jewish Holocaust, now four decades past. Do we prosecute an injustice to those who suffered if we fail to communicate the depth of the tragedy? Case 52 probes that possibility.

Are media practitioners oblivious to the violence they contribute to the culture? Hardly. 'The Storyteller" explores the problem from inside the industry. In "Comic Capers" we look at the perennial issue of violence in children's media.

50. "Born Innocent" and the Imitation Argument

On the evening of 10 September 1974, the National Broadcasting Company sent to its affiliate stations a drama depicting the life of an unwanted child and by so doing set in motion a legal and moral drama whose theme was the power of television to influence human behavior.[1]

The program, "Born Innocent," starred Linda Blair as a girl whose innocence is shattered through her experience in a girls' reformatory. Because the drama would include violent scenes possibly objectionable to some viewers, NBC ran a warning at the start of the program: "'Born Innocent' deals in a realistic and forthright manner with the confinement of juvenile offenders and its effects on their lives and personalities. We suggest you consider whether the program should be viewed by young people or others in your family who might be disturbed by it." As a portent of the show's later troubles, 15 sponsors withdrew shortly before the broadcast.

"Born Innocent" did, in fact, raise objections from viewers. Hundreds of calls and letters were received by NBC affiliates across the nation, 700 in New York alone. (Only a few callers, notably social workers familiar with reformatories, applauded the network for its realistic portrayal of a pervasive problem.) Particularly troublesome was one scene in which Blair was raped by four female inmates using a plumber's helper for penetration. The victim was shown naked from the waist up.

The program and its forthright realism would have been largely academic but for a real-life rape three days later. On Baker Beach near San Francisco, nine-year-old Olivia Niemi was attacked by three girls and a boy, ages 9, 12, 13, 15, who "raped" her with a beer bottle in a fashion similar to the attack on television. Olivia's mother secured the services of personal-injury attorney Marvin E. Lewis, who filed suit for $11 million against NBC and the owners of KRON–TV.

Lewis' brief charged that NBC was guilty of negligence in broadcasting the program during family viewing hours (8 p.m. on the West coast). He claimed that one of the assailants referred to the television show when she was arrested. The link between dramatic and real violence might not be strictly causal, but the network had not taken adequate precaution against the program's potential effects on young viewers. His case was strengthened by the absence of any similar type of rape on the casebooks of juvenile authorities. If Olivia's attackers had perpetrated a first-of-its-kind rape, their teacher and proximate cause was the television network which had prestaged the event.

NBC declined to argue the facts. Instead, defense attorney Floyd Abrams contended that the First Amendment protected his client from damages from alleged effects of a media program. California Superior Court Judge John Ertola agreed. In September 1976, he ruled in favor of NBC without calling a jury, claiming, "The State of California is not about to begin using negligence as a vehicle to freeze the creative arts."

Lewis went to the Court of Appeals, which overturned the ruling. Niemi had a right to a jury trial on questions of fact, the appeal judges contended.

Before the case was retried, NBC urged the U.S. Supreme Court to quash the trial. At stake, the network claimed, were basic constitutional rights. On behalf of NBC, the American Library Association filed an amicus curiae suggesting that the Appeals Court ruling might lead to libraries being sued by victims of crimes suggested in books. The Writers Guild of America wrote of the "chilling effect" on popular drama that a trial on the facts could have. For Niemi, the California Medical Association filed a friend-of-the-court brief. The Supreme Court declined to intervene.

Each side geared for the coming courtroom battle. NBC could argue that a warning had been given before the drama, that the four attackers had previous juvenile records, and that some testimony suggested none of them had seen the televised rape. Causal explanations for the crime other than the television show rested on stronger psychological evidence. One of the attackers, for example, had been molested by her father. In theory, NBC insisted, the plaintiff's case would shift accountability for criminal acts away from the persons responsible and toward the producers of televised drama.

Lewis could argue that the rape scene in "Born Innocent" ignored NBC's own production code and the NAB Code that proscribes graphic depictions of violence. The rape scene, in fact, had been abridged in telecasts after the first one. No one, Lewis contended, should be absolved of civil liability because of the First Amendment.

In August 1978 judge Robert L. Dossee ruled that "Born Innocent" was presumptively protected by the First Amendment. The sole issue in the upcoming trial would be whether NBC had intended to incite someone to an assault with a beer bottle. *Olivia Niemi v. NBC and Chronical Publishing* (owners of KRON–TV) was dismissed, the case made untenable by the court's decision that the First Amendment, and not negligence, was the central issue.

The court quashed the case on legal grounds, but the ethical question persists: Is graphic violence on television wrong?

Networks certainly cannot justify such violence on Kant's imperative. No reasonable person could will that such portrayals become standard television fare. Neither can Aristotle's mean or the Judeo-Christian persons as ends be summoned to the defense. And Rawl's veil of ignorance does not seem to fit the specifics of this case; networks cannot be expected to negotiate programming decisions with potential victims of crimes allegedly related to a show.

We are left with the principle of utility as apparently the only ethical ground on which to justify graphic violence on television. One might argue that artistic freedom is so vital that NBC's creativity ought not be curtailed in any form. Or one could conclude from the utility principle that reform of detention institutions is so urgent that "Born Innocent's" realism served the larger purpose of raising public awareness. But both of these beneficial consequences seem meager compared to the rape of Olivia Niemi. Both potential benefits stand against obvious personal harm. The principle of utility renders ambiguous results at best.

The courts undoubtedly ruled correctly on the legal question. But in the moral domain, no ethical principle can be reasonably located to defend "Born Innocent." Who, then, should be held responsible? On what grounds?

No evidence suggests that the program's writers and producers struggled with the issue, though they apparently did not sensationalize the actual conditions of juvenile reformatories. However, it is not obvious that their attempt at realism was morally adequate. NBC decided to air the program in early prime time, but did add a warning to viewers. Was this sufficient caution? The show's advertisers and carrying stations can claim a legal right, but in terms of ethics, they are guilty of negligence. The parents of the five juveniles who raped Olivia Niemi are morally culpable also. In this case, all decision makers bear some responsibility (producers, network executives, advertisers, local station, and parents) because each carried enough power to make a difference, that is, to eliminate violent scenes (or the viewing of them) and thereby deemphasize the lurid without sacrificing dramatic integrity.

51. *Papillon* and Prescreening

Chicago attorney Fred Howard (fictitious name) heard the radio ads plugging a family adventure film and noted the PG rating awarded to *Papillon* by the Motion Picture Association of America (MPAA). Satisfied, Howard chose the drama of a seamy French prison camp and its victims for a family evening with his three daughters, aged 7, 11 and 14.[2]

Following the show, however, it was Howard who felt like a victim: misleading ratings had not conveyed a true warning of the movie's violence. He filed suit in Cook County Circuit Court for seven dollars in compensatory damages (the cost of the theater tickets) and $250,000 in punitive damages. It was the first consumer action against the six-year-old MPAA rating system. Named as defendants were Allied Artists, the producers; General Cinema Corporation, the distributors and owners of the Highland Park theater where the Howards had viewed the film; and the MPAA. The suit charged that *Papillon* showed "in explicit detail" a decapitation, a homosexual assault, and various gruesome killings and beatings.

Federal Judge Richard B. Austin, in dismissing the suit, stated, "Plaintiff was accurately put on notice that he should exercise caution in letting children view this movie and he failed to do so." The MPAA attorney claimed that PG carries the warning that some material in a film might be unsuitable for preteenage viewers, and that the rating system contains no warranty—it is merely an expression of opinion by the MPAA.

We are rightfully suspicious of ratings issued by the MPAA, knowing how such decisions are frequently negotiated in the best interests of a film's investors. In the case of *Papillon*, if it could be established that the assigned rating was patently deceptive, we could summarily condemn the MPAA as ethically abhorrent under each and all of the five criteria described in the introductory chapter. But such condemnation would be too simple a solution, and not entirely deserved.

What happened in this case is an example of doing the least to satisfy a moral requirement. Movie producers (represented by the MPAA) do not wish to discourage box office patrons, and neither do theater owners. So ratings are issued in the most inoffensive manner possible: a single letter or two letters with a terse explanation of their meaning and in only four varieties. It is the least noxious deterrent for a paying customer.

What if producers and theaters owners were to treat customers as reasonable creatures responsible for the moral tenor of their viewing experiences? Synopses of plots, descriptions of the kinds of scenes in a film, even a more sophisticated set of rating symbols would show good faith toward the viewing public.

In this case, however, we cannot fault the movie industry entirely. With little investigation beyond notice of the film's rating, Howard took his children to see it. Was parental guidance a sufficiently active element in his decision? Probably not. The PG rating should have prompted him to ask questions of friends, read reviews, and perhaps even call the theater manager. The cursory nature of his investigation suggests that even if additional safeguards were provided by the industry, Howard would not have noticed them.

Proponents for greater liberty in television programming typically emphasize the viewer's right to turn off his set. The wider liberty of the magazine and book publishing industry also presumes that parents will monitor the reading material of their children and prevent their exposure to material too mature for them to accommodate. Surely the same supervisory responsibility must apply to children's selection of motion pictures. Howard has himself to blame for failing to do his homework on *Papillon*.

At each point from movie producer to consumer, application of the persons-as-ends principle would help in the responsible discernment of cultural fare. The movie audience surely needs more reliable, less laundered information on which to base viewing choices. Yet parents and others adults are responsible also. They still control the last, vital link in the movie market system. Changing money for tickets is the free act of a consenting buyer who, even in the course of collecting on his purchase, can decide to get up from his seat, go home, and read a book.

52. "Holocaust" and Television's Limits as a Medium

A generation plus has passed since the terror of Hitler's New Order was unveiled, and survivors of the Holocaust are concerned: when the last of them pass away, will anyone be able to tell the story in its full tragedy, passion, and horror? Perhaps the task will fall to the media, but that prospect is less than comforting to those most interested in preserving the memory and meaning of their suffering.

On 16–19 April 1978, NBC aired a nine-and-a-half hour docudrama called "Holocaust", the story of two German families from 1935 to 1945.[3] The Weiss family is Jewish. Josef and Berta are the parents of a typically close-knit clan which fails to interpret the first signs of Nazi persecution. Their oldest son, Karl, and his Roman Catholic wife, Inge, are sent to Buchenwald and Theresienstadt. Their daughter, Anna, is brutally raped, then killed in a "hospital" for the mentally ill. The middle son, Rudi, escapes the German net and after much hardship takes up arms against the Nazis.

The Dorfs, Erik and Marta, live in Berlin. He is an unemployed lawyer, she an ambitious wife who convinces Erik to join the German SS. He becomes an aide to "blond beast" Reinhard Heydrich and in that capacity travels the breadth of Europe engineering schemes for ridding the Reich of the Jewish "menace." To add realism to the drama, writer Gerald Green included portrayals of such personages as Adolf Eichmann, Heinrich Himmler, and Heydrich.

NBC took unusual pains to generate an audience for the financially risky mini-series. The network invited prominent churchmen from the three major faiths to preview the series, and it encouraged the preparation of study guides for school and church discussion on the meaning of the Holocaust and the means of avoiding another. Rabbi Irving Greenberg of New York wrote the introduction to the interfaith guide.

Such careful preparation—and a lot of advertising—worked well. An estimated 120 million Americans saw some part of the four-night series. The first installment drew a 43 share; the third evening drew a 49 (59 in New York City).

Reviewers across the country applauded. The Washington *Post* called it "the most powerful drama ever seen on television." Rev. William L. Weiler, executive director of the Office of Christian-Jewish Relations of the National Council of Churches, called the program a "very effective, engaging drama." Rabbi Marc Tannenbaum, director of national interreligious affairs for the American Jewish Committee, who served as a consultant for NBC, remarked: "I have seen it three times and found myself crying each time. The impact of the series is greater than anything I have witnessed since the end of World War II."

Only in one corner of the country was a dissenting opinion raised, but that corner happened to be the most important one—New York City. Two days before the mini-series began, *Times* critic John J. O'Connor concluded that the production staff of "Holocaust" had faced "a massive problem and were unable to find satisfactory solutions." The plot was contrived, the actors sterile, and the effect superficial. Perhaps commercial television was simply not the medium capable of telling the terrible story, he mused. To throw Jews and Nazis, fictional or historical, into a

second-rate dramatization that will be seen with interruptions for inane commercials is to enter automatically a process of diminishment. Incredible horror is reduced to 'effective' on-location settings in Austria and West Berlin. Unprecedented pain is mixed up with the choosing of 'correct' costumes. . . . The very barbarity of Nazism is whittled down to an image not dissimilar from the fad for a touch of sadism in lingerie ads. No matter the good intentions of the production staff, the inevitable trivialization is fatal.[4]

Also writing in the *Times*, Boston University historian Elie Wiesel lashed out at the stereotyped characters, historical errors, the obsessive theme of Jewish resignation, and errors in the portrayal of Jewish life and liturgy. He called the series "untrue, offensive, cheap: as a TV production, the film is an insult to those who perished and to those who survived. . . . It transforms an ontological event into soap opera. Whatever the intentions, the result is shocking." Wiesel wrote with the passion of one who had seen and survived the Nazi terror:

We see naked women and children entering the gas chambers; we see their faces, we hear their moans as the doors are being shut, then—well, enough: why continue? To use special effects and gimmicks to describe the indescribable is to me morally objectionable. Worse: it is indecent. The last moments of the forgotten victims belong to themselves.[5]

On the day after the series concluded, O'Connor followed up his earlier review with a scathing attack on the "shocking insensitivity" of a network's exploiting such serious material for commercial gain. "A monstrous historical fact has been put through the peculiar process that is called commercial television. In its more extreme moments, that processing proved to be almost as obscene as the Holocaust itself."[6]

Letters from viewers poured in. Many were outraged at the commercial interruptions; others were resigned to them. Some abhorred what they perceived as trivialized history; others were gratified that, whatever the shortcomings, the series had raised the consciousness of millions toward the evils of anti-Semitism.

In the course of the debate, the network lost one of its most important allies: Rabbi Greenberg. For him the series "lacked the insight and touch of survivors," especially on the question of Jewish resignation. "Holocaust" had portrayed as heroes those Jews who took up arms, as they did in the Warsaw Ghetto. The drama was critical, especially through the character of Inge, of the many who grimly walked in front of the machine guns or into the deadly showers. Why did so many submit? Here was a problem that defied the quick cuts and surface storyline which television requires. Greenberg pointed to the "overwhelming force and cruelty that made death inescapable and often a relief; the collective responsibility and the way family and children tied the hands of those who would have fought. . . . [Real survivors] realize that just living as a human being, refusing to abandon family or religion or dignity was the true, incredible everyday heroism of millions who died and the few who survived. The absence of this insight may be the gravest flaw of 'Holocaust.' "[7]

Television, by its physical dimensions alone, is a limited medium. It cannot convey the grandeur of vast tracts of landscape; it cannot hope to show finely detailed art.

Is the medium limited, too, in the drama its format can adequately portray? Plots that need only stereotyped characters and move along to predictable conclusions are obviously television's strongest trump. Intricate plots and extended character development are much more hazardous, especially where continuity must be sacrificed for sponsors' announcements.

A television producer exploring the idea of a mini-series on the Holocaust would have to consider the potential audience, but satisfying the business criterion ought not determine his decision. Does he have writers, actors, and other support personnel to do justice to the script? Presuming these resources would be available, the decision to produce is still not certain.

Once the technical and financial means are in hand, the producer must ask: Is this a story I really want to do? He may be drawn to the story (or repelled from it) by hopes for recognition and advancement in the field. He may have a native interest in the story: the plot or theme strikes a creative nerve and he feels compelled to do it because of the inner resonance the story provokes.

Typically a producer's decision process ends at this point. If the program idea is marketable, and if staff and equipment are available, and if he personally wants to produce (for whatever reason), then why not—let's do it!

Has an important criterion been overlooked? Are there ethically sensible reasons why a producer of a mini-series on the Holocaust might choose, in the final analysis, to respect the limitations of his medium, preserving the dignity of those who endured the bitter grief?

This is another form of the question: to whom is moral duty owed? In the case of "Holocaust," network producers were admirably sensitive to duties toward their audience. Providing study aids and enlisting the help of concerned agencies could be seen as a public relations ploy, but on the surface it must be applauded as above and beyond the normal concern given a docudrama.

But Rabbi Greenberg, Elie Wiesel, and John O'Connor were raising the matter of duty owed the subject of the drama itself: the victims of the actual Holocaust. Were their concerns given sufficient attention? Perhaps this is a question only victims themselves can answer. At a minimum, Holocaust victims viewing the docudrama must not feel exploited, simplified, or divinized. They must not feel compromised by the inherent limitations of the television medium. Most importantly, network producers must not be open to the charge that they used the setting of the Holocaust to create just another human-interest stock drama, imposing familiar plot devices onto the Jewish story.

Assistance from survivors at every stage of the process might have produced a more realistic "Holocaust." Turning the project over to creative talent in Jewish heritage agencies might have given a more realistic, less stereotyped rendering. More sensitive allocation of commercials would have shown greater respect to the victims.

Moral duty in this case is also owed the German people. Few Germans today are not repulsed at the heinous human-rights violations of Hitler's Reich. Modern attempts to dramatize the gigantic moral lapse of their fathers and grandfathers must do justice to the economic and political context which made that nation so vulnerable to Hitler's rhetoric. Simple portrayals of 1930s–40s' Germany as brutish and barbaric do injustice to the moral agony of the perpetrators, and contribute nothing to the healing that intervening years have allowed to happen, to some extent at least.

If such moral considerations—based soundly on the persons-as-ends principle—are too costly, too time consuming, or too idiosyncratic, then the network should have faced up to the boundaries of its own universe. Perhaps commercial television, due to time constraints and institutional demands, cannot recreate in dramatic form the intense human feelings and tragedy that after more than a generation still stretch the limits of credibility.

53. "The Storyteller"

In primitive oral cultures, "storyteller" might connote the village historian or tribal sage, the person responsible for interpreting the outside world to kindred with lesser vision, the personal repository of a culture's myth and wisdom. With perhaps the same idea in mind, scriptwriters Richard Levinson and William Link, creators of the police drama "Columbo," gave the title "The Storyteller" to their introspective drama about the crisis of conscience faced by a television scriptwriter whose work, aired one evening on network television, portrayed several acts of arson. In the story, the show is seen by a youth who immediately after viewing leaves his home to try to burn down his school. The youth dies of smoke inhalation in the fire.[8]

Levinson and Link broke into television writing just as the industry came face to face with questions of the influence of televised violence on the real world. The many studies, essays, and investigations following the Kennedy assassinations, however inconclusive, at least established the intuition that television can be a factor in why real people do some things and not other things. Not that violence was new to popular drama. Levinson and Link grew up on Dashiell Hammett, Zane Grey, the squeaky door of Dr. Frankenstein's laboratory, and "survived not only intact but also enriched." But the decade of the 1960s brought a new fascination with the "actual moment of slaughter," slow-motion carnage, and the chilling spectacle of audiences cheering the cinematic bloodlust. Whose was the moral burden?

The purpose of "The Storyteller" was, in Levinson's and Link's words, to "analyze our own feelings and attitudes, not only about the violence issue, but also about the responsibilities, if any, of those of who enter so many homes and minds each night of the week." To the consternation of some viewers, the drama did not follow predictable television denouement. Instead of taking a point of view and suggesting answers to their dilemma, Levinson and Link were satisfied to "explore the problem . . . to present the audience with the incredible tangle of pros and cons involved." Yet their sense of moral accountability comes through when the mother of the dead boy asked the writer, "You come into peoples' homes, the homes of people you don't even know. Do you think about that every time you sit down at your typewriter?" The primitive village sage never faced a question like that.

This kind of self-reflection is a big step toward responsible media; it stretches the mind and draws out the issues, even if it reaches no conclusions.

Perhaps it falls to agencies such as the Screen Actors Guild (SAG) to coalesce opinion and reach positions on these matters. Its members and board formally passed an antiviolence resolution in 1974 (updated in 1977) that reads, in part:

> While various studies do not lead to absolute conclusions, there is reasonable cause to believe that imitation of violent acts seen on television is a potential danger and examples of this phenomenon are well documented. There is reasonable cause to believe that the excessive violence viewed on television can also increase aggressive behavior patterns and that repetitive viewing of violence leads to greater acceptance of violence as a norm of societal mores.... What is disturbing in television programming is the emphasis on violence and the degree of violence portrayed.... The extent and degree of violence in television programming is excessive.... Degrees of violence can be lowered in entertainment just as we hope to reduce such excess in our society.... We challenge those who are responsible for the programs aired to make the effort—and for the sake of all—the sooner the better.[9]

Someone might object to these sentiments, of course. The statement assumes a reasonable cause connects media violence with real behavior. This, someone might argue, is the same kind of speculative hearsay that makes up the rhetoric of media watchdog groups.

And another objection: The SAG statement purports to recommend change "for the sake of all," a clear appeal to the utilitarian principle of the greatest good for the greatest number. But that principle can never demonstrate the difference between too much and appropriate violence. Would the SAG suggest that violence is appropriate if and only if no one in real life is physically harmed in any way? Unlikely. Everything from eating bacon to brewing moonshine has some inherent risk. And such a prescription would be too late to help the victims anyhow. Would the SAG preclude violence that harms a significant number in a significant way? Impossible. Who could calculate such an application? Ergo, the SAG statement and all others like it are mere rhetorical flourishes and soap-box oratory. The only workable principle is to give writers and producers a free hand in the scripts they develop. True art is achieved only in the context of free expression. Artificial or arbitrary constraints will keep television drama forever immature.

True it may be that art is achieved only in the context of free expression. The question for media ethicists is to what extent art is accountable to moral principle. Is art good because it is free, or is it good when it captures in poignant and resonant ways a slice of the human search for meaning. The latter avoids the facile pairing of art and freedom that excuses so much tripe, and brings art squarely into the moral domain. Art and ethics are not mutually exclusive categories. It should be possible, then, to conceive a policy for the portrayal of television violence that will remain true to the aspirations of creative talent without violating the genuine moral claims of actors, viewers, and others drawn into the process after major decisions have already been made.

Place yourself in the role of writer, producer, or distributor. Does the golden mean provide a basis for responsible violence? Appropriate violence must steer away from that which would make humans into mere beasts, or portray humans as unrealistically angelic. Can specific policies be drawn from such an appeal to principle? Try your hand at formulating your own national policy on television violence. While such statements often turn into dead letters uniformly ignored, on occasion intelligent manifestoes, conscientiously promoted, have aroused attention and changed opinions.

54. Comic Capers

From the greatest of the old-time crime chasers (Superman) to the most bizarre of change agents (Incredible Hulk), the comic heroes press on from chase to mace in their pursuit of daring and virtue. Often the denouement involves overpowering some dastardly character, defusing some devastating explosive, or derailing a hunk of heavy machinery—all in the name of protecting the innocent and winning the war against cruelty (see figure 11.1).

But what of the cruelty required of the heroes themselves? Is it possible that the comics' depiction of cruel means to virtuous ends confuses young minds by suggesting that anything is okay if some good is served in the end?

Recent concern about the violence menu of young children has focused largely on television programming, but for the purposes of ethical reasoning, the issue is significant in any medium.

Figure 11.1

Everything the cover promises. . . .

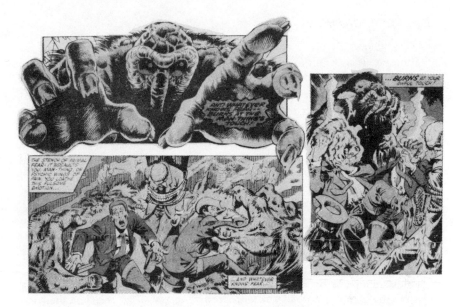

... The inside pages deliver: skull-crushing monsters, prehistoric battles, beatings, and the savagery of war.

Violence is a dominant theme in the comics. In 1974, John Di Fazio analyzed the comic book treatment of fourteen American values and found that "peaceful resolution of conflict" was one of the values least often portrayed.[10] Our own quick review of a grocery store comic rack revealed plot resolutions involving a woman blowing herself up with a shotgun while trying to save an infant from a monster, the crashing of a boulder on the cranium of a muscle-bound cyclops, and the blinding of a Rebel soldier by a "blue belly" bullet.

Such unrestrained violence was not always the rule in children's literature. Note, for example, the ethic of restraint that characterized the popular Nancy Drew detective series:

There was an abundance of violence in the Nancy Drew series, but it was controlled violence. Clubbings, wrecks, assault and battery were common. Attacks fell indiscriminately on many types of characters with Nancy often the target. Despite this violence no one was murdered. Criminals who assaulted their victims did not go beyond beatings. In a decade [the 1930s] when sensational real life kidnappings stirred the population, these fictionalized kidnappings ended happily and no victim of abduction was killed. Guns were used but were either fired as warnings, and not directly at persons, or used as clubs.[11]

One concern that ethicists cannot avoid is the question of the effects of the violence on impressionable consumers. And here, as media researchers are well aware, the evidence is both solid and gaseous; advocates line up on both sides. The 1969 Media Committee Report to the National Commission on the Causes and Prevention of Violence summarized the typical disclaimers and rejoinders:[12]

Disclaimers

1. Cartoons are fantasy, not reality.
2. Children know the difference between fantasy and reality.
3. Fantasy has no harmful effects on children.

Rejoinders

1. There is no conclusive evidence that children can differentiate between fantasy and reality in television programs.
2. It remains to be proven that fantasy programs have no effect upon child viewers.
3. Television has properties of perceptual reality which blur the distinction between fantasy and reality.

4. For many children, the first contact with violence probably occurs while viewing television.

Researchers at Texas Tech in 1980 found no support for the hypothesis that reading violent comics leads to greater aggression among children, but admitted "it is possible that the effects of comic book reading may be long-term and cumulative."

The ethicist is faced with puzzling questions: Who is hurt by reading or viewing fictional violence? Would the harm attributed (by some) to media programming come about anyhow, in which case violence in media becomes an insignificant part of the equation? Who should assume moral responsibility for children's media menu: publishers, writers, television directors, sponsors and advertisers, parents?

A reasonable argument could be made that children would read comics and watch cartoons regardless of the style of the conflict and the means of its resolution. Children do not demand violence in media; they are entertained with or without clubs and knives and pistols. Producers, then, cannot argue that they must provide violence to secure an audience. "Mister Rogers" and "Sesame Street" give muscle to the argument that low-level violence or none at all do not diminish a child's loyalty to the program. Producers might well be confronted with the Potter Box technique and faced with the question about their ultimate loyalties. Certainly they cannot reasonably choose a concern for their own pocketbooks over service to their juvenile audience. In any case, it seems apparent that production people could move toward more humane conflict resolution without jeopardizing their enterprise.

Ultimate moral duty must fall to those who are most directly involved in the guidance and growth of children. While not absolving producers and writers, moral reasoning assumes that the parent/guardian-child relationship is primary for the teaching of values. In Western democracies the public marketplace is kept relatively free, while each family exercises the closer selection of what will become part of their perceptual experience.

At the level of family, the ethic of persons as ends is given most prominent play. Here moral duty is to the child first and foremost, not to the marketplace; each child is the most valued part of the sender-channel-receiver process. Here the concerns of the individual rise to prominence as the values of free and unimpeded media programming recede. Resolving the issue of violence in children's media is chiefly a matter of recovering the notion of family as a moral institution. Only on this intimate level can the ethic of persons as ends truly flourish.

Notes

1. Material for this case was drawn from "TV Wins a Crucial Case," *Time*, 21 August 1978, p. 85; T. Schwartz and others, "TV on Trial Again," *Newsweek*, 14 August 1978, pp. 41–2; "NBC's First Amendment Rape Case," *Esquire*, 23 May 1978, pp. 12–13; "Back to Court for 'Born Innocent,'" *Broadcasting*, 1 May 1978, pp. 37–8; "Judge restricts 'Born Innocent' case to First Amendment issue," *Broadcasting*, 7 August 1978, pp. 31–32; Karl E. Meyer, "Television's Trying Times," *Saturday Review*, 16 September 1978, pp. 19–20; *New York Times*, 18 September 1978; *Wall Street Journal*, 25 April 1978.

2. This case follows a true story described in the *Wall Street Journal*, 1 June, 6 and 12 December 1974.

3. "Holocaust" was analyzed in the *New York Times*, 14–30 April, 4–7 May, 24 June 1978.

4. John J. O'Conner, "TV Weekend," *New York Times*, 14 April 1978, p. C26.

5. Elie Wiesel, "Trivializing the Holocaust: Semi-Fact and Semi-Fiction," *New York Times*, 16 April 1978, sec. 2, p. 1.

6. John J. O'Conner, "TV: NBC 'Holocaust,' Art Versus Mammon," *New York Times*, 20 April 1978, p. C22.

7. Irving Greenberg, Letter to Editor, *New York Times*, 30 April 1978, sec. 2, p. 30.

8. Richard Levinson and William Link, "A Crisis of Conscience," *TV Guide*, 3 December 1977, p. 6.

9. "SAG Position Re Excessive Violence on TV," Minutes of the Special Meeting of the Executive Committee of the Screen Actors Guild, 29 November 1976, p. 9919.

10. DiFazio's study is cited in Alexis S. Tan and Kermit Joseph Scruggs, "Does Exposure to Comic Book Violence Lead to Aggression in Children?" *Journalism Quarterly* 57 (Winter 1980): 579–83. This is the Texas Tech study referred to later in the commentary.

11. James P. Lones, "Nancy Drew, WASP SuperGirl of the 1930s," *Journal of Popular Culture* 6 (Spring 1973): 712.

12. Robert K. Baker and Sandra J. Ball, "Mass Media and Violence," A Report to the National Commission on the Causes and Prevention of Violence, November 1969, p. 330.

Chapter Twelve

Financial Improprieties

Entertainment media in American are 90 percent business and 10 per-cent public service. Or are these figures too lopsided toward public service? Only the most unrepentant idealist would argue that public service or social responsibility is a major consideration in most entertainment media decisions. If such social benefits show up in the product, all well and good. But woe is the producer, director, editor, or recording executive whose product shows a financial loss, whatever may be the social gain. The profit motive is the most compelling concern in entertainment industry decisions; some observers would insist it is the only concern.

As Parts One and Two in this volume indicate, the bottom line of profit and loss affects media of all types; but the entertainment media feel the impact most directly. A recent major survey of executives in the motion picture industry confirmed the intuition that here was a media system operating on essentially amoral criteria. A vice-president of a major production and distribution company commented: 'There are no ethical decisions in the movie business. In a word, the profit motive renders ethics irrelevant. The only counterbalance is that certain individuals—and precious few at that—live their personal and professional lives according to some reasonably high standard."

The cases in this chapter are all part of the public record. We raise them here not to bring "criminals" to trial, to perpetuate rumor and innuendo, but to explore the kinds of ethical pressures typical of the entertainment business in its various media and to ask whether, despite the arid climate, ethical considerations have any hope of taking root. The Begelman case raises the question whether entertainment executives live under such pressure as to redraw the boundaries of legal or moral behavior. The "Payola" case suggests that the entertainment gatekeepers are in a position to benefit from several sources, and the audience could be the loser. "The Purpose is Profit" wonders if the business ethos is ever sufficient for a creative media person, however necessary it may be. "Blind Bidding" explores whether traditional practices in the entertainment business need to be reformed with a more responsible ethic in mind, whereas "Corporate Takeover" highlights the dilemma between business efficiency and creative independence. Finally, "Super Strip" points to an example of humane fairness that may carry the seed of hope for fairness and justice apart from legal constraint.

55. David B. "Steals" $80,000

Actor Cliff Robertson was puzzled. He had received an earnings statement from Columbia Pictures for $10,000 in the early months of 1977, but the money itself had never been sent, nor had Robertson rendered service to Columbia that year. When he investigated, he was told by Columbia's senior executive vice-president David Begelman that a young man at the company had forged Robertson's name on a check. The company was willing to handle the matter internally. Would Robertson extend the same generosity to a misguided youngster, Begelman asked.

On the advice of his accountant, Robertson asked for and received a copy of the forged check. The bank officer who had handled the transaction had initialed the check, and Robertson's accountant called the official to verify the story. Yes, the official did remember the person who cashed the check: it was David Begelman.

Begelman's subsequent confession to misusing about $80,000 in Columbia funds (three forged checks, overbilling on company-funded home improvements, and other irregularities) touched off a widely reported Hollywood scandal. Why should an executive earning $234,000 a year plus generous benefits risk his reputation and freedom on such relatively small change? And why should the company ultimately retain the executive at a new position and a higher salary than before?

When the forgeries and other mismanagement became known, Begelman was asked by Columbia to repay the $80,000 and take a six-month leave. Begelman did resign as executive vice-president and he also resigned from the board of directors of the parent company. He took a leave from his post as head of the television and movie units, and he paid back the money. All this in good faith. The question then plaguing the Columbia board was whether to accept the word of the psychiatrist who pronounced Begelman cured of self-destructive tendencies after six weeks of treatment, or to permanently oust the wrongdoer.

Alan J. Hirschfield, president and chief officer of Columbia Picture (CP) Industries, wanted Begelman out. Matthew Rosenhaus, board member and largest single stockholder, favored Begelman's return, as did Herbert Allen, the New York investment banker whose firm controlled CP Industries. At one point, it appeared that Hirschfield himself might be on the way out due to his lone opposition to Begelman. But eventually Hirschfield accepted the majority view and Begelman returned to his desk as chief of television and movie production (though not as a director and executive vice-president).

Rosenhaus defended the move as decent and humanitarian: "If I thought Begelman was a thief, I wouldn't have him around Columbia. But we're not defending a thief but a sick man who did some stupid things . . . who had psychological problems that have now been corrected." Herbert Allen accented the same approach: "This is not a moral issue. It's a story of a breakdown. And since when is a breakdown immoral? After three months of investigation, I don't think we found one fact that Begelman had materially hurt the shareholders of this company." Hirschfield, on the other hand, was not so generous: "The whole business showed a lack of respect for authority, for values, for the company. It was 'public be damned, shareholders be damned, S.E.C. be damned.'"

Begelman claimed that while his actions were not responsible, they were not malicious either:

My misdeeds, my misappropriation of funds . . . were aberrational, bearing no sense to reality. I had neurotic displays of self-destructiveness. While everyone considered me very successful, apparently subconsciously I didn't have the same high regard for myself. Therefore, I was determined to do something that, if it didn't destroy me, would hurt me badly.[1]

Complicating the issue for Columbia were charges that Herbert Allen defended Begelman in order to stave off a collapse in Columbia stock that the Allen firm was attempting to unload. Allen denied these claims.

In December 1977, David Begelman resumed his duties at Columbia. But pressures from law enforcement agencies and the media continued to make life difficult for him and for the board. In February 1978 he resigned his position but was retained by Columbia as an independent producer.

The tale has an epilogue. John Vande Kamp, the Los Angeles district attorney who filed charges against Begelman, also formed a task force "to determine the extent of white collar crime in the entertainment industry."[2] He found quite a lot, and indictments came down. The supervising investigator of the task force commented:

It's not that there are more bad people in Hollywood. It's just that studios are not the typical mom and pop grocery store where you work hard for forty years and there's never more than a few dollars in the till. Deals have to be made in a hurry—hundreds of thousands of dollars rushed somewhere. The common thread is that all the employees [who committed crimes] had a position of some authority and could use their position to steal.[3]

The task force, after one year, had sent only one person to jail. Against the hunches of the district attorney, Begelman claimed, "I am not the tip of the iceberg. I am the iceberg."[4]

Forging checks and falsely reporting company expenditures are obvious breaches of the law. Begelman's plea of innocence was not his denial that he had perpetrated such activities, but only his effort (and an altogether customary one) to negotiate a lighter sentence from the court. It seems clear that the law was broken in this case, and that such outright lying for selfish gain is morally wrong.

Yet the file should not be closed too quickly. Several parts of this drama raise questions that an ethicist will want to ponder. Hirschfield seems to have argued his point on the strength of the Kantian imperative: theft is wrong. The movie industry ought not, as a whole, flaunt the standards of shareholders, the government, and the general public. Consequently, no one individual should violate them either. The CP Board appealed to the utilitarian argument: no one was materially hurt. Begelman's talents, despite his wrong actions, are necessary to the fulfillment of company and stockholder objectives; hence the greatest good for the greatest number warrants reinstatement of Begelman to a position in which he can produce profitable films but not make company policy decisions.

The fact that Hirschfield's Kantian appeal was less persuasive in determining policy than Allen's utilitarian position (Judeo-Christian forgiveness was a sham in this case, was it not?) might say something about the difficulty of challenging the industry with ethical absolutes. (Hirschfield, incidentally, was fired by the Columbia board six months after Begelman pleaded 'no contest' to a felony charge of grand theft. Begelman was fined $5000 and put on three years probation).

If ethical principles played a role here, were they rightly applied? Would a utilitarian ethic necessarily lead to the decision to reinstate Begelman, or might the long range interests of the greatest number be better served by making an example of the woebegone executive, even to the point where Columbia would aid public prosecutors in their attempt to bring an indictment?

Any application of the utility principle in this case must ask: to whom is moral duty owed? To Begelman certainly, since he is a colleague who needed help to overcome a problem. Also to shareholders, whose investment in CP Industries is entrusted to the Board. And to the public, represented both by customers of CP products and by the government on behalf of the interests of all the people.

Begelman's needs are addressed in the Board's lenient treatment and through the services of a professional counsellor. But beyond that, the Board's actions are suspect. It would appear that their greatest concern was to protect their own personal interests: their investments in CP Industries, and perhaps their own reputations as movie business managers. Various Board members stood to gain personally if CP stock remained high. Their motives in dealing with the Begelman affair were personal, and their style more concerned with public relations and stock prices than principles.

The success of no big business hinges on the talents of one man. CP Industries could have applied the Kantian imperative here, given Begelman fair severance pay, and found a replacement. But to do so would have stirred speculation on the stability of the corporation, or so the Board surmised. They chose to settle the matter in the least disruptive way. The long-range results may be more disruption than they faced here. A corporation not able to apply the rudiments of a principled ethics is vulnerable for repeated offences. Certainly its stock in the public's eye takes a big slide downward.

56. Payola

Just when the furor over quiz show scandals seemed to be cooling and a cleansed television industry was returning to normalcy, a new form of shady business emerged: payola, gifts of cash or merchandise to disk jockeys in return for the airing of a song.

Payola was nothing new. In the 1890s music publishers paid to have songs played in beer gardens. In the 1920s popular singers were the beneficiaries, and the 1930s saw big band leaders cut in. But in the fall of 1959, it was America's disk jockeys who were allegedly enriching themselves on the largesse of record producers. And among the DJs, 30-year-old Dick Clark, host of the weekday "American Bandstand" and the Saturday night "Dick Clark Show," was by far the nation's most popular.

Clark began his rise to fame in 1957. Two years later his shows had an audience of 16 million viewers, mostly teenagers. Clark alone accounted for 4 percent of ABC's advertising revenue at the time. Little wonder that the House Special Subcommittee on Legislative Oversight, which began payola inquiries in the fall of 1959, felt that Clark's testimony in April 1960 would lead to their prize catch.

Clark had already undergone the scrutiny of an ABC investigation by the time he faced the House Subcommittee. During the previous December ABC had instructed Clark to sell his interest in 33 music firms or leave the network. Clark had agreed, and ABC concluded its investigation "with renewed faith and confidence in Dick Clark's integrity."

To the House Subcommittee Clark claimed innocence: 'I have never agreed to play a record in return for payment in cash or any other consideration." But the Subcommittee's findings and subsequent media reports did not paint such a virtuous picture:

- A Memphis record manufacturer told the New York *Post* about a deal he had made a year earlier. The firm, Sun Records, had just released "Breathless" by Jerry Lee Lewis. According to the terms of the deal, the record would be sent by Clark to all viewers who mailed in five Beech Nut gum wrappers (his television show sponsor) plus fifty cents. More than 38,000 responded to the offer, and the publicity contributed to "Breathless" selling over 1 million copies. Sun provided the records for the promotion without charge, and Clark was given half of Sun's subsequent sales profits.
- In 1958 songwriter Orville Lunsford signed with Fraternity Records for 400,000 copies of his "All-American Boy." He testified that a Fraternity representative told him Clark would plug the record if Mallard Pressing Company received an order for 50,000 disks. When the order was placed, the song was heard every other day on "American Bandstand" and was

second on national sales charts for a time. Clark was part owner of the Mallard company.

- Assigning copyrights to DJs was another form of payola. The 1958 hit "Sixteen Candles" was spun four times in ten weeks on Bandstand; sales floundered. Late that year Clark was named the song's copyright owner. It was played 27 times in the next ten weeks and became a hit.
- Among Clark's business interests was the talent firm SRO Artists and the record company Jamie Records. SRO managed singer Duane Eddy and Jamie pressed his recordings. During a 27-month survey that became part of the House Subcommittee's findings, Clark had played songs by Frankie Lane once, likewise for Bing Crosby, Perry Como four times, Frank Sinatra not at all, Elvis Presley 173 times, but Eddy was heard 240 times. Clark testified that he had not consciously favored Eddy over other artists.
- Clark did admit, however, that performers on Bandstand regularly kicked back a percentage of their earnings for appearing on the show. It was common practice, Clark explained, due to the terribly high union scales for live music performers.
- When ABC sent out an affidavit for all their DJ's to sign, Alan Freed, a New York disk jockey, refused on principle and was fired. Clark did not sign either, but rather submitted his personal revision of the affidavit to the company; he was exonerated.

At the time of the investigation, Clark had made nearly $500,000 in outside profits. The Subcommittee called the money "Clarkola," but some critics wondered if Clark and fellow DJs were taking the heat for business tactics which permeated American enterprise. How many Congressmen themselves held undisclosed financial interests? How many of the 600 record producers putting out a total of 200 new cuts every week could survive without some way, however questionable, of gaining access to the airwaves? Payola was such an accepted practice that record distributors claimed "payments of appreciation" to DJs as business-related tax deductions. In all, the House Subcommittee found evidence of $263,245 in payola payments to 207 disk jockeys in 42 cities.

Payola was a problem. Jack Gould wrote in the New York *Times*: "Most hanky-panky in the business world is a relatively private moral problem. But in the case of radio and television, payments made in the dark may have a strong cultural influence affecting the nation as a whole."[5] Other critics were less confident of payola's cultural repercussions. Wrote Paul Ackerman in *Nation*: "Payola may be ethically deplorable, but it is unlikely that it has ever changed, or ever could change, the course of popular American music."[6]

Problem or not, payola was a persistent market strategy. A CBS News documentary, "The Trouble with Rock," revealed in 1974 that the recording industry was rife with drugs, underworld contacts, and payola. A year after the documentary, federal grand juries in three cities indicted six companies and 16 persons for bribing radio station personnel with money, clothes, and cars to plug records. An FCC investigation in 1977 revealed that payola was still happening but according to one newspaper report, the Justice Department was not interested in prosecuting those petty types of misdemeanors.

One approach to the ethical issue would be to ask: who is hurt by payola? Unlike many kinds of ethical problems, this one seems to have no victims. The record producer considers payola a business expense, the DJ obviously benefits, and the recording artist watches royalties roll in from the increased popularity of his disk. Unless we define the roles of these parties to include some thread of social responsibility rather than pure showmanship, it is difficult to locate any victim. It might therefore be appropriate to legalize and regulate payola.

But if DJ's, for instance, fulfill a social role more important than the mechanics of turn-table operation, if in fact a DJ is a cultural gatekeeper whose judgments are respected by an audience of rock music devotees, then the suspicion that his aesthetic judgment is biased by payola is too strong to dismiss. The integrity of the DJ as a judge of musical art is severely compromised.

Results of such compromise could be profound, and merit condemnation on both Kantian and utilitarian grounds. In Kant's framework, we should never permit for ourselves what we do not wish to become universal. Notice, then, that our society depends on the (supposed) independent judgment of many people at all levels and functions: courtroom judges, newspaper correspondents, pharmaceutical specialists, school textbook buyers, auto mechanics. What chaos would result if a carburetor company were to pay mechanics a special fee for each one of their products installed, or if drug companies engaged in competitive kickbacks to pharmacists for pushing syrups and pills. The independent judgment upon which we depend would no longer be reliable. A common core of assumptions about how people relate to others would quickly vanish, and with it much of the social organization that makes our lives pleasant and civilized. In utilitarian terms, the greater good for the greatest number is served when people responsible for exercising skilled judgment follow professional standards in a spirit of comradeship and filial concern for others.

"Do unto others" is an ethical assumption that guides many of our social and business relationships. When we lose it, we cease to trust;

we retreat into our own (often unskilled) judgment; we surrender the caring motive that transforms our energies from "I-me" to "I-thou." Financial kickbacks such as payola directly conflict with the social role of the disc jockey. Even if no law is broken, a valuable trust is betrayed.

57. The Purpose Is Profit

Larry Dowd (fictitious name) was in his mid-twenties and already had three million books in print. He held a two-year contract with Argo Publishers (fictitious name) which called for eight more books and several cross-country promotional tours.[7]

Dowd's themes came from the news (political scandals, Hollywood affairs) salted with a shrewd instinct for the offbeat twist. One reviewer called his work "very soft-core porn—sex viewed from the soap-suds angle." His books, all mass market paperbacks, were written in a single draft while the author listened to country music or watched television. Dowd told one interviewer, "Yea for TV. I belong to the church of television watchers of America." His editor at Argo said, "Some doctor ought to look at his thyroid to see where he gets all that energy."

Dowd is pleased that his books sell fast even if they die young. "I write stuff I'd like to read, and if it isn't timely any more, I'm really not interested in reading it. I have the attention span of a puppy. Besides, my books are entertainment. They're meant to be read, then exchanged for the next one. Or even thrown away. I'm a very impatient person. I like my books to come out fast. I take a filmic approach to a book. Writing's only part of it; marketing's an important part, too."

Dowd's first novel enjoyed a hefty initial printing of 600,000. He had six other books under the belt by that time, two of which had sold over a million copies. "I like to work," Dowd told a reporter. "It pays me to work hard. Hardcover reviews would be nice, but meanwhile I like my royalty checks. I look on my career as a business. . . . All I want is to be free and comfortable and not bored."

At one point, his first novel held prospects of a motion picture contract, a possibility that prompted the comment, "I'm going to be in the movies! In pictures! Yea for me!"

The writing and publishing of books has traditionally enjoyed a degree of respectability that places its people and products a notch above most others in the creative arts field, perhaps because books and writing have a long and dignified history, because great books live from generation to generation, and because the manufacture of books is a relatively drawn-out process with several check points. Moreover, the enduring nature of a book makes it all the more subject to reflective criticism. An author or publisher guilty of a non sequitur, for example, would likely endure more prolonged embarrassment than a popular singer whose voice quivers during a live performance.

Authors of books, along with symphonic musicians and composers, painters, and sculptors have been considered less commercially motivated, less transient and ephemeral than, for instance, writers of pulp magazine tales and illustrators of advertising material. But these stereotypes have shifted with the coming of high-speed offset printing and inexpensive paperback binding. Yet, to find a writer of books who is thoroughly given to mass market commercialism still provokes a sense of dissonance, as though a sacrosanct profession has been invaded by a crass profiteer. Perhaps competition for the pop-culture dollar makes commercialism in all media inevitable. But wholesale commercialism? It sounds demeaning, exploitative. On the other hand, a writer oblivious to the audience may starve for lack of sales. Clearly, the business element cannot be ignored.

This line of reasoning is based on the assumption that a creative professional, in addition to owing something to the public, also owes a debt to his profession, to his colleagues, and to the professional tradition from which he profits. A creative talent who turns art into the science of marketing, whose short-term gain is his only measure of success, is unfairly trading on a tradition that he is doing nothing to uphold; rather, his actions, as a Kantian would notice, if copied by enough of his colleagues would subvert the art side of his business completely.

Dowd cannot will that his own standards become the accepted norm. If they were, writers would be public jesters, fools deserving a scornful laugh, but nothing more. Dowd might find his own market significantly smaller. Conceivably, universal application of his standards would do a slow self-destruct. Dowd needs a more mature, more responsible ethic than he currently has. He needs to read a good book before he tries to write one.

58. Blind Bidding

The ad appeared in the Gastonia (North Carolina) *Gazette*, placed there by R.L. "Sonny" Baker, owner of the Webb Theater, who had

Figure 12.1

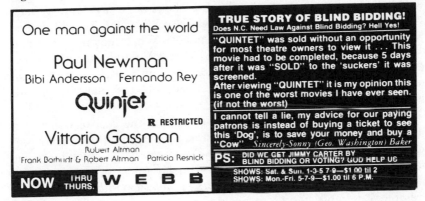

One man against the world

Paul Newman

Bibi Andersson   Fernando Rey

Quintet

R RESTRICTED

Vittorio Gassman

Robert Altman
Frank Barhudt & Robert Altman   Patricia Resnick

NOW THRU THURS. **W E B B**

TRUE STORY OF BLIND BIDDING!
Does N.C. Need Law Against Blind Bidding? Hell Yes!

"QUINTET" was sold without an opportunity for most theatre owners to view it ... This movie had to be completed, because 5 days after it was "SOLD" to the 'suckers' it was screened.
After viewing "QUINTET" it is my opinion this is one of the worst movies I have ever seen. (if not the worst)

I cannot tell a lie, my advice for our paying patrons is instead of buying a ticket to see this 'Dog', is to save your money and buy a "Cow" *Sincerely-Sonny (Geo. Washington) Baker*

PS: DID WE GET JIMMY CARTER BY BLIND BIDDING OR VOTING? GOD HELP US

SHOWS: Sat. & Sun. 1-3-5 7-9—$1.00 til 2
SHOWS: Mon.-Fri. 5-7-9—$1.00 til 6 P.M.

made a blind bid on the film, informed of its contents by a hype-filled circular (see Figure 12.1). Baker lost $2,500 on the engagement, a modest sum compared to the risks taken by big-city theaters for blockbuster movies, some of which require hundreds of thousands in advance guarantees and a commitment of up to 16 weeks of showing time.[8]

The practice of blind bidding (theater owners making bids on a film they have not seen) and its counterpart, blockbooking (high-quality films sold in a package with poorer ones), has been the subject of legislative dispute since the 1920s. During that decade, public-interest groups negotiating with local theaters over which films to show were thwarted by trade practices which shifted responsibility for film selection away from the community and toward the Big Eight producers. The problem still lives, claims the National Association of Theater Owners (NATO), which has been pressing state legislatures to outlaw the blind bid.

The blind bid, running roughshod over community values, can make trouble for theater owners. One owner scheduled *Slap Shot*, a hockey film starring Paul Newman, for his family chain in South Carolina on the basis of the producer's plug sheet, "but when we got it, we found it was a rowdy picture with atrocious, foul language, and we were embarrassed."[9]

The Motion Picture Association of America (MPAA) represents the producers' side of the question. Its general attorney, Barbara Scott, has called the local-standards argument an example of the use of a moralistic veneer to avoid the financial risks inherent in the industry. "Sure they [exhibitors] scream about *Slap Shot's* bad language," Scott said, "but you don't hear them complaining about *Saturday Night Fever's* [unexpectedly bad] language, which was also blind bid. The difference is that *Saturday Night Fever* made money. What they're concerned about is money, not offensive language."[10] Jack Valenti, executive director of the MPAA, echoed the same response in a *Wall Street Journal* interview: "Blatant hypocrisy," he charged, "They'll play any picture that makes money."[11]

The MPAA's case for blind bidding rests on the cost of delaying a film's premiere and on the impossible financial burden that pre-screened bids would place on small theater owners. So much money is tied up in feature films that a six-month delay for prescreening by exhibitors could easily cost a film's backers $1 million in interest payments. Prescreening rights, therefore, would spell the end of the spectacular, big-budget movie. On the second point, the MPAA insists that bids for a really great movie, if prescreened, would shoot through the roof. Small theaters could never compete for the best films. Box office prices would skyrocket to keep pace with the escalated bids. Chiefly, however, the MPAA claims that state legislatures have no right to interfere in what is essentially a marketing dispute between two sectors of private industry. Valenti has said, "The end of blind bidding will destroy this business by crippling the distribution process."

NATO obviously disagrees. "The producers don't want us to see the turkeys," one exhibitor said. Another claimed that blind bidding was the "culprit behind the big-name, big-budget flops now polluting the nation's theaters." To press their case, some 450 theater owners in New York and New Jersey have shown a two-minute trailer depicting a young couple at a car dealer's lot. The dealer insists on money down before the couple may peek at the auto they wish to buy. Movie patrons are then asked to sign an anti-blind bid petition in the lobby after the show.

The momentum of the legal battle is slowly shifting toward NATO, despite vigorous MPAA efforts to lobby against bills before state legislatures. No anti-blind bid bill has yet been defeated once on the floor of a state senate or house; committee pigeon holing has been the MPAA's most successful strategy, but that has not stopped nineteen states plus Puerto Rico from passing anti-blind bid statutes.[12]

The legal arena can only address specific grievances between the disputants. What a popular culture industry ought to provide, to whom should it be accountable, and what structural modifications might enhance cultural diversity are questions that few holding the reigns of corporate power are likely to ask. But others—theatre owners like

Sonny Baker, citizens concerned about pluralistic culture, and students of the media—might well ask those questions. It is clearly against the interests of local theater owners, presumably responsive to their communities, to receive films containing they know not what. Short of pre-screening the entire film, theater owners could expect more detailed information (perhaps film segments) on the explicitness of the film's violence and sex, and the blueness of its language. No patron walking into a theater should be surprised, and theater owners bear much of the obligation to inform them of the entertainment they are purchasing. A golden mean between costly prescreening and hyped movie company circulars could be found. Movie companies alert to their ethical obligations toward consumers will not balk— or shout "free enterprise"—at these fair concessions.

59. Corporate Takeovers of Media Companies

The irony was remarkable. The feature story in *Business Week* claimed that American Express "seems determined to acquire a big company soon." Little did the editors realize that American Express had ambitions toward their own parent company, McGraw-Hill.

The acquisition of one company by another is hardly uncommon. Media companies frequently come under conglomerate ownership, or themselves become conglomerates through acquisitions of nonmedia companies. Occasionally the transfer is miniature warfare—a hostile takeover in which a conglomerate buys large blocs of a company's stock until it holds controlling interest.

American Express did not plot a secret hostile takeover of McGraw-Hill. An offer was made in January 1979 to pay thirty-four dollars per share ($830 million) for McGraw-Hill stock, which was then selling for twenty-six dollars. The offer represented an acceptable profit to share-holders, under most corporate circumstances.

But not to the family-controlled board of McGraw-Hill. Chairman Harold McGraw Jr. had no interest in selling the four television stations, sixty trade magazines and newsletters, Standard and Poors rating service, *Business Week*, and the nation's second largest book publishing company—all of which comprised McGraw-Hill. There would be no takeover without a fight, assured Harold McGraw. The board "strongly believes in the preservation of the independence of the communication media as well as the independence of securities' ratings activities," he said.[13]

One part of the effort to block the takeover was an appeal to the

Federal Communications Commission. McGraw-Hill's four television stations could not change hands without FCC approval, a bureaucratic formality that could buy valuable time for the threatened company. American Express countered. It would set up a trust such that the broadcast operations would have their own independent management and board of directors. Furthermore, American Express promised that the independence of McGraw-Hill's media divisions would not be compromised. "Editorial and media integrity are as respected by and as important to us as I know they are to you," wrote the American Express board chairman to Harold McGraw.

Despite the assurances, the McGraw-Hill board turned down the offer. Five days later one of the board, Roger H. Morley, resigned. Morley was also president of American Express and had been instrumental in conceiving the deal.

Angry over the appearance of corporate spying, Harold McGraw ran a two-page ad in the New York *Times* (January 17, 1979) reproducing his letter to the American Express board:

The background and manner of your proposal demonstrates that American Express lacks the integrity, corporate morality, and sensitivity to professional responsibility essential to the McGraw-Hill publishing, broadcasting, and credit rating services relied upon by so many people. . . . The obvious conflict of interest created by your secret plan to pursue acquisition of McGraw-Hill while Mr. Morley remained a director is an unprecedented breach of trust.[14]

Amexco countered again, this time with a suit accusing McGraw-Hill of "libelous, false, and misleading statements" designed to deprive stockholders of a "fair opportunity to evaluate" the American Express offer. McGraw-Hill's petition to the FCC was called a "diversionary, shotgun tactic" with the same purpose in mind. Many McGraw-Hill stockholders (including some McGraw family members not on the board) were, in fact, eager to realize the profits of such a sale, and some brought suit against the McGraw-Hill board.

On January 30, American Express raised its bid to forty dollars per share. Again the McGraw-Hill board unanimously rejected the offer, claiming that to sell would compromise the editorial integrity and independence of its properties. A month later the American Express offer expired: the battle was over. McGraw-Hill stock, which had climbed to thirty-two dollars in anticipation of the merger, plummeted to twenty-four dollars.[15] Millions of dollars in potential profit to stockholders were wiped out.

American Express felt that its offer had been generous and its guarantees secure. McGraw-Hill viewed the takeover as a devious, illegal maneuver in which one of its own board had "violated fiduciary duties" to the company and had "misappropriated" confidential company information.

In the midst of the takeover bid, media critics voiced concern. The president of the Authors Guild wrote: "There is no kind of corporate move that the Authors Guild opposes more strongly than the takeover of book publishers by companies with no previous interest in books."[16] Columbia professor Fred Friendly wondered "whether four centuries of press struggles to break the licensing bonds of censorial governments could end with a new variety of restraints, where the gatekeepers of information are a handful of super conglomerates not steeped in the ethos of the news business."[17] He did admit that many media operate independent of the interests of their conglomerate parents. NBC and CBS had both covered the Vietnam war without interference from the corporate hierarchy, he noted, despite the fact that each parent conglomerate had been awarded large Department of Defense contracts. One question he did not address was whether the networks had covered the war better (or whether, by application, publishers could offer even more diversified cultural fare) because of the enormous resources available to them as part of a complex, profitable conglomerate enterprise.

Two principles were in conflict. Harold McGraw and the Authors Guild were operating on a principle flavored by Kant's categorical imperative: independence is essential to the purpose of a media company. The pro-merger faction probably had something like the principle of utility in mind: more people (shareholders) are directly served (in terms of appreciated stock value) by the planned merger.

Harold McGraw's appeal is based on a belief that profit, while essential to the survival and health of a media company, is not sufficient as an explanation of its purpose. The purpose of the company, in this view, is service, and service requires independence from the kinds of commitments a corporate merger would demand. Mr. McGraw might view the privilege of shareholding as an opportunity to participate in the purpose of the company as well as in the profits. Whether shareholders would agree does not alter the ethical weight of Mr. McGraw's appeal.

Is such a position hopelessly idealistic? Is profit an end in itself? If McGraw-Hill set as its goal the establishment of a reputable publishing house that contributed vigorously to the stock of ideas in our culture, then profit would be pointless unless it furthered that end. The final decision, then, cannot turn on the greatest profit for the greatest number, but on the corporate structure best suited to meet the company's stated goals.

60. Super Strip

Jerry Siegel and Joe Shuster were high school teenagers in Cleveland, Ohio, when they came upon the idea of a cartoon figure who, born in a distant galaxy, would escape to earth as a baby, grow up in an orphanage, and as an adult, impervious to gravity and mightier than a locomotive, would aid the forces of justice in their battle against evil.

Siegel actually conceived the idea. His buddy Joe Shuster liked to draw, so the two fledgling cartoonists set out to sell their story. Five years of pounding on doors finally won them a contract with Detective Comics, and the first "Superman" strip appeared in 1938. Siegel and Shuster were paid ten dollars a page for their work, about fifteen dollars a week per man.[18]

The contract favored the company. The more popular Superman became, the clearer was Siegel and Shuster's loss. Finally they brought suit against Detective, were awarded some money, but still had no rights to their hero. When the legal dust settled, Detective fired Siegel and Shuster, and the two creators were left to watch others get rich and famous off their idea. More lawsuits proved futile. Late in 1975, with legal routes exhausted, the men defied the advice of their attorneys and went public with their story.

Their tale was one of sadness and struggle. Neither man had received any money from Superman since 1948, though profits from the Man of Steel were in the multi-millions. Shuster now was legally blind, living in Queens with a brother who supported him. Siegel was ill and lived with his wife in a tiny apartment in Los Angeles where he worked as a government clerk typist for $7000 a year. The men appealed to Superman's current copyright owner "out of a sense of moral obligation," said Shuster. The National Cartoonists Society and Cartoonists Guild lent their full backing to Siegel and Shuster's moral claim.

The appeal brought results. Warner Communications, which owned movie rights to Superman, claimed "no legal obligation," but "there is a moral obligation on our part." Two days before Christmas Shuster and Siegel signed a contract with Warner. They would each receive $20,000 yearly for life, and heirs would also be helped. The creators' names would appear on all Superman productions. At the signing, a

Warner executive commended the two cartoonists. The contract, he said, was "in recognition of their past services and out of concern for their present circumstances."

The financial prize awarded Siegel and Shuster presented no threat to the profits of Warner Communications. The sum of $40,000 a year may be less than the company spends in processing receipts from Superman sales. But as a gesture neither required by law nor essential to public relations, it represents an application of the Judeo-Christian ethic of other mindedness.

Consider the dynamics of the award. Shuster and Siegel had sold their idea under the duress of the Depression and at a time in their youth when neither could be expected to negotiate a contract with business savvy. Events had changed dramatically since then. One was now handicapped, and the other ill; both were living on a bare-bones income. Exhausted by fruitless legal efforts, they claimed a moral right to some relief.

Warner could have called their appeal a nuisance. Business is business, after all. Investors who cash in stock certificates, for example, never qualify for post-facto profits. Farmers who sell a corn crop in November may not appeal for extra payment when the bushel price rises in January. Buyers and sellers each assume part of the risk, and each understands that one could emerge from the deal a clear winner. Because the terms are understood, the bargain is fair.

But contracts are not independent from the economic milieu in which they are made. Were they selling a cartoon character today instead of in 1938, Siegel and Shuster might negotiate for a compensation clause should their idea become a bonanza. The economic climate of the late 1930s was not ripe for such risk-reducing appendixes.

So the recognition awarded Shuster and Siegel was for the cartoonists a humanitarian gesture of life-sustaining aid, while to Warner it represented no loss to shareholders and no risk to corporate solvency. Perhaps a thorough application of "others as ourselves" or Rawl's ethic of undifferentiated negotiators would have resulted in larger awards, or royalties for Shuster and Siegel, or a cost-of-living adjustment in their $20,000 annual amount, or life insurance policies to establish an estate for each man. Maybe so. It may be argued that Warner hemmed and hawed until it was expedient for them to make a gesture, quite apart from what was fair for the two penniless cartoonists. But the award, such as it was, points to a residual sense of group solidarity and caring, a dissonant but hopeful interlude in the normally amoral entertainment business.

Notes

1. Quoted in "Why Begelman Stole," *New York*, 16 January 1978, p. 9.

2. Quoted in Aljean Harmetz, "Prosecutors Zero In on White-Collar Film Crime," *New York Times*, 26 March 1979, p. C12.

3. Ibid.

4. Quoted in Charles Schreger, "Task Force Looking at Hollywood," *Los Angeles Times*, 8 August 1979, sec. 4, p. 10.

5. Jack Gould, "TV: Assessing Effects of Life Under the Table," *New York Times*, 20 November 1959, p. 63.

6. Paul Ackerman, "Payola: Sing a Song for Sixpence . . .," *Nation*, 5 December 1959, p. 415.

7. This case is based on J. Howard, "Yea for Me!" *New Times*, 2 November 1973, pp. 46–47.

8. Material for this case was drawn from Earl C. Gottschalk, Jr., "Theater Chain Revolts," *Wall Street Journal*, 9 August 1979, pp. 1, 29ff; Steven Brill, "Litigating Bad B.O.," *Esquire*, 26 September 1978, pp. 17–20; and Fred Bratman, "Theater Owners Seek End to Blind Bidding," *New York Times*, 24 February 1980, sec. 22, p. 17. A staff person at the Gaston County (N.C.) Public Library kindly located and sent a copy of Sonny Baker's advertisement.

9. Jack Fuller, Sr., quoted in Steven Brill, "Litigating Bad B.O.," *Esquire*, 26 September 1978, p. 17.

10. Ibid., p. 18.

11. Quoted in Earl C. Gottschalk, Jr., "Theater Chains Revolt Against Hollywood's Method of Marketing," *Wall Street Journal*, 9 August, 1979, p. 1.

12. In a letter from Joseph G. Alterman, vice-president and executive director, National Association of Theatre Owners, 29 July 1980.

13. Quoted in Robert C. Cole, "$830 Million in Cash Bid for McGraw-Hill by American Express," *New York Times*, 10 January 1979, p. D16.

14. *New York Times*, 17 January 1979, p. 12.

15. Quoted in Robert C. Cole, "McGraw Draws Suit on Merger," *New York Times*, 19 January 1979, p. D1.

16. John Brooks, quoted in Herbert Mitgang, "McGraw-Hill Bid Stirs Editorial Fears," *New York Times*, 14 January 1979, p. 51.

17. Fred Friendly, "McGraw-Hill and a Free Press," *Wall Street Journal*, 26 January 1979, p. 14.

18. Material in this case is from the *New York Times*, 22 November, 10 and 24 December 1975.

Chapter Thirteen

Triviality and Escapism

For every medium there is a scale; it can be called an aesthetic scale. On the one end are the serious artists and serious producers, careful about the integrity of their craft and insistent that their labors give audiences a better insight into meaningful existence. On the other end are writers and producers who want to provide the most popular product possible. The latter care little if lofty artistic visions are part of their work; theirs is the task of attracting the largest possible share of the audience, because if they do not, the competition will. Success is measured by the best-seller lists and the top ten Nielsen rankings.

The pull of the media's commercial base may inevitably lead to television programs, movies, and books that trivialize human dilemmas or escape entirely from them. Perhaps the forces resisting such trends are too weak to mount much of a counterthrust. Yet only the cynic will claim that money is really all that matters in popular culture and only the most cloudly idealist will assert that money does not matter at all.

Between the demands of art and the marketplace are a host of moral questions that media practitioners face every day: Must art be compromised when it passes from one medium to another? Are stereotyped characters fair to real people? How far should commercial concerns dictate cultural products?

These cases bring media aesthetics and ethics closer. Questions that initially might be taken to involve merely aesthetic preferences may in fact require hard ethical thinking. In the first case a serious artist turns his skill from print toward the electronic media (with benefits of greater prestige and money) and must work through the moral implications of what at first might be considered an aesthetic change.

The second case deals with cinema. Who besides film critics and cinema aesthetes should care whether the resolution of film drama is contrived or realistic? Yet there may be ethical obligations even in the construction and execution of popular film fare. The third case, involving television game shows, ponders whether a typical show's gambling incentive contributes to social health, or to escaping adult responsibility by playing Lady Luck for instant prizes.

Surely one of our most pernicious habits is entertainment at the expense of someone else's self-respect. Here is triviality at its extreme— the trivializing of someone's ethnic or peer-group identity. Can the media avoid it? To compress dramatic action into a thirty-minute television show or a two-hour movie demands some degree of stereotyping, but how much is too much, and is any amount right at all? The cases on black exploitation movies and ageism explore those concerns, one from the viewpoint of a recognized minority group, the other through the eyes of a group attempting to coalesce into a minority-type movement.

61. A Serious Writer Faces the Lure of Electronic Popularity

Joseph Wambaugh grew up in East Pittsburgh, Pennsylvania, a sooty steel town where nobody ever had enough. Small wonder that his father decided to move the family to California when Joe was 14.

After a stint in the Marine Corps, Wambaugh entered college to study for a teaching career, but shortly before graduation decided to join the Los Angeles police force—more money, more excitement. Once a cop, he continued work toward a master's degree in literature. Then at age 30, Joe Wambaugh began to dovetail his literary interests with his police work, and the results were a financial boon for him and new style of police drama for the American public.

Wambaugh's first novel, *The New Centurions*, was compiled from notes collected during his years of police work. It became a successful movie starring George C. Scott, but Wambaugh was only moderately happy with it. He aimed to show what police work was really like, not the typical shoot-em-up excitement, but the emotional price a policeman pays for the stresses and strains of his work. When his second book, *The Blue Knight*, was being planned for a four-part television mini-series, Wambaugh fought harder for its integrity.

For Wambaugh, literary integrity meant projecting a realistic picture of police work. For the televison producer, success meant providing enough raw excitement to keep the networks interested.

Wambaugh was not an easy writer for the television people to cope with. "If they get hokey with the series—phoney it up—then I'll quit," he told them. He was described as obdurate, unbending, and indifferent to Big Sell. He explained: "People who want to see rape, fire, pillage, and murder in the first three minutes should try another program. That's not our show. If this series is going to die, at least it should die with a little grace."[1]

Later Wambaugh became consultant for a television series built around stories of Los Angeles policemen—not police files à la "Dragnet," but policemen talking into a recorder, and then a writer building a story around the incident. "Police Story" was a successful series for several years, but Wambaugh had to fight for every inch of the show's integrity. He told one interviewer:

They pay me a lot of money to use my name and be a consultant and all that business, but they're not listening to me. I'm trying to tell them what a police show should be about, what police life is all about. And so far they are giving me cops-and-robbers stories. What I've gone through with television has been unreal. They brought me in to give them the first true-life television shows about police. Good drama, strong in plot, strong in character, adult shows. And I sit there . . . and they nod their heads and say "Yes, but there's the real world and then there's the real world of television. The folks like lots of shooting and chase scenes." And I keep telling them, that is not what I'm here for. But they can't really free themselves from that misconception yet, and I was terribly naive to think that they could.[2]

The problem of balancing artistic integrity against the lure of a financial windfall is nothing new, though certainly the high prices commanded by talent in television and cinema balloon the problem beyond any previous scale. Before the dominance of the electronic media, a writer might have been persuaded to spice his pages with an eye to the popular audience, but in the past twenty years a tendency has grown to regard a good novel as a mere basis for television screenplays, the latter being the arena of real financial success. The writer who regards his craft as a vehicle of truth must negotiate with a television industry that imagines viewers frothing after murder scenes and car chases. Wambaugh faced such negotiation.

Certainly he could have refused all overtures from film and television producers. Since his message was intact in book form, one answer to its threatened dilution, or worse, its popularization, would be to keep the story in a form he could manage. Why allow the message to be watered down for the sake of a mass audience? Better, perhaps, to let one's message find the medium appropriate to it, and not assume that crossing to a new medium could do it justice.

The conflict of opinion here is best understood in terms of the fourth quadrant in the Potter Box regarding ultimate allegiances. Wambaugh steadfastly sees his first obligation as the demands of high-quality art. Second, he considers himself morally bound to represent honestly his colleagues on the police force. Should either of these be compromised significantly in the negotiations, Wambaugh would be rightly judged as selfish and greedy.

The producers return persistently to the viewers. They argue, in effect, that nothing of a novel's message would reach the mass audience unless certain concessions were made. But such blind appeal to audience taste seems to be motivated by a selfish thirst for ratings and financial rewards. Producers are ethically justified only if they can demonstrate that the television production is satisfactory drama in which a major part of the original has been maintained while rearranging other parts to fit the demands of television. They might contend, and plausibly so, that the only alternative is to communicate nothing at all.

62. Are Fake, Unhappy Endings Any Better Than Fake, Happy Ones?

The motion picture *Chinatown* has little to do with the Los Angeles ethnic quarter but much to do with political and moral corruption. The city is in a drought, and a powerful city boss, Noah Cross, is buying parched Los Angeles county farmland while at the same time arranging for the dumping of reservoir water into the ocean to force farmers to sell cheaply.

Private detective J. J. (Jake) Gittes has been hired by Evelyn Mulwray. Her husband, Hollis Mulwray, chief water engineer for the county, has been murdered after discovering the land/drought scandal. Evelyn wants to find the killer.

Gittes does his job. Hollis was killed by Cross, who is also the dead man's father-in-law and former business partner. Evelyn hates her father for an earlier act of incest, and, in the last scene, wants only to escape the sordid web with her feeble daughter-sister, Katherine, whom Evelyn has thus far shielded from her past. Cross likewise hates Evelyn for hiding his younger "daughter" and forces Gittes to take him to the girl.

Gittes' former police partner, Lou Escobar, is the police lieutenant assigned to the case. Earlier the pair had been together on the force in Chinatown, where supervisors had discouraged them from honest police work because the corruption was too deep—hence the symbol of complete moral collapse. Escobar believes Evelyn to be the murderer, although his mind has likely been purchased by Cross. At least Escobar knows Cross to be a powerful man in city politics.

The principals all meet at night on a busy street in Chinatown. The only chance for justice to prevail is Evelyn's escape. As the scene opens:

Gittes is held at gunpoint by Cross and a henchman. As they walk to Evelyn's parked car, they are intercepted by Escobar and his police team. Gittes' associates, Walsh and Duffy, are also there. Gittes begins to speak, but stops short when he sees Walsh and Duffy handcuffed.

Escobar: You're under arrest, Jake.

Gittes (relieved to be rescued from gunpoint): Good news.

Escobar: Withholding evidence, extortion, accessory after the fact!

Gittes (protesting): I didn't extort nothin' from nobody, Lou. This is Noah Cross, if you don't know. Evelyn's father, if you don't know. He's the bird you're after, Lou. I can explain everything if you just give me five minutes . . .

Escobar: Shut up!

Gittes: Five minutes is all I need. He's rich, you understand?

Escobar (yelling): Shut up! (*Now whispering*) Shut up or I'm going to lock you to the wheel of that car.

Cross: Lieutenant, I am rich. I am Noah Cross. Evelyn Mulwray is my daughter—

Gittes: He's crazy, Lou. He killed Mulwray because of the water thing. If you'll just listen to me for five minutes . . .

Escobar (to a subordinate): Lock him to the car.

Gittes (being moved away): Lou, you don't know what's going on here, I'm telling you.

Evelyn and Katherine rush past the crowd, heading for her car. Cross approaches.

Cross: Katherine! I . . . I am your . . . your . . . grandfather.

Evelyn blocks his approach.

Evelyn: Get away from her! Get away!

Cross: Evelyn . . . please, please be reasonable. How many years have I got? She's mine, too!

Evelyn (angrily): She's never going to know that!

Evelyn draws a small pistol. Cross backs away.

Cross: Eveyln, you're a disturbed woman. You cannot hope to provide—

Gittes (from off camera): Evelyn, put that gun away. Let the police handle this.

Evelyn (irate but under control): He *owns* the police!

Evelyn circles the car to the driver's side, while Cross approaches again.

Evelyn: Get away from her!

Cross: You'll have to kill me first.

Evelyn: Get away! Get—

She fires at Cross. He clutches his arm.

Evelyn (frantically): Katherine, close the door.

The car takes off down the street.

Escobar (yelling): Halt!

He fires twice at the car, missing. A third shot is deflected by Gittes, who grabs his arm. Another detective steps up, takes aim, fires three shots. The car, now a hundred yards away, stops in the middle of the street, the horn blaring. All the men—police, Gittes, Cross—run toward the vehicle. Katherine screams.

Escobar arrives first and opens the driver's door. Evelyn's body falls away from the horn to reveal blood streaming from her left eye. The men are stunned. Meanwhile, Cross has opened the passenger door and is comforting the hysterical Katherine in a grandfatherly manner. He cups his hand over her mouth and leads her away from the scene. Escobar, recovering his senses, turns to a uniformed policeman.

Escobar: Turn 'em loose, turn 'em all loose.

Handcuffs are released.

Escobar (to Walsh and Duffy): You want to do your partner a big favor? Take him home.

The men are too stunned to move.

Escobar (yells): Take him home! Just get the hell out of here!

Duffy (whispering, trying to coax Gittes from the scene): Come on, Jake.

Escobar (*whispering*): Go home, Jake. I'm doin' you a favor.
Duffy: Come on, Jake.
Walsh (*as he, Duffy, and Gittes move slowly away from the car*):
Forget it Jake, it's Chinatown.
*The crowd disperses as the camera pans the street and a policeman is
heard yelling, "All right, come on, clear the area, get on the sidewalk,
clear the street . . ."*

Back in the good old days of the 1930s, 1940s, and 1950s, American
films were characterized by their happy endings, writes film critic John
Simon.[3] So buoyant and optimistic were Hollywood's productions that
a neologism appeared in several European languages: "Happyend." It
meant a "joyous resolution of complicated intrigues and overwhelming
problems, allowing the hero and heroine to fall in the last shot, against
all probability, into each other's arms and live, by implication, happily
ever after."

The "happyend" formula is well stated in a recent interview with
Lucille Ball, who first appeared in movies in 1934. Said Miss Ball:

I hate all the graphic violence and sex in movies and on TV. I miss the big,
beautiful musicals and nice love stories. Now it's hard to find stories or stars
who could do the marvelous, glamorous movies . . . that let audiences dream
and fantasize. What television and movies give you is glaring red, running
blood and foul words, and it leaves everybody without hope. Poverty and sick-
ness and psychos and wierdos are coming out of the closet—and doing it all on
television. I think that comedy and drama ought to let us have a little escape
from our troubles. . . . There's no difficulty understanding my shows. They
always had a beginning, a middle, and a happy ending.[4]

Simon notes that the tide of films began to change in the 1960s, and
the tidal wave of change came in the 1970s. What troubles him is not
that former optimism was challenged by present realism, but that the
new tide merely replaces fake happy endings with fake unhappy ones.

Consider the neofascist genre in which the armed hero virtuously
kills off his opponents for the sake of justice. Every man his own gun-
man, films such as *Death Wish* exhort. "In an indiscriminately vicious
world, the only release and relief comes from beating up or killing,
from taking the law into one's own hands and becoming Superman,
Superblack, Superwhatever. In the old days, it was the victory of the
forces of right over those of wrong; now, however, it is I (or my alter
ego) against everyone else," observes Simon.

Or consider the cinema of unbeatable darkness. In *The French Connection, Serpico, The Godfather I and II*, and *Chinatown*, there are

only losers in the end. Old bad values have given way to a new bad value: total despair effected by contrived, manipulative endings such as *Chinatown*'s, where the villain is lightly wounded at close range while the heroine, in a car speeding away from a nervous cop, takes a bullet between the eyes.

Or consider the films of political and social commentary. American filmmakers barely scratch the surface of tough, complex problems. An individual politician may be corrupt, but the system as a whole is okay. A war may be vile and pointless as long as the enemy is also cruel and immoral.

Do American films accurately reflect our society? "No," Simon answers, "if you mean honestly coming to grips with the difficulties we face, the insufficiencies of the society that we have fashioned and that in turn, molds us."[5]

Scriptwriters might be culpable if we assume that even entertainment programs should contain something of educational value, something to illuminate the paradoxes we humans face or something to aid us in solving them. To conclude that no solutions are available—that we can only walk away in perplexity and resignation—may be to abrogate a crucial responsibility and to discourage the kind of painful problem solving that humans must undertake to work through troubling problems. On the other extreme, denouements which fail to grapple at all with complex problems, choosing instead to wish one's troubles away in a scene of superficial merriment, seem equally to miss the mark of educating viewers toward responsible living.

Thus, enlightened discussion of the happy-unhappy motif centers largely on step two in the Potter Box where underlying values are exposed and debated. Beyond that, appealing to an ethical principle, the Aristotelian mean could be used to call media producers to realistic drama. Many examples, from foreign filmmakers to dramatic television epics such as "The Autobiography of Miss Jane Pittman," suggest that stirring drama and the honest portrayal of human problem solving need not be mutually exclusive.

63. Dreaming Ourselves into Middle-Class Comfort

"Fabulous prizes" yells the announcer to open a popular television game show in which a lot of chance and a bit of consumer knowledge combine with cutthroat tactics against other contestants to win entry to games featuring bigger prizes—mostly household items in the $500–$1000 price range.

The pacing is quick. Contestants are on their way from studio seats to the front before the host is introduced. "Come on, down," yells the announcer off camera as each of four names is called. The audience cheers enthusiastically.

The first contestant, a nicely dressed black woman, wins a grandfather clock. The camera catches the happy reaction of her family in the audience. "I came to win, I came to win," she yells on stage to celebrate her good fortune. "I want you to win," the host assures.

To the next contestant the host says, "Ours has been described as the most exciting show on television. Don't you think it would be exciting if you should win that!" Curtains open to reveal a sparkling red sports car, adorned with a female model who could make an army jeep sparkle. The car is worth $10,800, the contestant is told, and to win it she must answer a couple of questions and putt a golf ball into the hole. She misses. She turns to the host to say "Thank you," but the host is speaking to the audience and does not hear her. Someone in the orchestra lets go with a trombone groan.

The chance games include a simulated bank safe, the combination to which opens the door to the "fabulous prizes." Contestants guess for correct numbers while the studio audience yells their hunches. The host, jovial yet paternal, calls the crowd fickle for groaning when their guesses miss the mark. His chiding is all part of the fun.

The next contestant races to the front. "I even dreamt about you last night," she tells the host. His reply: "What were we doing?" She hardly caught the nuance. "I had to spin that big wheel and I was so small you had to hold me," she said. The host retorts quickly, "If you get up here, baby, I'll hold you." The audience cheers.

Not everyone wins, of course. Losers retreat graciously and quickly to their seats. Winners cup their hands in disbelief and anticipation. The chance for immediate possession of expensive furnishings is a rare moment—the middle-class dream coming true.

What social benefits accrue from the television game shows? Do they serve as an outlet for people who like to gamble a little for fun? Or are they entertainment programs pure and simple with no social benefits required?

In a society where the gambling instinct is becoming more and more acceptable (most states now allow some form of it), it may seem academic to discuss the merits of television shows which play to those risk-taking drives. Yet the point raised by critics still challenges the prevailing ethos. A sociologist at the University of Colorado has suggested that television game shows perpetuate irresponsible expectations of economic and social ladder climbing.[6] A rich, upper-class lifestyle is touted as unquestionably desirable, and the achievement of it is shown to ride on the winds of chance. No greater counterpoint to the Puritan work ethic could be imagined.

"Where do we draw the line between social entertainment and more serious activities that lead to pathological behavior such as compulsive gambling?" the researcher asks. What if the overall effect of television game shows is to achieve instant success through chance. Can any amount of innocent pleasure atone for that dangerous undertow?

64. Blaxploitation Movies

Junius Griffin, president of the Beverly Hills-Hollywood chapter of the NAACP, was ready for a fight. He had seen enough of the macho black antihero playing on movie screens before adventure-hungry teenagers. To him the battle against blaxploitation films was a battle for the moral fiber of the younger black generation.

On a summer night in 1972 he secured a room in the sumptuous RCA building on Sunset Boulevard—a world removed from days when he marched through the South with Martin Luther King Jr., but appropriate for the occasion. Representatives of major black organizations came to hear Griffin castigate the new black films. "These films continue taking our money, while feeding black people a forced diet of violence, murder, drugs and rape. Yet we go on paying millions of dollars for our own cultural genocide at the box offices of white folks' movie houses," he told them.[7]

Griffin's program for improvement was two pronged: stop dramatizing blacks as pimps, dope pushers, and other forms of social degenerates; then hire blacks in all phases of movie production and distribution. To initiate his reforms, Griffin called for a coalition of "community organizations that will launch a local confrontation with this nation's movie industry," a confrontation not without "street demonstrations and other means necessary."

From that meeting emerged a coalition of civil-rights groups called the Committee Against Blaxploitation (CAB). With recruits falling into ranks, Griffin's demands to the industry expanded. Now he wanted movie companies to seek black investors, to open accounts at black-run banks, and to submit scripts to the CAB for screening.

The industry would not be cowed by such demands. Nor were producers as culpable as Griffin claimed. Indeed, three years before any

CAB was around to demand it, most production companies were implementing affirmative action plans to recruit and train minority workers.

Problems plagued CAB from the outset. Most of the NAACP chapter board and some members of CAB earned their living in the industry as actors, stunt men, booking agents, or were formerly so employed. Some of those inside the industry wanted a minimum of confrontation and restructuring; to them collective bargaining rights for blacks could be victory enough. Some blacks in Hollywood organized against CAB, using an ad in *Variety* to disavow CAB's program.

Only months after its organizing meeting, CAB fell apart. Griffin resigned his leadership, remonstrating that "no other race has been degraded in the movies like the black man has. We are the only minority who has been used as the instrument of our own degradation."[8]

A year after CAB's demise, black films were still rolling out of Hollywood with such titles as *Foxy Brown; Sugar Hill; Scream, Blacula, Scream; Truck Turner; Slaughter's Big Rip-Off;* and *Hell Up in Harlem.* Said the producer of these movies: "Black films are simply a market."

A vice president at Warner Brothers, makers of *Super Fly* and the *Kung Fu* series, commented:

We give the public what it wants. The market for black films is the inner-city market. They want action and adventure movies. *Super Fly* was financed by two black dentists. The images? Blacks who know tell us that in the ghetto, the pusher is a hero to the kids. Street blacks and nonbleeding-heart blacks say this is the only reasonable goal that black youths can aspire to. We sneak previewed *Super Fly* in several cities. Audiences loved it. Only a loud minority protested—the glory seekers who want the headlines. We try to be sensitive to what people think of the movies. We won't do anything that we think is offensive.[9]

Those remarks are similar to the feelings of movie-colony blacks who opposed CAB. "You're trying to tell black folks what to see," was the common complaint.

Yet an informed feeling persists that movies like *Super Fly* are—however subtly and indirectly—socially dangerous. Said a black psychiatrist at Harvard:

These movies glorify criminal life and encourage in black youth misguided feelings of machoism that are destructive to the community as a whole. Their message is: blacks are violent, criminal, sexy savages who imitate the white man's ways as best they can from their disadvantaged sanctuary in the ghetto. Movies of any type teach cultural values and influence behavior. Black youth in Brooklyn dramatically increased their use of cocaine after *Super Fly* glamorized the narcotic.[10]

Blaxploitation is a loaded term raising a series of puzzling questions: Are the ethical problems in those movies simply a figment of someone's overly sensitive conscience? Is the social problem simply a mirage, the result of an emotionally laden term? Are the psychiatrist's observations so forceful that, even without concrete evidence, they should warn us against the social evils that such movies could provoke?

CAB argued that white producers and distributors were turning out movies that exploited antisocial forces in the urban black community. CAB's solution proposed greater participation by blacks in the business and creative phases of film making. Some of Griffin's steam was let out of the balloon when Warner argued that blacks were financing certain of the movies in question. Griffin's implied charge that racism is to blame cannot be fully established. But that commercialism is a big part of the problem can hardly be disputed. Commercialism, unless it is subordinate to a social ethics, is another name for hedonism, where loyalties are solely to self. As the Potter Box reveals, an ethics based heavily on self-benefit runs afoul of its own introverted loyalties. A common procedure in ethical thinking is to justify one's action before those potentially injured by it. In this situation, it seems unlikely that a moviemaker could defend his film before the parent of a black school-age viewer.

65. A New Group of Longstanding Members Demands Respect

The Gray Panthers' Media Watch asks volunteer television monitors to evaluate a program's "ageism." The following reproduces the Media Watch's criteria:

Stereotypes

Any oversimplification or generalization of the characteristics and images of old age that demean or ridicule older people. Examples:

1. Appearance: Face always blank or expressionless; body always bent over and infirm.

2. Clothing: Men's baggy and unpressed; women's frumpy and ill fitting.
3. Speech: Halting and high pitched.
4. Personality: Stubborn, rigid, forgetful.
5. In comparison to others, are older people depicted as less capable?

Do they have less to contribute? Are their ideas usually old-fashioned? Is the rocking chair image predominant?

Distortions

The use of myth or outright falsehoods to depict old age as either an idyllic or moribund stage of life. Examples·

1. Are older people depicted as intruders or meddlers in the relationships of others?
2. Are old people ridiculed when they show sexual feelings?
3. When there is an age difference in romantic relationships, are older women accorded the same respect as older men?
4. Are old people patronized and treated as children?

Omissions

The exclusion or avoidance of older people, of their life concerns and of the positive aspects of aging. Examples:

1. Are the oppressive conditions under which older people must live in society analyzed? Are alternatives to existing conditions presented?
2. In any discussion of social and economic issues, are the perspectives of older people included?
3. Are older people directly involved in writing, directing, and producing the program?
4. How about the acting? Are there valid reasons for young actors to play the roles of older people?[11]

Comedian Johnny Carson has done a skit portraying a doddering old lady, Aunt Blabby. The semi soap "Mary Hartman, Mary Hartman" featured a secondary character called Fernwood Flasher, who took up the perversion in his elderly years. Countless television dramas have portrayed post-65ers as soft headed, dependent, impotent, decrepit, and sentimental. Whether in humor or in serious drama, the portrayals share a common flaw: ageism, or "discrimination on the basis of chronological age."

The Media Watch is determined, vocal, and not without success. A comedy segment performed by Carol Burnett portrayed the elderly as cranky, stubborn, crumbling human beings, according to the Gray Panthers. Their complaints eventually reached the ears of the National Association of Broadcasters, that has, as a result, included age as an area to be handled with the same sensitivity accorded race, sex, and creed.

But professional codes notwithstanding, the elderly may be television's most stereotyped demographic group. A major study conducted by the Annenberg School of Communications at the University of Pennsylvania found that heavy television viewing

makes a consistently negative contribution to the public's image of the personal characteristics of the elderly, and the quality of their lives. We did not find watching television to be associated with *any* positive images of older people. Heavy viewers believe that the elderly are unhealthy, in worse shape financially, not active sexually, closed-minded, not good at getting things done, and so on.[12]

The study concluded that these patterns of social stereotyping are the "creation of a system of broadcasting and of story-telling with deep historical, cultural, and commercial roots. This system allows very few degrees of freedom" in which producers and directors can work.

An earlier study found that characterizations of successful persons decrease with age, just as the number of personal failures on television increase with age. "Aging in prime-time drama is thus associated with increasing evil, failure, and unhappiness. In a world of generally positive and happy endings, only 40 percent of older males and even fewer female characters are seen as successful, happy, and good," the study claims.[13]

While the goals of the Gray Panthers may appear commendable and the findings of social scientists deplorable, not all television decision makers are enthusiastic about the implications of either. The concerns of the Panthers constitute a potential danger to free expression, some media people contend. A director for the Mary Tyler Moore company said about the problem of ageism on television: "I have heard a lot of complaints. I understand how these people feel. But I came away wondering if they aren't really after creative control. I'm not going to have any group tell me what I can do. I won't let any pressure group tell me how to be creative."[14]

Such responses are not unlike the sentiments of some free press advocates of the 1930s, a decade when pressure groups were particularly successful in influencing the content of popular entertainment. Newspaper editor Ralph Ingersoll said in 1941:

All pressure groups and special interests . . . are antagonistic to the whole truth and nothing but the truth. Quite legitimately, for their own purposes, but still hostile to the objectives of a really free press. . . . No pressure group regards itself as an enemy of truth . . . and I'm not thinking of greedy monopolists with paid lobbies in Washington, but of wholly respectable and sincere organizations such as labor unions, churches, *people over sixty*, of people who fought in the last war. Yet from the journalist's point of view they are all enemies, because they try to impose their orientation of the facts.[15]

Perhaps the Gray Panthers are too thinskinned when they object to exaggerated depictions of the elderly on the Carson or Burnett shows. Humor lives on exaggeration of human foibles and exploitation of stereotypical behavior. If we cannot laugh at ourselves, are we taking ourselves too seriously? One possible answer: We do not violate the dignity of another person or group until we are unable to convince them that our depictions are innocent and without malice. When the butt of the joke can no longer be persuaded that the depiction is sympathetic, then we have cause to reexamine the message. Our use of Rawls' principle in this case finally hinges on whether possible personal offense is that important compared to the need for a free, unrestrained drama industry.

Notes

1. Quoted in "Wambaugh Gets Script Control of 'Blue Knight,'" *TV Guide*, 14 February 1976, p. A1.
2. Quoted in Steven V. Roberts, "Cop of the Year," *Esquire*, December 1973, p. 153.
3. John Simon, "From Fake Happyendings to Fake Unhappyendings," *New York Times Magazine*, 8 June 1975, pp. 17–19.
4. Quoted in *U.S. News and World Report*, 26 September 1977, p. 58.
5. Simon, "From Fake Happyendings," p. 35.
6. Tomás Martinez, "Gambling, Goods, and Game Shows," *Society*, September/October 1977, pp. 79–81.
7. Quoted in "Filth vs. Lucre: The Black Community's Tough Choice," *Psychology Today*, February 1974, p. 98.
8. Ibid., p. 102.
9. Ibid.
10. Alvin F. Poussaint, "Cheap Thrills That Degrade Blacks," *Psychology Today*, February 1974, p. 26.

11. "Media Watch Criteria" was sent to the authors by Lydia Bragger, national media coordinator for the Gray Panthers.

12. George Gerbner, Larry Gross, Nancy Signorielli, and Michael Morgan, "Aging with Television: Images on Television Drama and Conceptions of Social Reality," *Journal of Communication* 30 (Winter 1980): 47.

13. Craig Aronoff, "Old Age in Prime Time," *Journal of Communication* 24 (Autumn 1974): 86.

14. Jay Sandrich, quoted in "Nobody (in TV) Loves You When You're Old and Gray," *New York Times*, 24 July 1977, sec. 2, p. 21.

15. Ralph Ingersoll, "A Free Press—For What?" in *Freedom of the Press Today*, ed. Harold L. Ickes (New York: Vanguard Press, 1941), p. 142.

Chapter Fourteen

Morally Offensive Material

Cases in this chapter cut a wide swath across the field of ethics in entertainment programming. And a dangerous one. On one side is the threat of prudery and its consequence: programming that portrays a false sense of innocence about human affairs. On the other side is moral anarchy, the abandonment of all moral principle except that of absolute freedom. It is our conviction that responsible media can ill afford the danger of either terrain. Society is not served by mindless dumping of its moral traditions; nor do we explore the moral life intelligently through casuistry or naiveté.

These cases, therefore, present one of the most perplexing issues for a pluralistic culture: how to achieve moral continuity and, at the same time, moral exploration. If "culture" means anything, it means a common ground of moral understanding ordering the lives of diverse people. Media should both respect and challenge that common ground.

"Bigotry as Debate" asks whether attacks on race or religion violate ethical judgment, even if cast in the form of public debate. Lawbreaking as acceptable behavior comes to the fore in "High Times." Does this kind of media legitimize activity not in the best interest of social life?

Offensive language in programming surfaces in "Seven Dirty Words," and the perennial dilemma of what to do about sex is approached in "Soap" and "The Cable is Blue." All together, the cases make this chapter a scintillating adventure in ethical reasoning.

66. Bigotry as Debate

"Black Perspectives on the News" was typically a 30-minute talk show produced for distribution on the Public Broadcasting Service by WHYY, Philadelphia. But the show scheduled for the last week in September was not the ordinary half-hour.

Bring together the head of the American Nazi Party and the Imperial Wizard of the Ku Klux Klan. Cast them with three black interviewers. Result: sixty minutes of largely uncontrolled, rambling conversation that included several sharply anti-Semitic remarks.

When word of the show leaked out, many viewers in Philadelphia were upset that a publicly funded station would produce such a diatribe. Three Nazi prison camp survivors living in the city filed suit to prevent the station from putting the show on the air. A local judge found in their favor on the day the broadcast was scheduled, and only a reversal from the state's Superior Court kept the 9 p.m. program on schedule. Even then, about 2000 Jewish, Polish, and Black demonstrators protested outside the studio that evening.

The Jewish community was not about to sit by while shades of the Third Reich danced on the screens of the nation's television sets. Especially at WNET, New York, the American Jewish Congress (AJC) actively protested the up-coming show in a letter accusing station management of gross irresponsibility.

When the AJC letter of protest was released to the press, WNET perceived it as a claim by the AJC that it had won cancellation of the show. Now the station was in a dilemma. Said one executive: "If we are perceived as yielding to the wishes of one pressure group, we'll be asked to give in to others and there'll be no end to it."[1] WNET's final decision: the station would produce its own version of the show, to be called "The Extremists: American Nazis and the K.K.K.," and this revised version would include about a half-hour from the original "Black Perspectives" production. "We almost had no choice," said the WNET executive.

Two sides were lined up for battle. The AJC vigorously denied that it had claimed credit for a programming decision at WNET. However, it would not retract its belief that the show was reprehensible and that its cancellation was the only right decision. In Cleveland the AJC protested: "There is no legal or democratic necessity to publicize falsehood." A New York *Times* critic, pondering the role of the public in media decisions, commented: "The American Jewish Congress is only one of many groups in this country which knows itself to be in possession of the truth, and if television producers did not resist the constant pressures, the world of television would be an even blander place than it is. One group's falsehood is another's truth."[2]

WHYY felt deserted. Only 105 of the 207 PBS stations aired the program, even when WHYY tacked on a 30-minute follow-up featuring spokesmen from the American Jewish Committee, the National Jewish Community Relations Advisory Council, and the Pennsylvania Human Relations Commission. James Karayn, president of WHYY, criticized PBS affiliates for succumbing to pressure: "I thought the whole reason for public television was to air public issues that commercial TV wouldn't. . . . Even if our judgment was wrong in this case, the station broadcasts over 5000 hours of programming a year, and we are not going to allow a few people who object to one program to destroy the whole thing."[3]

The American Civil Liberties Union (ACLU) fully supported the position of WHYY. "The danger of prior censorship by pressure is greater than the danger of irresponsibility by the press," said the ACLU.[4]

On what moral grounds could the AJC object to "Black Perspectives" being aired in New York City? Perhaps a closer look at the letter sent from Mrs. Naomi Levine, executive director of the AJC, to WNET management will cast light on the reasoning involved. The letter read:

What is involved here is Channel 13's program judgment—not censorship. Obviously TV and radio stations have the right to decide what shows they believe are worthy of public viewing. . . . The community . . . has an equal right to question the wisdom of their decisions.

In this instance we believe that any decision by Channel 13 to broadcast a program admittedly racist and anti-Semitic in content, a discussion which has been described by . . . the station which originated it . . . as containing "contradictory and factually inaccurate" statements, would be an act of irresponsible journalism and wretched program judgment.

We do not object to this program because its subject matter is controversial. We do not believe there is anything "controversial" about racial and religious hatred. . . .

We are confident that Channel 13 is not so bankrupt in program ideas that it must give precious air time to a program that projects racial and religious hatred and whose only result can be to inflame interracial and interreligious relations in our city. We recognize your right and authority to decide upon your own programs; we are grateful that in the exercise of that judgment you have understood that carrying this program would be an irresponsible act and a serious abuse of public trust.[5]

The AJC seems to be arguing that the content of the show is so demeaning to human dignity that it does not deserve the protection normally accorded to controversial debate. At the point where humans become the subject of race hatred, speech has passed into the intolerable, purely destructive zone. Certainly the Judeo-Christian ethic of persons as ends plays a large role in their thinking.

But nearly all other ethical foundations can be brought to bear on the AJC's case as well. The golden mean might argue that vigorous programming avoid the extreme of inflammatory demagoguery. Utility could contribute the point that no one is served by bigotry. The categorical imperative could never allow racism as a universal good, and the veil of ignorance would equalize the power of a national network and the relative smallness of a religious-cultural protest group.

WNET's response to the AJC points to an underlying adversity between media producers and public interest groups. Is it unrealistic to hope that the interests of both factions would be better served by proceeding from a foundation of mutually acceptable moral principle?

67. *High Times* Magazine and Drug Market Information

The promotional blurb read:

7,000,000,000 JOINTS! Yes, it has been estimated by the government that over 7 billion joints will be rolled in the United States this year. That's the equivalent of thirty joints for every man, woman, and child in the country. Of course, there are lots of highs, legal, semilegal, and illegal. Everything from herbs to meditation, and laughing gas to mushrooms.

High Times is written for that High Society.

With its authoritative columns, timely news and reviews, fascinating features, and beautiful appearance, *High Times* is a magazine that people read, take seriously, show their friends, and keep around a long, long time.

High Times is one of those magazines that goes under the rubric "underground press." Despite the label, it has a slick, above-ground appearance, evidence that a lot of people are buying. Articles range from the kinky Christmas wishes of Truman Capote to life histories of the gurus of punk rock and pot. A regular feature gives market quotations on drugs from Madrid, Melbourne, Moscow, and other worldwide trading posts. Printed on every two-page market spread: "The TransHigh Market Quotations are intended solely for comparative purposes and in no way are meant as an inducement to illegal activity, nor as an endorsement of any drug or drug usage or trafficking."

Ads are mostly for paraphernalia, but occasionally even these take an exotic turn. A full-color page shows the handles of two umbrellas, with the caption: "Better Smoked Than Soaked. Nosy narcs will change their minds, if they have any left, after they sustain a cranial impact equal to eight g's from the flexible metal blackjack on this hand-carved wooden handle. Only $150."

A parent from a Chicago suburb wrote about *High Times* to a Chicago *Tribune* columnist:

We tell our children that drugs are dangerous, and this magazine tells them how to grow them. How can drugs be illegal and yet a magazine like this be sold? Is there no limit to freedom of the press? It's strange that this junk is protected by the courts, but when we try to raise our children to be good and decent, and they wind up in court, then it's the parents' fault. We need help.[6]

In response the columnist spoke with the chairman of the department of psychiatry at a Chicago medical school. The doctor commented: "All kinds of people market the youth culture. There is a natural experimenting with what you can do with your body, and if they want to feel goofy, they can feel goofy. You'll never be able to control your child."[7]

If the psychiatrist is right, we should give up and return to the caves. His comment, of course, hinges on the meaning of "control." We agree that parents (or surrogate parents) cannot *determine* the behavior or value system of children, but enlightened guidance is something different. Upon the possibility of careful direction rests, in fact, the whole point of ethical analysis: reasonable beings can know the good and knowing, should follow it. So to swallow the psychiatrist's advice is to opt for the "terrain of anarchy" which was called an unacceptable extreme at the outset of this chapter.

The problem of *High Times* is the difficulty of cultural inconsistency. What the society declares to be illegal in deed is not illegal in print. A conflict exists between the commonly accepted mores of the culture and its institutions, in this case, the media and the courts. Yet the golden mean, a consensus-seeking principle, suggests the existence of extremes. At the moral frontier of any free culture will be advocates whose ideas, if widely accepted, would subvert moral order. The mean's strength is in its persuasive appeal to rational control, not in elimination of the extremes themselves. In this case, rational control rightly begins with family units and progressively relaxes as it proceeds through larger social institutions.

68. Seven Dirty Words

On 30 October 1973, a man driving with his young son in New York City was tuned to WBAI when the announcer warned that material to follow included sensitive language which some persons might regard as offensive. That material was a monologue from the album "George Carlin, Occupation: Foole" devoted almost entirely to the use of seven words depicting sexual or excretory organs and activities. It was broadcast as part of a discussion on society's attitude toward language.

Five weeks later a letter of complaint arrived at the Federal Communications Commission in Washington. The man in New York was incensed that his son had been exposed to such a fusillade of indecent language in the middle of the day on a major broadcast station. The FCC took the complaint as an opportunity to clarify its definition of "indecent." The result was a Declaratory Order issued in 1975 which defined as "indecent" language that which describes "in terms patently offensive as measured by contemporary community standards for a broadcast medium, sexual or excretory activities and organs, at times of the day when there is a reasonable risk that children may be in the audience." The Carlin broadcast, deemed the FCC, so fit this definition and was therefore prohibited.

Underlying the Order was the FCC's view that broadcasting is unique among modes of communication by virtue of its intrusive nature. Unlike other media, television and radio come directly into the home without any "significant affirmative activity" on the part of the listener. The privacy of the home and the medium's ease of access to children demanded special precaution. At times of the day when children might constitute a minimal audience segment, broadcasters could exercise more latitude.

The Pacifica Foundation, license holders of WBAI, took a different view. Before the District of Columbia Court of Appeals, Foundation counsel argued that the Order was unconstitutionally vague unless the term "indecent" were equivalent to "obscene" as defined in *Miller v. California* (1973).[8] Against those criteria the Carlin monologue was not obscene since it did not appeal to any prurient interest and because it had literary and political value. Neither the Carlin monologue nor the seven dirty words themselves may be prohibited, claimed Pacifica. An amicus brief filed by the Committee for Open Media further argued that the Order would have an especially harsh effect on the broadcast of minority literature.

Before the case came before the Court of Appeals, the FCC issued a clarification of its earlier order. It was not the Commission's intent to place an absolute prohibition on the broadcast of indecent language. Such language could be broadcast when children were a minimal audience segment, if sufficient warning were given to unconsenting adults, and if the language in context had serious literary, artistic, political, or scientific value.

In a two-one decision, the Court of Appeals agreed with Pacifica. "The direct effect of the Order is to inhibit the free and robust exchange of ideas on a wide range of issues," wrote Judge Edward Tamm. "In fact the Order is censorship, regardless of what the Commission chooses to call it."[9] The Order would proscribe the uncensored broadcast of many of the great works of literature as well as passages from the Bible. The Order was vague in that it failed to define children. The "intrusive nature" of the medium is inconsequential since, as the Supreme Court noted in *Lehman v. City of Shaker Heights* (1974), "the radio can be turned off"; listeners are not captives who cannot avoid exposure. The Order's assumption that apart from FCC action filth would flood the airwaves has no empirical foundation. Moreover, broadcast licensees are businesses dependent on their respective markets. "If the Commission truly seeks only to enforce community standards, the market should limit the filth accordingly," wrote Tamm.

Judge Harold Leventhal dissented. "Every society has special vocabularies appropriate only for special groups, times and places," he wrote. "The abhorrence of censorship is a vital part of our society. But there is a distinction between the all-out prohibition of a censor, and regulation of time and place of speaking out." Leventhal argued on principle rather than on empirical grounds:

A concept like 'indecent' is not verifiable as a concept of hard science. Its acceptance by and application by the FCC does not necessarily reflect, or depend upon, a determination by the FCC that this material would be dangerous to the children. What it reflects is a determination concerning a broad consensus of society, the view that the great bulk of families would consider it potentially dangerous to their children, and the further view that in our society, with the family as its base block, it is the family that should have the means to make that choice. With the pervasiveness of TV-radio and its reach into the home the choice made by broadcasters precludes an effective choice by the family.[10]

A year later, the Appeals Court decision was reversed by the Supreme Court. Accepting the FCC's rationale concerning the intrusive nature of broadcasting and the need to protect children from this "uniquely accessible" medium, the Supreme Court (five to four) agreed with the FCC's appeal to nuisance law which achieves social control not by absolute prohibition but by channeling behavior into appropriate contexts. (The FCC Order had argued that no one is absolutely prohibited from keeping a pigsty; rather, the prohibition is against a pigsty in the wrong place, like a neighborhood.) The Court found Carlin's monologue to be indisputably "vulgar," "offensive," and "shocking," without the political or artistic significance that would call forth First Amendment protection. Under the authority of 18 U.S.C. 1464 that prohibits the broadcast of "obscene, indecent, or profane language," the FCC was acting properly even though Carlin's words in context did not fall under the *Miller* definition of obscenity.

In his dissent, Justice Brennan lamented the majority's "depressing inability to appreciate that in our land of cultural pluralism, there are many who think, act, and talk differently from the Members of this Court....It is only an acute ethnocentric myopia that enables the Court to approve the censorship of communication solely because of the words they contain."[11]

In democratic societies, people are constantly bumping into each other. Because our spaces overlap, part of one person's terrain is also part of another's. Laws regulate what is deemed permissible on the common ground, and moral norms, in an even broader sense, help set the boundaries within which societies can function. Therefore, when moral norms are not held in common, cultural conflict results.

Would not Aristotle's golden mean rule out a devilish contempt on Carlin's part for anyone else's conscience on the one hand, and on the other an immovable set of cultural standards which refuses all compromise? Between these two ditches, the virtuous path gives license to

Carlin and consenting adults where they can express disapproval if necessary or walk away. Use of a medium open to children for scatological word salads would be unacceptable. The golden mean forces imaginative compromise from both sides.

69. "Soap" and Explicit Sex

Whatever else the ABC network planned for the new fall season, it was assured that one of its new series would not come and go unnoticed. Program themes would range from adultery to impotency to transvestism—nothing new to prime-time television, claimed ABC programming chief Fred Silverman, just an "innovative form of character comedy."

Writers for "Soap" had created two middle-aged sisters, the first married to a wealthy lecher, the second to an impotent blue-collar worker. From that starting point the intricacies developed. The wealthy husband is being blackmailed by his secretary-mistress while his wife and daughter are each having their own affairs with the same tennis pro. His son is in puberty and obsessed with pornography. His daughter is puritanical—according to one network description, a "latent nun." An old curmudgeon of a grandfather trades ethnic jibes with the family's abrasive black servant. In the second family, one son is a member of the mafia. The other is a homosexual who wants a sex change operation; in the meantime, he likes to model his adoring mother's gowns.

Public reaction to the serial began to surface long before its scheduled September debut. In mid-June, the archdiocese of Los Angeles attacked the program as indecent and called for a boycott of its advertisers. Everett Parker of the United Church of Christ's Office of Communication expressed the concern of many viewers: "Even if 'Soap' is done in good taste, it's going to be the opening wedge for sexually explicit material in primetime and then will come the deluge."

Even some within the network family had reservations. After prescreening the pilots, a spokesman for WOWK, Huntington, West Virginia, said: "We considered the first two episodes one long dirty joke. Our attitude is: we don't need it. We feel it's bad for television, bad for the industry."[12] The president of KMVT, Twin Falls, Idaho, was reported as saying: "It's not a new frontier; it's a new sewer."[13] And the president of Westinghouse, owner of WJZ, Baltimore, explained why that station would not pick up the first two shows:

It presents a variety of subject matter which I feel does not lend itself to the casual episodic comedy form. I believe that all of the subjects treated on "Soap" should be able to be handled by television effectively in an adult manner in serious dramatic programming. Presenting such subjects in a serialized comedy simply tends to lend an aura of insensitivity that I believe will be offensive to significant portions of the audience and a number of institutions. It appears that the series intends to break new barriers with constantly increasing leering sensationalism under the guise of comedy and satire on an ever expanding basis.[14]

ABC's first reaction was to dismiss interest-group concern as Victorian sentiment. The network's director of program information wrote in the New York *Times*: "Most if not all of the special interest groups attacking the show have not seen it. They are engaging in prior censorship, a pernicious type of censorship that has a chilling effect on free speech."[15] What he failed to also mention is that ABC denied all requests made by religious agencies to prescreen the show. Some watchdog groups were, in fact, able to see the pilots through the courtesy of local ABC affiliates.

To its credit, the network did begin to take note of criticism from inside the family. Revisions in the first two episodes toned down the more salacious aspects: a scene of adulterers in bed was eliminated, as were their musings about a slang term for fornication. A young girl's husky command to her lover—"Take your clothes off"—was also cut. But the main ABC defense was a strong offense. A network statement issued in August read: "In a pluralistic society, it is imperative that we maintain the freedom as broadcasters to present responsible entertainment programs and that adults have the similar freedom to watch or not watch the programs."[16]

The latter point was picked up in a New York *Times* editorial. Does the PICON formula (public interest, convenience, and necessity) that supposedly informs news and documentaries also apply to entertainment programs? The situation is unclear, said the *Times*. Yet it is the "right of all citizens to object as strenuously and effectively as they can to whatever they deem offensive on the public airwaves." And it is also the right of broadcasters to offer whatever they think will attract a market and make a profit, the editorial concluded.[17]

All these efforts—cosmetic, rhetorical, or genuine—did little to pacify the watchdogs. In late August, a consortium of four major religious bodies (National Council of Churches, United Church of Christ, United Methodist Church, and the National Council of Catholic Bishops) representing 138,000 churches formed to combat the introduction and spread of sex-oriented shows during primetime. They appealed to local stations not to simply accept whatever the network offered. The responsibility for program selection rests with local licensees who are accountable to the interests of their own communities, claimed the consortium.

The show did debut on schedule and during prime viewing time (9:30 p.m. in the East). Mr. Silverman hypothesized that "Soap" would run the gamut of public opinion in much the same fashion as "All in the Family": first outrage, then acceptance. "When TV networks stop trying to do things that stretch the boundaries of the medium, we're all in trouble. 'Soap' is an intelligent show written and produced by intelligent people, and in time it will be perceived as a moral show," he said.[18]

It is, of course, in ABC's best interest to have "Soap" perceived as "a moral show," in the sense of morally adventuresome and pathbreaking. On what ground "Soap" is morally acceptable is a question its producers did not choose to expound upon, unless the old saw of television as a mirror of society is pulled out of the barrel with a grin that betrays its essential buck-passing utility.

To suggest that moral criteria should enter into judgment of a program like "Soap" is itself to open a veritable can of worms. Perhaps the most sensible approach is to laugh it off as comical farce, the product of some television exec's wildest Freudian daydreams. All the fuss generated by watchdog groups seems, in retrospect, to be like pulling out the cannons to hit a gnat. But the important point to remember is that guardians felt they were confronting the first wave of a trend, a new threat to the already dismal television schedule. In prospect rather than retrospect, their concerns and actions are reasonable expressions of moral concern.

Even if "Soap" had survived, perhaps for consenting adults it would have answered some unmet program preferences. Children and teenagers, who have enough questions about sexual orientation without the added confusions of a "Soap" to bubble the brew, would have needed some protection.

Future television programs may make "Soap" appear innocuous in comparison, and concerned groups may in time reconcile themselves to the idea of parody. But a coherent approach to sex comes as close as anything to the wellsprings of healthy human personality, and a public parade of sexual incoherence only postpones trauma. Comedy in the long run is not exempt from the claims of a social ethic. Since comedy trades on the bizarre, one cannot reasonably force it to comply with a golden mean. Since comedy swipes at people's idiosyncracies, a Kantian imperative seems too staunch and stern to afford much light either. But what of the veil of ignorance? Comedy writers, behind the veil with the persons who are the butts of their jokes, might soften the sarcasm when they consider the sensitivities of the other parties. Comedy that ridicules a person's identity, scorns his sacred symbols, or discredits his hard-won achievements is comedy at the price of human dignity. When the butts of jokes can also laugh, and laugh heartily, then comedy is respectful of persons. No one should be above chuckling at his or her own foibles. But no one laughs when his "ground of being" is the cynic's joke. Media producers behind the veil with blacks, Catholics, Italians or whomever would emerge with a surer sense of what is funny and what is trash.

70. The Cable Is Blue

Academy Cablevision (pseudonym) began service in their midwestern city of a half million in the mid-1970s. A year later they began to offer "Telecinema." For a monthly fee of three dollars customers could get a converter box and key enabling them to pick up four extra channels: one a children's channel, two offering neighborhood cinematic fare, and then Channel F, described by Academy's program director as their "R-rated service."

"It was pretty soft stuff," said Debra MacDonald, who reviews and purchases movies for Channel F. "Nudity and innuendos, nothing more. Our policy was to show no graphic or oral sex, no penetration, and no male frontal nudity or erections. Those were the guidelines our lawyers advised, and the city's police vice squad went along with it. Sure, they monitored us. And if the vice officers didn't like a movie, we pulled it." That happened only once, said MacDonald.[19] A movie called *Cartoon* featuring animated characters and explicit sexual material drew a phone call from the vice squad after it had been on the wire for three days. Academy dropped the movie without protest.

"Our typical titles were things like *Campus Playmates* and *Swinging Playmates*, the stuff you might see at a drive-in. We definitely stayed away from the movies shown in art theaters, although several of our customers actually wanted more males and more explicit sex. I remember a letter from a 65-year-old woman who said that she and her husband enjoyed the adult movies, but they would like to see more male frontal nudity. So we had all kinds of people watching, but many of them wouldn't have been caught dead walking into an adult movie house," said MacDonald.

Because Telecinema used a converter box with a key, parents could control family viewing. Children could not inadvertently (or purposefully) tune in adult movies. But the main reason for the box and key was not protection of children, said MacDonald. It was the protection of the customer's monthly bill. "Our subscribers didn't want a babysitter coming over and rolling up a twenty dollar bill on Telecinema," she explained. If a parent really wanted to protect the children, they had the option of getting a filter on the box that would eliminate Channel F altogether. But no one ever requested that, said MacDonald.

Academy stirred up a little community reaction when Telecinema was first offered, but according to Debra it was positive, not critical. Even when the city became troubled about a local skin magazine, there was no spillover of antiporn sentiment to Academy.

Unfortunately for Academy's owners, the lack of community reaction showed up on the company's ledger, and Telecinema was dropped after five years on the wire. "We were losing money on that part of our operation," said Debra, "though Channel F accounted for about 50 percent of our Telecinema income. Our two [cable television] competitors in this area still offer blue movies, but they don't like to talk about it. One of them is trying to get franchises in the South where skin flicks would not be accepted.

"We don't talk about it a lot, either. It was part of our service for awhile. When we cancelled, some people complained. We still get letters asking when the service will resume. And we might do it again under a one-time monthly charge system. Under the pay-as-you-watch system, we had people spending $100 to $200 a month on Channel F, but not enough of them to make it go."

An ethicist might initially ask whether the viewing of such programs by informed adults constitutes a genuine dilemma at all. If the blue channel is properly controlled and the viewer sufficiently informed, there should be no unconsenting viewers.

Control and information become two key elements in the ethicist's approach to the question. Unlike a movie house, cable television has no brightly colored marquees alerting every passerby to the promiscuity of the product. But cable is more intrusive than a movie theater, more accessible, less ritualistic; watching cable requires less of a commitment from its viewers than going to a theater. Control of the product so only those who want it get it (and then after certain other minimal conditions such as age or parental supervision) is satisfied here.

An ethicist might also argue that a cable company issue a specific policy regarding its blue channel. How blue is blue? A stated policy would alert viewers to the product permitting many to use other entertainments, allowing some the freedom of informed choice.

No ethical framework except hedonism would advocate that the values portrayed in the skin flicks become the social norm. And hedonism, because it focuses on greed and denies the individual's responsibility to the social whole, is not a moral option. Under any moral framework, control and information become minimum conditions for blues on the air.

While a viewer's personal ethics may argue rigorously against sexual brutishness, imposing a sex ethic on the public raises other concerns. Our society permits prostitution and gambling—business ventures that make no claim to moral foundations. These we regulate, recognizing that to permit them the same freedom of enterprise we give to ice cream shops would be to expose ourselves to dangerous and destructive impulses. If we cordon off a red-light district, can we not by the same logic give moral sanction to blue movies on the tube, assuming sufficient control and information to protect against violating the unsuspecting viewer?

Perhaps the greatest good for the greatest number is a principle that would allow us this option. If viewers are consenting and informed adults, and if nonviewers are not being intimidated, let the buyer beware. The golden mean might also justify a blue movie, after safeguards are observed. Some might argue that scintillating R-movies are a reasonable compromise between the truly obscene and the altogether sexless.

The television is less adept, perhaps even negligent, at developing sexually mature drama that respects the persons as ends principle. Here is where the ultimate test is rendered. Movies without a responsible sex ethic may pose little public menace, but the viewer is the loser; the one who feeds an appetite for brutality is the tragic victim. The persons as ends principle, or "do unto others," assumes that the self also be well cared for. The principle cannot condone self-injury, even if the self wills it and no one other than the self is intimidated.

Notes

1. Quoted in Les Brown, "7 PBS Stations Reject Klansman and Nazi Interview," *New York Times*, 1 October 1977, p. 48.

2. Walter Goodman, "How Should Public TV Handle the Inflammatory?" *New York Times*, 11 December 1977, sec. 2, p. 39, and Goodman's reply to a letter, *New York Times*, 25 December 1977, sec. 2, p. 35.

3. Quoted in Walter Goodman, "How Should Public TV," sec. 2, p. 39; and in Brown, "7 PBS Stations," p. 48.

4. Quoted in Brown, "7 PBS Stations," p. 48.

5. Undated press release issued by the American Jewish Congress, headed: "New York's Public TV Station Won't Share Panel Discussion with Nazi, Ku Klux Klansman."

6. Quoted in Jack Mabley, "Magazine Pushes the Drug Culture," *Chicago Tribune*, 3 September 1976, sec. 1, p. 4.

7. Ibid.

8. The *Miller* standard: a) whether the average person, applying contemporary community standards, would find that the work, taken as a whole, appeals to the prurient interest; b) whether the work depicts or describes in a patently offensive way, sexual conduct specifically defined by the applicable state law; and c) whether the work, taken as a whole, lacks serious literary, artistic, political or scientific value.

9. Pacifica Foundation v. Federal Communications Commission, 556 F. 2d 9 (1977).

10. Ibid.

11. Federal Communication Commission v. Pacifica Foundation, 438 U.S. 726 (1978) at 775.

12. Lewis Klein, quoted in Les Brown, "'Soap,' ABC's Explicit Comedy, Has Critics in Lather," *New York Times*, 27 June 1977, p. 53.

13. Dale Moore, attributed in John J. O'Connor, "TV: Stir Over 'Soap' Continues," *New York Times*, 12 July 1977, p. 59.

14. Donald H. McGannon, quoted in O'Connor, "TV: Stir Over 'Soap'," p. 59.

15. Tom Mackin, Letter to Editor, *New York Times*, 15 September 1977, p. A26.

16. Quoted in Les Brown, "Catholic Conference Assails 'Soap'," *New York Times*, 12 August 1977, p. C21.

17. "'Soap' or No 'Soap'?" *New York Times*, 4 September 1977, sec. 4, p. 14.

18. Quoted in Brown, "'Soap,' ABC's Explicit Comedy," p. 53.

19. This case is based on an interview with a cable company official who wished to remain unidentified, along with her company. Names used in this case study are fictitious.

Chapter Fifteen

Censorship

Censorship, one of the ugly words of the English language, speaks of the repression that democratic beliefs officially and inexorably condemn; it warns of the consequences of state tyranny, church tyranny, union tyranny, corporation tyranny—the strong hand of any institution silencing the dissenting voice. "Liberty," on the other hand, provokes cherished feelings that resonate with our deepest human longings—an elusive goal, perhaps, but eminently worth the sacrifice required for each step in its advance.

So by our ideals we set the stage for the great paradox of democratic theory: liberty can never be absolute, censorship can never be absent. Liberty requires constraints at every level—speech, sex, movement, health care, business, religious practice—for man to create an ordered society. That which we prize most must be taken in measured portions.

Few of our essential constraints partake of the spirit of Star Chamber repression in seventeenth-century England. Jailing and hanging writers no longer occurs at the whim of the monarch. Yet many contemporary restrictions are nonetheless called censorship. One of our fundamental questions, then, is where to draw the lines—a question of ethics.

At the end of World War II, the Hutchins Commision on Freedom of the Press struggled over the question as they deliberated toward a theory of press freedom that would promote social responsibility as a new and important concept in media studies. All of the commission members were ardent democrats; some might even be called dreamy-eyed in their praise of democratic virtues. True liberals in the historic sense, they held free inquiry to be a paramount ideal. Yet they struggled with the question of censorship. The chief philosopher of the commission, William Ernest Hocking of Harvard, captured the dilemma poignantly in an essay written as plans for the commission were being laid:

Are . . .thoughts all equally worthy of protection? Are there no ideas unfit for expression, insane, obscene, destructive? Are all hypotheses on the same level, each one, however vile or silly, to be taken with the same mock reverence because some academic jackass brings it forth? Is non-censorship so great a virtue that it can denounce all censorship as lacking in human liberality?[1]

The cases in this section attempt to point out a few of the dimensions of those questions. *Baby Doll* probes the role of agencies that assume guardianship over the morals of a large constituency, and hence indirectly over the public as a whole. *Cruising* approaches the problem from the viewpoint of a counter cultural programming. "The Artist Censors Himself" looks at the influence of ideology on free communication from a personal perspective. *Show Me* moves out of the theater and into the library, but the issue transcends any one channel: should local communities have a say in the kinds of messages which become part of that community's currency of ideas? Finally, "The CIA Caper" raises the perennial issue of government censorship parading under the banner of public good.

While the reader puzzles with us over these democratic conundra, we may be encouraged in the knowledge that to do so—to read this book and think about these questions—is testimony that we are at least on the way to answers. It becomes apparent in these cases that ethical guidelines are the only responsible framework for constructing and defending any boundaries on free expression.

71. Moral Guardianship: *Baby Doll*

Time magazine called *Baby Doll* "possibly the dirtiest American-made motion picture that has ever been legally exhibited" up to that time. It was the story of a 19-year-old blond (Baby Doll Carson McCorkle) and her frumpy husband—a balding, inept, middle-aged owner of a cotton gin. Unfortunately, Archie's gin had been run out of business by an interstate syndicate. Adding to his trouble, Carson insisted that their marriage not be consummated until she turns twenty. Frustrated in business and pleasure, Archie takes careless revenge by burning down the syndicate's gin. The rest of the picture describes how the syndicate's manager seduces Carson and persuades her to give evidence connecting Archie to the fire, all on the day before her twentieth birthday.

The Catholic Church in New York City had endured a humiliating setback in the "Miracle Decision" (Burstyn v. Wilson) just a few years earlier. Nevertheless, Cardinal Spellman called for a boycott against *Baby Doll* and a six-month boycott against theaters that exhibited the film.

The Catholic Legion of Decency was not a boycott-organizing group. It rendered ratings through an elaborate system of lay reviewers and clerical supervisors, including means whereby film producers could argue a Legion decision. While the Legion attached no activist protest to its ratings, the Cardinal's boycott was consonant with the Legion's opinion that *Baby Doll* be condemned as "morally repellant both in theme and treatment. . . . Its unmitigated emphasis on lust and the various scenes of cruelty are degrading and corruptive."[2]

Around this same time, two allocutions (now jointly known as "The Ideal Film") from Pope Pius VII insisted that motion picture themes respect human dignity, treat human trials sensitively, and honor the institutions of family and state.[3]

All of this activity generated a call for the revival of the purposes of the Legion in a year when one-third of all movies rated were assigned a "B" (morally objectionable in part), an 11 percent increase over the previous year.

The renewed campaign against the movies drew the full spectrum of response. *Commonweal*, a liberal Catholic journal not accountable to the church's hierarchy, both praised and criticized the movement: "In this real world where greed and violence constantly menace society, it is the role of the church to concern itself . . . with keeping greed and violence in check."[4] Concerning the Cardinal's punitive boycott, however, *Commonweal* noted with regret the church's use of "naked economic pressure . . . to achieve a worthy spiritual goal. In the long run, the flourishing of such power never works out well for the Church. The Church loses in meaningful influence to the degree that it hides behind swagger and cockiness."[5]

This case encapsulates several important issues not easily resolved.

Should agencies committed to a clearcut moral tradition have a voice in film, television, and book production? Is an authority figure such as Cardinal Spellman using his power legitimately in starting his campaign? In the interest of democratic life, should his ideological opponents have supported his right and privilege to do what he did? The debate that evolved from *Baby Doll* clarified at least some aspects of these questions.

Moral guardians have been wary of the motion picture industry ever since John C. Rice administered a prolonged kiss to Mary Irwin in the 1896 production of *The Widow Jones*, a dramatic moment that gave the International Reform Bureau initial steam. But the largely Protestant protest lacked central authority and failed to develop a comprehensive moral argument.

When the Catholic church stepped into a major guardianship role in the 1930s, they suffered no such handicaps. Through the Legion of Decency, the church mustered the most vigorous and populous protest against cinema fare (and media fare in general) of this century. Catholic thinking was at the foundation of the Motion Picture Production Code of 1930 and much of the Hays' Office effort to enforce self-regulation for the industry. A Catholic layman, for instance, was given charge of the Production Code Administration, the industry's own script review and code enforcement bureau.

The Catholic apology for intervention in the nation's entertainment business was delivered most cogently by a Jesuit priest in *Catholic Viewpoint on Censorship*. Harold C. Gardiner placed the Legion's guardianship role in the context of Catholic political philosophy which viewed the state as a natural (meaning God-ordained) institution and therefore to be respected. Yet custom and tradition are also important social forces and these are the domain of the many groups that comprise the larger nation. While law serves as a final arbiter in civil disputes, the first court of appeal is the informal constraint of group custom and values. This primary arbitrating and civilizing force needs protection.

Given Gardiner's portrait of the state, individual freedom can never be merely doing as one pleases. True freedom is freedom to act as one ought: "The fundamental 'oughtness' under which a man can alone act with full freedom is ... an 'oughtness' that is handed to man by the faculty of his reason." The Legion, argued Gardner, is not a censoring agency able to coerce behavior, but a guide to the reasoned "formation of public opinion, and whatever supression of material (films or books) follows as a result of the formed opinion is secondary and accidental to their main purpose." Here is a kind of control, but in the open marketplace apart from legal constraints and dependent on the support of a significant public. Any attempt to suppress the Legion "is an attempt to shut off the channels of free opinion and debate that make for a socially, intellectually, and morally stronger America."[6]

The rebuttal to Gardiner came in 1960 from the pen of unitarian Robert W. Haney. The Legion was wholly wrong, he contended, "too puritanical and restrictive," devoid of compassion, presenting "self-righteous fantasy as moral truth. . . . Governmental restraint of culture is being replaced by a smiling, genteel dictatorship of private citizens who seek to do what the law cannot do."[7]

Not all liberals shared Haney's all-condemning tone. Moral guardianship by nongovernment agencies is not equivalent to state censorship, argued John Hospers in *Libertarianism: A Political Philosophy for Tomorrow*. Catholics may censor a film, but no one is required to join the church. Without an army to enforce its dicta, the church "can only use moral suasion on its members, as any private citizen can do."[8] Two of America's foremost communications scholars, William Rivers and Wilbur Schramm, exonerated the role of the Legion "as long as it controls only its own members."[9]

Though no champion of the church, C. Wright Mills laments the modern trend toward mass society and finds the decline of the "voluntary association as a genuine instrument of the public" to be one of the most important structural causes of the trend. Modern power, he writes, is in the hands of the "the huge corporation, the inaccessible government, the grim military establishment." Between these institutions (which contradict notions of traditional democratic pluralism by their bureaucratic control over formerly active "publics") and the primary institutions of family and community, there are no "intermediate associations" for the coalescence of socially responsible public opinion. Mass media have "helped less to enlarge and animate the discussions of primary publics than to transform them into a set of media markets in mass-like society."[10]

Doubtless Mills would have taken serious issue with many of the guardians' positions. Nevertheless, his concern for the recovery of community level publics able to speak powerfully to their political and social milieu is one of the important issues in democratic life.

72. *Death Wish* and Television Violence

A telex message was sent to all CBS affiliates on November 8, 1976:

WE HAVE JUST VIEWED THE EDITED VERSION OF DEATH WISH AND BELIEVE THAT ITS THEME OF VIGILANTE REVENGE, TOGETHER WITH THE

SCENES OF BRUTALITY AND VIOLENCE, IS AN INCITEMENT TO INHUMAN BEHAVIOR AND SOCIAL TERRORISM. EACH CBS AFFILIATE HAS THE LEGAL AND MORAL OBLIGATION TO DETERMINE WHETHER THIS FILM SHOULD BE BROADCAST INTO THE LIVING ROOMS OF ITS SERVICE AREA. WE BELIEVE IT SHOULD NOT. HOPE YOU AGREE AND WILL DRAW THE LINE HERE.

REV. PATICK J. SULLIVAN, S.J.   REV. WILLIAM F. FORE
DEPARTMENT OF COMMUNICATION   COMMUNICATION COMMISSION
U.S. CATHOLIC CONFERENCE (USCC) NATIONAL COUNCIL OF CHURCHES (NCC)
1011 FIRST AVE., N.Y., N.Y.   475 RIVERSIDE DRIVE, N.Y., N.Y.

In a joint statement issued the same day as the telex message, the agencies explained their mutual action:

Death Wish is a blatant and cynical example of television's constantly escalating lesson to young and old that violence is the acceptable solution to most problems: a view we reject. We reject it as Christians and as citizens of a nation that is struggling to maintain its principles of democracy and the value of the individual in a world that increasingly violates those principles.

We believe that a decision on the part of the CBS network and its affiliates to broadcast the film *Death Wish* is immoral. In addition to the many moments of brutality and violence, the greatest problem is that the theme of the film teaches violence: the solution to brutality is even more brutality and the taking of the law into one's own hands. This theme is socially irresponsible, and when it is portrayed in an exciting way as a model for others to follow, and then is made available to virtually every home in America, it becomes an incitement to the worst kind of inhuman behavior and social terrorism.

We do not question the right of the CBS network and local stations to decide to broadcast *Death Wish*. We do question the morality and the social responsibility of the decision. We have asked CBS not to show the film. We commend those stations which already have refused to carry it, and we encourage others to join them.

In the 1960s, Catholics abandoned the effort to censor or boycott films, opting instead for a strategy of film education and, at the same time, expanding considerably the tolerance limits of an approved film. The change in tactics was not a full-scale surrender in the battle for morality in media. Neither Protestants nor Catholics were suggesting that dehumanizing, gratuitous sex and violence were now acceptable cinematic themes; rather, they were insisting that the proper and only place to register protest against cultural products in a free society was at the box office: individuals should not pay to view bad movies.

Then came the problem of morally objectionable motion pictures appearing on television. The theater is one thing—away from home, an admission price to discourage the indifferent, a ratings system to protect children. But television is that lackadaisical box in the center of the home, available to children and adults for nothing more than a flick of a switch. Apparently this difference prompted the National Council of Churches and the U.S. Catholic Conference to act.

Few stations acknowledged receipt of the telex communiqué. Four stations had already decided not to take the feed, but none canceled *Death Wish* because of the NCC/USCC request. William Fore explained that the "main value of protest was to call attention to the public that television was moving into ever increasing violence."[11]

Guardian agencies are not fussing over media fare to broaden their profit margin. Rather, they seem to be motivated by something akin to Rawl's principle that finds justice done by decisions made in the best interests of the politically weakest participant or the participant who would most likely suffer reproach from the decision. In the producer-distributor-sponsor-viewer matrix, the weakest link (in terms of determining which shows are aired) is the viewer.

If decisions about television programming were made in a room where negotiators shared equal voting power and did not know which of the four principal roles (producer, distributor, sponsor, viewer) they would assume upon leaving the room, television programming might be vastly different. Delivering markets to advertisers might be less important than in our current commercial system. Protecting the absolute right of the distributor to make a free decision would still be important, but freedom might include notions of responsibility and obligation to the society as a whole.

73. *Cruising* for Survival

During the summer of 1979, film director William Friedkin brought a crew to Manhattan's gay district to do location shots for a film depicting the sado-masochistic leather fringe of the homosexual subculture. Entitled *Cruising*, the film starred Al Pacino as an undercover detective out to find a sadistic killer. While investigating, Pacino becomes confused about his own sexual identity and finally, maybe, commits a murder in the same bloody mode used by the man he stalked. Scenes from the film show torture, mutilated genitals, men urinating on other men as a kind of erotic exercise, and several murders of gays by gays.

Soon after Friedkin arrived in New York, *Village Voice* writer

Arthur Bell obtained a copy of the screenplay and reacted with a column that urged gays to stop the filming at once by whatever means
necessary. The film, claimed Bell, was dangerous to the homosexual
community; it would inspire brutality from oppressive straights; it
would legitimize violence against gays.

Homosexuals in New York took the warning. Several hundred conducted nightly protest marches, often where film crews were working.
Gay bars that had contracted with Friedkin were damaged; many cancelled their contracts. Friedkin and his staff were targets of cans, bottles, and Gay Rights Task Force pressure.[12]

This latter began on July 25 when representatives of the National
Gay Rights Task Force (NGRTF) asked New York's Mayor Edward I.
Koch to withdraw Friedkin's film permit. Ethan Geto, a spokesperson
for the NGRTF, insisted that his group was not advocating censorship,
only that "the mayor respond to a large segment of his constituency
and withdraw the support of the city."[13]

On July 26 Mayor Koch rejected the demand for a license cancellation. "To do otherwise would involve censorship," Koch explained. "It
is the business of this city's administration to encourage the return of
film making to New York City by cooperating to whatever extent feasi-
ble with film makers. . . . Whether it is a group that seeks to make the
gay life exciting or to make it negative, it's not our job to look into
that, and we are not going to do it."[14] Koch's statement drew a
thousand demonstrators into Greenwich Village, blocking traffic in the
Avenue of the Americas. Two arrests were made.

Charges and counter-charges came from the filmmakers, the gays,
and the press. Geto likened the film to the Ku Klux Klan "making a
movie about the black community on 125th Street in Harlem." Film
producer Jerry Weintraub argued that *Cruising* was a true depiction:
"what is really there."[15] The New York *Times* editorialized on July 28:
"We understand the fears of the demonstrators but think they erred in
seeking any official discrimination against the film. Anyone has the
right to try to embarrass or boycott another's speech. But to enlist government in the protest invites unacceptable censorship. Those who are
often denied their rights by official action ought to appreciate that better than most."[16]

On August 6, after a week of loud protest to "raise the consciousness" of Friedkin and Weintraub, the Gay Task Force withdrew its demand that the city revoke the film license. The demand, they admitted,
smacked of censorship.

However, street demonstrations kept the matter of self-censorship
alive. Vigorous protests continued. On August 20 nearly one hundred

policemen were called out to restrain the demonstrators after Weintraub was hit by a bottle. Two arrests were made. Pickets followed the film crew to most of their eighty locations throughout the city, using whistles and noisemakers to try to disrupt filming. Efforts to establish dialogue between the two sides repeatedly failed, each claiming that the other was simply out to parade his or her self-interested position.

Reaction to the film was varied. General Cinema Corporation cancelled thirty-three bookings, claiming that the film should have been rated "X." Friedkin's statement after location shooting was finished: "I don't make a film because I'm against something. For that matter, I don't make a film because I'm for something—I don't make propaganda. If anything, all the films I've made are enormously ambiguous."[17] The Gay Task Force responded to Friedkin's disclaimers in a letter to the *Times*: Demonstrators, much more peaceful than if blacks or Jews had been the subject of a bigoted film, hope they have shown the need "for our inclusion in the system of industry self-censorship that is now applied to all other minorities."[18] The public was fascinated. *Cruising* led *Variety's* list of top-grossing films for six weeks.

In the cases of *Baby Doll* and *Death Wish*, traditional and broadly accepted pressure groups had sought, unsuccessfully, to stem what they considered detrimental film fare. For *Cruising*, the group was a countercultural force, or at least a counter-lifestyle one.

Nevertheless, it was a group, not a lone crusader, which saw in the movie the potential for harmful effects. And the effects it foresaw were ones involving actual physical harm, not merely psychological or moral perturbation. The Gay Task Force considered *Cruising* a direct physical threat. In retrospect, we might regard those perceptions as overly reactive, but a group responding to a crisis cannot be held accountable to every even-minded rationalization that, from our own vantage point, seems the wiser path of action. (As it happened, of course, cooler heads in the Task Force eventually prevailed and the demonstrations subsided.)

The ethicist's task is to evaluate the moral claims advanced by the Task Force (who held the welfare of its public uppermost), the mayor of New York (who must make political decisions based on the interests of the city as a whole though not without regard to requests of the city's people), and the filmmakers (who feel responsible for creative and artistic integrity).

The Task Force can hardly object to the film merely because it exposes the distasteful, violent side of one of its fringe subcultures. Initially, the gay community felt that Friedkin was creating a sensationalized version of truth, but eventually these objections were waived. Indeed, a public examination of any culture—whether the deviant brutishness of sado-masochism or the redemptive idealism of Boystown— is fair game for the movie industry. Dramatization of cultures should be true to the spirit of the group under examination, and if the film is critical, the criticism should be fair, not based on wild exaggerations or naive stereotypes. In the case of *Cruising*, the jury was divided. *Time* argued that the film genuinely reflected the violence of homosexual homocide.[19] *New Yorker* film critic Robert Angel called *Cruising* a "slovenly, bruising sort of movie....It scares us in a dishonest way."[20]

New York's mayor seemed to base his argument on the utilitarian principle. A healthy city budget serves the interests of all the people, and film licenses contribute to that end. The moral content of the film is not the city's concern. While the prospect of a city official censoring filmmaker's work is ominous and unacceptable, neither can the mayor's confusion of means and ends stand up to ethical scrutiny. A healthy city budget is indeed laudable, but not at the expense of common decency. For example, a city would be condemned for importing and selling slaves in order to raise revenue. Slavery is understood to be a demeaning, inhumane condition, and no amount of benefit justifies slavery today. Sadomasochism per se, though it involves supposedly consenting adults, partakes of the same kind of moral condemnation and should not be the means of public revenuemaking. Can films about S-M barbarity claim immunity from the same moral charges?

The filmmaker's concern for integrity and freedom is a social value that needs jealous guarding. Artistic freedom has been a long time in coming, and its legal status today is reasonably secure. Its moral status is more difficult to evaluate, simply because it enjoys legal sanction. Friedkin's arguments focus on the purpose of art. At a minimum, one could argue that the purpose of art is to explore the meaning of humaness, its qualities and ambiguities, in such a way as to move the quest for meaning toward an ethically justifiable goal. This restriction excludes art for the sake of exploiting an audience; it even argues against art for the sole end of profit making. Friedkin and others may quarrel with the "in such a way" clause, but an ethicist would insist that all creative effort is goal directed. Friedkin should make his true goals a part of his defense.

74. The Artist Censors Himself

Eric Hurlbert, a respected playwright from Western Europe and a recognized voice of the New Left, was a student of countries that had undergone popular revolutions. His own intuition was that social change only happens through forceful confrontation, and that populist movements carry the greatest likelihood of translating confrontation into real social gains. Cuba held special interest for him, for here was a revolutionary movement in the backyard of a powerful ideological and economic adversary. How had the revolutionary movement changed the landscape and lifestyle of Cuba? Hurlbert determined to find out.

His trip through Cuba was intense. For three months he visited local leaders, ate with common people, worked alongside farmers and laborers, and visited every conceivable cultural setting Cuba had to offer from Havana saloons to back-country folk festivals. Eric did not conduct any public seminars or give public lectures while in Cuba. He had made no commitments to editors or producers for material following his trip. He was not financed by any interested party. He had gone to learn, not to further an international career.

All this was fortunate from Eric's viewpoint, for the trip revealed much that he had not anticipated. In a word, he had become disillusioned. The agrarian reforms had not raised farmers' living standards; no vital intellectual movement undergirded the peoples' crusade; tradition and culture had suffered under the standardizing influence of bureaucracy and a weak national economy. Eric had found the country poor and the people lethargic, their government riddled with patronage and impervious to citizens' needs. Regrettably, Eric could see little difference between present-day Cuba and life there before the revolution except that military uniforms were simpler and the political rhetoric was of a different ideological hue.

When Eric's trip was over, he struggled for weeks about how, or even whether, to give literary expression to his impressions and feelings. As a serious writer, he felt obligated to tell an honest story—not to gloss over the revolution's imperfections. At the same time, he was identified with and emotionally committed to the ideology behind the Cuban regime. How would an honest dramatic description be interpreted?

After much soul-searching, Eric decided not to write his play or any other piece for publication. His reason: such a piece could be used polemically by the Right.

———

In this case, we presume that no official coloration of the facts distorted Eric's literary judgment, that he had succeeded in exploring Cuban society as it is lived by the natives, and that Eric was indebted to no party for favorable results. The pressure to censor his creativity was internal—a felt pressure not to speak lest his words be distorted or misused.

Hulbert's motives were internal, yet he cannot be automatically cleared of moral blame. Consider the point raised by Archibald Mac-Leish, a prolific writer who was never himself accused of pulling punches: "No writer worthy of the name ever refused to make his position clear for fear that position might be of service to others than himself. The further truth is that the man who refuses to defend his convictions for fear he may defend them in the wrong company has no convictions."[21] Writer André Gide has likewise been criticized for his decision to stay mute about abuses he had observed in the Soviet Union. A strong, public stand by a respected man of letters could have influenced public opinion—might even have saved lives.

On the other hand, Hurlbert reckoned that a creator of literary or visual art has liberty to decide whether or not to create. One can hardly be faulted for a personal decision to not produce. Judgment can be rendered only on what exists, not on images and intuitions still in the creator's mind. Partly on this basis Hurlbert had decided to lay aside his pen.

The question could easily be situated at most every level of media work—writer, editor, producer, cinematographer. Is ideological commitment a sufficient reason to withhold a work of art that might add perspective and depth to the human pursuit of meaning and value? Is the possibility of distortion by one's ideological opponents sufficient cause for censoring entertainment material?

Hurlbert's struggle was with his own conscience. His actions had direct influence only on his own creative work. As in the case of Gide, Hurlbert's writing might have aided some people, and if it was within his power to provide aid, he would have been obliged to do so. But in this case he had no constituents pleading for his writing, no innocent victims begging that their untold suffering get a hearing. We cannot presume that Hurlbert could identify any specific persons or groups who would suffer loss for his silence. He has not snatched bread from starving children by his decision to not write.

Since no one was directly injured by Hurlbert's decision, no moral blame is involved. But we might accuse Hurlbert of failure of nerve; we might insist that he get out of the writing business if he can no longer "tell it like it is." Certainly his subsequent writings, whatever they might be, will be less powerful if the public discovers the reasons for his silence on Cuba. Hurlbert has traded away some of his independence and some of his critical edge by sparing his ideological colleagues an incisive public exposure. As a creative writer, Hurlbert will have to be on guard that his writings do not degenerate into mere propaganda. Hurlbert himself could not ethically wish that all writers with an ideology become publicists, for that would result in just the sort of deconscientization which has frustrated him about the so-called free world.

75. *Show Me* and Pressures on Libraries

Folks in Oaklawn and Evergreen Park, south Chicago suburbs, were incensed. The book *Show Me* was now available in the local public libraries, and worse, it was being read by teenagers.

Show Me is a picture book. Full-page photos of teenagers in various sexual acts—masturbation, oral sex, and so forth—are used to teach reproduction and anatomy. Younger models are shown exploring each other's genitals. According to protesting parents, the actual use being made of the book by its mostly younger readers had little to do with academic physiology. Parents demanded the book be removed; library officials refused. Finally, a compromise was reached: the book would remain, but minors could not check it out.

While local negotiations were underway, protesting parents were at work on another level. A petition signed by about 800 residents was delivered to State Senator Jeremiah Joyce, who subsequently introduced a bill into the Illinois General Assembly that would make librarians liable for criminal prosecution under obscenity laws. Joyce believed that something had to be done to keep the book away from impressionable teenagers (though he did not really want to incarcerate librarians). *Show Me* would enjoy healthy sales if it were on bookstands on south State Street, Chicago's porn district, said Joyce, "and it would be obscene if it sold there."[22]

Response from professional librarians and others concerned about censorship was understandably strong. Judith Krug, executive director of the American Library Association's Office of Intellectual Freedom, claimed that the bill would have a "chilling effect" on librarians' rights.[23] The Chicago *Sun-Times* called Joyce's efforts a "stupid bill . . . insidious . . . . It lets book-banners bare their fangs and it could intimidate librarians and library boards into censoring good literature."[24]

Whether by design or coincidence, Joyce introduced his bill on the day before the close of the legislative session. It was easy, therefore, to pass by the opportunity to debate a growing concern among both professional librarians and parents of vulnerable readers.

The issues surrounding book censorship have a long and complicated history. The liberal reaction in seventeenth-century England was against book censorship primarily. Limiting the reproduction and distribution of heretical books was, long before that, the domain of established religious bodies. Many contemporary political regimes exercise a censorship over books as vicious and complete as the most tightly controlled monastery ever was. So the battle still rages between an unrestrained freedom of expression, full-fledged censorship, and a middle ground wherein freedom is given wide berth, but restricted for reasons that appear to be in a community's public interest.

When professional librarians are asked for an opinion, the debate often turns acrimonious. Feelings are strong and accusations are not always helpful in moving toward principial answers. An article in the *Library Journal*, for example, uses ad hominem tactics to explain the rationale of those who would keep certain books from general circulation. The article suggests that a censor is a person with "some suppressed impulses which he often wishes others to suppress also."[25] Modern-day censors keep alive the spirit of Puritan New England, with its oppressive tangle of dark, subliminal, masochistic drives, the writer states.

The American Library Association (ALA) has been extremely cautious over the influence of groups like Citizens United for Responsible Education and the National Congress for Academic Excellence. The ALA has characterized such public interest groups as right-wing do-gooders who seek to encroach on the librarians' professional domain. Said the ALA: "The crucial point is that these educational pressure groups, like other right-of-center pressure groups, view 'the others'— be they professional educators, students, women—as unable to reason, unable to choose from the bewildering array of often contradictory material on a given issue. They seem to see themselves as the guardians and proponents of the correct idea."[26]

The pressure groups hold that professionals have imported liberal values not indigenous to the communities they serve. To return control of educational and library facilities to parents and communities seems to them a reasonable demand, however threatening it may be to the outside professional.

A socially responsible public library system cannot be oblivious to the tastes and sensitivities of its community of patrons. To claim that professional privilege or expertise should dominate library policy decisions is to circumvent Rawls' rule that justice is approached only in negotiations which have excluded the social differences factor. That principle might be implemented by asking a third party to negotiate between competing value groups. Many times such third parties could well be professional persons such as teachers, social workers, clergy-men, or librarians themselves. Third-party groups might be more successful in finding ways to offer reading material that challenges traditional ideas without subverting deeply held values.

Certainly books on sexual practice for adults are considered legiti-mate for most community libraries. But youngsters receiving first train-ing in the meaning of sexuality need the inheritance of values that many parents still make it their goal to provide. Public libraries should not write their mission so broadly as to compete against the value sys-tems of families in this delicate matter. *Show Me* is such a book. It can-not provide the moral framework for sexual instruction that a family can. The book, like sex itself, should not be a matter of idle and super-ficial curiosity, available to any youngster who knows of its presence. The persons as ends principle is not upheld when the sexual imagina-tion turns exploitative, and no reasonable person could wish that all youngsters (the Kantian imperative) imitate the apparent freedom of the models used in *Show Me*.

76. The CIA Caper

"I don't see why we need to stand by and watch a country go Com-munist due to the irresponsibility of its own people," said Secretary of State Henry Kissinger in a conference in 1970 concerning Chile and Salvador Allende. Victor L. Marchetti reported the quotation in the manuscript of his book, *The CIA and the Cult of Intelligence*. How-ever, when the book was issued by Alfred A. Knopf in 1974, the Kissin-ger quotation and 167 other sensitive passages appeared as nothing more than white space on the page. The edits had been made by CIA officials acting under court order and in compliance, they felt, with Marchetti's oath not to reveal any secrets he learned during his tenure with the Agency. The lengthy incident opened new questions concern-ing government meddling in the free flow of ideas through books pub-lished by private companies.

Marchetti signed with the CIA in 1955 and resigned 14 years later. When he began to write articles critical of certain CIA activities, the Agency obtained a court injunction requiring him to submit manu-scripts to the CIA for selective editing. About the book Marchetti coauthored with John D. Marks, a trial judge found that 142 of the 168 edits made by the Agency concerned material not classified during Marchetti's employ.

But the 4th U.S. Circuit Court of Appeals set aside this ruling without looking at the evidence. Any classifiable document must be considered classified, the Court held. Every sentence in a volume marked "Secret" must be considered as legally secret as the next sentence. Marchetti's lawyers argued that their client was the first case of a writer being required by permanent court injunction to submit proposed books and articles to a government agency for advance clearance. The Appeals panel judged that Marchetti had waived his right to invoke the First Amendment when he signed contracts with the Agency.

With only Justice William O. Douglas dissenting, the Supreme Court declined to review the Appellate decision, thus strengthening the power of the executive branch to keep certain information from reaching public eyes.

The case hinged on the need to protect national security, according to government arguments, but New York *Times* columnist Anthony Lewis felt the real fear was that publication would embarrass someone.[27] If either argument could be established, the case would appear to be closed.

An ethicist committed to free speech and press still asks whether everyone needs to know everything, and of course the answer is negative. Much information is trivial, hurtful, and utterly unnecessary for the making of an informed electorate. Other information (lists of CIA operatives, for example) would jeopardize lives if widely disseminated. Information is frequently suppressed by the media until its danger passes, as in an abduction where police efforts to free the hostage would be hampered by early release of the details.

The Marchetti book, then, hinges on two double questions. First, who is harmed by the material he includes, and is a greater amount of harm done to more people if his material is withheld? And second, what was the nature of his promise when he signed with the CIA, and can such promises be perpetually binding? No one implied that Marchetti purposely lied on his CIA contract in order to become privy to information for later publication. But Marchetti's own dissatisfaction with CIA activities apparently overruled his earlier promise of silence. Yet the commitment to honor contracts rationally and fairly negotiated seems to come close to an ethical absolute, a categorical imperative. We would quickly freeze social intercourse if we could not depend on the veracity of our verbal commitments, written or spoken.

Notes

1. William Ernest Hocking, "The Meaning of Liberalism: An Essay in Definition," in *Liberal Theology: An Appraisal*, ed. David E. Roberts and Henry P. Van Dusen (New York: Charles Scribner's Sons, 1942), pp. 54–55.

2. *Motion Pictures Classified by National Legion of Decency, 1936–1959*, (New York: National Legion of Decency, 1959), p. 13.

3. Gerald Kelly, S.J., and John C. Ford, S.J., "The Legion of Decency," *Theological Studies* 18 (September 1957): 406–8.

4. "Catholics and the Movies," *Commonweal*, 3 June 1955, p. 220.

5. "Move on Baby Doll," *Commonweal*, 1 February 1957, p. 465.

6. Harold C. Gardiner, *Catholic Viewpoint in Censorship* (New York: Hanover House, 1958), pp. 106–7.

7. Robert W. Haney, *Comstockery in America: Patterns of Censorship and Control* (Boston: Beacon Press, 1960), p. 177.

8. John Hospens, *Libertarianism: A Political Philosophy for Tomorrow* (Los Angeles: Nach, 1971), p. 27.

9. William Rivers and Wilbur Schramm, *Responsibility in Mass Communications*, rev. ed. (New York: Harper and Row, 1969), pp. 126–27.

10. C. Wright Mills, *The Power Elite* (New York: Oxford University Press, 1956; Galaxy Books, 1959), pp. 306–11.

11. William Fore, personal letter, 10 July 1980.

12. "Protesters Call the Film 'Cruising' Antihomosexual," *New York Times*, 26 July 1979, p. B7.

13. Quoted in Les Ledbetter, "1000 in 'Village' Renew Protest Against Movie on Homosexuals," *New York Times*, 27 July 1979, p. B2.

14. Ibid.

15. Quoted in "Protesters Call the Film 'Cruising' Antihomosexual," p. 137.

16. "Between Expression and Suppression," *New York Times*, 28 July 1979, p. 16.

17. Quoted in Janet Maslin, "Friedkin Defends His 'Cruising'," *New York Times*, 18 September 1979, p. C12.

18. Letter to Editor, *New York Times*, 27 September 1979, p. A18.

19. Frank Rich, "Cop-Out in a Dark Demimonde," *Time*, 18 February 1980, p. 67.

20. Robert Angel, "Mean Streets," *The New Yorker*, 18 February 1980, pp. 126, 128.

21. Archibald MacLeish, "Communists, Writers, and the Spanish War," in *A Time to Speak* (Boston: Houghton, Mifflin, 1940), p. 99.

22. Quoted in "'Obscene' Book Bill Shelved," *Chicago Tribune*, 3 December 1980, sec. 1, p. 6.

23. Quoted in Karen Koshner, "Librarian Obscenity Law Asked," *Chicago Sun-Times*, 3 December 1980, p. 16.

24. "A Stupid Boost for Book-Banners," *Chicago Sun-Times*, 5 December 1980, p. 51.

25. Eli M. Oboler, "Paternalistic Morality and Censorship," *Library Journal*, 1 September 1973, p. 2397.

26. American Library Association statement quoted in Susan Wagner, "Right-of-Center Censorship Increasing, ALA Finds," *Publishers Weekly*, 13 February 1978, p. 58.

27. Anthony Lewis, "The Mind of the Censor," *New York Times*, 7 April 1980, p. A19. Other material for this case is from the *New York Times*, 22 and 28 May 1975.

Epilogue

Ethics is news. ABC News "Nightline" interviews entertainment personalities Joan Baez, Jane Fonda, and Martin Sheen. Are the ethics they project in films and TV programs and popular songs the same as those they champion in real life? Could their real advocacy of political and social ideals conflict with the demands of their profession?

The *Wall Street Journal* gives front-page play to Ed Asner, or is it Lou Grant? The story's subhead: "Actor With a Public Identity as a Conscientious Editor Aids Many Liberal Causes." CBS kills the series; has the program worn thin or is Ed Asner too politically active?

Walter Cronkite's retirement sparks a new round of debate on whether network anchorpeople are journalists or actors. Between their dual responsibilities of truthfulness and attractiveness, which takes priority?

A dramatic investigative report from the "Mirage" tavern in Chicago reveals corrupt city services, documenting with photos and quotations the extent of the payoffs. But the reporting team is denied a Pulitzer. Said Pulitzer judge Ben Bradlee: "Newspapers should operate in the open. We instruct our reporters not to impersonate themselves, period." This second story, the one on ethics, gets nearly as much national press play as did the investigation itself.

A reporter for the Washington *Post* constructs a series on a poor young addict named Jamie. He turns out to be fictional. Bradlee and the *Post* are deeply embarrassed; Janet Cooke, the reporter, is fired. The public wonders anew about "unnamed sources" and "official spokespersons" and whether the highest and mightiest, the paper that helped nab a president, can be counted on to tell the truth.

Procter and Gamble, which spends more than any other corporation on television advertising, commends the Coalitian for Better Television for its grassroots crusade against television prurience. Ad people, mindful of P & G's $486 million contribution to their business in 1980 alone, began to wonder whether ad placement strategy should depend on more than Nielsen numbers.

Such examples of ethics as news can only underscore the need for journalists, advertising specialists, creative producers, and the public to take account of their ethical foundations and perspectives. When Charles Sieb, former Washington *Post* ombudsman, spoke to journalism educators about the training of journalists, he urged less emphasis on such skills as copy editing, editorial writing, even news writing, and "more emphasis on more basic matters, personal integrity, the making of ethical judgments. . . . Ethical quandaries are much more significant aspects of the [journalist's] real world" than journalism schools have realized. "And," Sieb added, "much more difficult matters."[1]

The media serve a broad purpose in democratic life. As our technological society becomes increasingly complex, we expect the press to inform us fully on all issues. We need accounts of our common public life, enlightened consumer information, and entertainment programs with redeeming value. Newspapers, magazines, radio, and television together form a paramount social institution, so deeply embedded we label our present era "the information age." In order to measure and critique this social enterprise meaningfully, we have operated in this volume from the perspective of social ethics. With the Potter Box as springboard, we have advocated here a wide-angled type of moral reasoning compatible with the media's informational and entertainment missions.

The ethical issues surveyed in these chapters reflect a common stock of problems in society at large. Especially in convoluted and stressful times, a continuing stream of questions and debates will catch news, advertising, and entertainment in its wake. As long as law-bending, stereotyping, and violence subvert our democratic experiment, media will find themselves in the storm-center. Understanding communication ethics may be hard work with few direct incentives and no immediate material gains. But the media professional whose career involves its probing is serving the audience well: doing the good work of building a socially responsible press. On that premise this book is offered. Toward that end this book is only a short installment.

Notes

1. Speech to the Association for Education in Journalism, East Lansing, Michigan, August 11, 1981.

Recommended Reading

Introduction

Bayles, Michael. *Professional Ethics*. Belmont, Calif. Wadsworth, 1981.
   Overview for upper level undergraduates of ethical issues faced by professions as a whole. Bayles examines the meaning of professional obligation and challenges the traditional norms that usually go unquestioned.

Callahan, Daniel and Bok, Sissela. *Ethics Teaching in Higher Education*. New York: Plenum, 1980.
   Essays prepared for the Hastings Center Project on the Teaching of Ethics. Includes important chapters on the goals of ethics instruction, whistleblowing, and the history of ethics in university curricula.

Frankena, William K. *Ethics*. Englewood Cliffs, N.J.: Prentice-Hall, 1963.
   A summary of ethical theory for general readers. This familiar classic, though brief, is a virtual encyclopedia of major concepts and thinkers in philosophical ethics.

Gert, Bernard. *The Moral Rules*. New York: Harper Torchbooks, 1973.
   Addressed primarily to the ordinary reader, Gert nonetheless develops a sophisticated theory of moral obligation. The heart of the book is a set of

ten moral rules that can be justified for all rational persons, rules such as don't kill, don't deceive, don't deprive of pleasure, and so forth.

Goldman, Alan H. *The Moral Foundations of Professional Ethics*. Totowa, N.J.: Rowman & Littlefield, 1980.
Intelligent and careful defense of a rights-based theory of professional ethics in the liberal tradition. Focuses on the key issue—whether professions are governed by special moral principles that differ from our common moral framework.

Jones, W.T.; Sontag, Frederick; Beckner, Morton O.; and Fogelin, Robert J., eds. *Approaches to Ethics*, 3rd ed. New York: McGraw Hill, 1977.
A venerable anthology of representative Western philosophers from Plato to John Rawls. Excellent opening chapter on ethical theory; useful outlines and index.

Long, Edward LeRoy, Jr. *A Survey of Christian Ethics*. New York: Oxford University Press, 1967.
Typically rated as the best available introduction to Christian ethics, including both historical and contemporary materials.

MacIntyre, Alasdair. *A Short History of Ethics*. New York: Macmillan, 1966.
Outlines in a readable manner the history of moral philosophy in the Western tradition, from Homer in ancient Greece to twentieth century ethicists.

Wellman, Carl. *Morals and Ethics*. Glenview, Ill.: Scott, Foresman and Company, 1975.
Textbook in which the chapters alternate in pairs—the first analyzing a special moral problem and the second a related theoretical issue. Demonstrates that the study of ethics can aid in making intelligent moral choices.

News

Christians, Clifford G. and Covert, Catherine L. *Teaching Ethics in Journalism Education*. New York: Hastings Center Monograph, 1980.
Survey of state-of-the-art in ethics teaching and substantive issues in journalism ethics today. Outlines four instructional objectives.

Hulteng, John L. *The Messenger's Motives: Ethical Problems of the News Media*. Englewood Cliffs, N.J.: Prentice-Hall, 1976.
Built on a series of cases and illustrations which show how the media operate. Questions how successfully they live up to contemporary codes of ethics.

Merrill, John C. and Barney, Ralph, eds. *Ethics and the Press*. New York: Hastings House, 1975.
Collection of articles and addresses. Part I deals with theoretical issues. Part II presents ethical dilemmas of everyday newsgathering.

Rivers, William L.; Schramm, Wilbur; and Christians, Clifford. *Responsibility in Mass Communication*. 3rd ed. New York: Harper and Row, 1980.
A classic text on media ethics that argues for the social responsibility option.

Rubin, Bernard, ed. *Questioning Media Ethics*. New York: Praeger Special Studies, 1978.
Several general articles on journalism ethics, plus coverage of specific problems such as smalltown journalism, third world, fairness doctrine, and stereotyping of women.

Swain, Bruce M. *Reporters' Ethics*. Ames: Iowa State University Press, 1978.
Readable summary of the ethical problems faced by 67 reporters from 16 metropolitan dailies who were interviewed by the author.

Thayer, Lee, ed. *Ethics, Morality and the Media*. New York: Hastings House Publishers, 1980.
Twenty-seven essays and speeches—mostly by practitioners—on the current status of media ethics, with a long introduction by the editor ("Notes on American Culture").

Vander Meiden, Anne, ed. *Ethics and Mass Communication*. Utrecht: State University of Utrecht/The Netherlands, 1980.
Fourteen original essays from selected authors in such countries as the Netherlands, Korea, United States, Finland, Belgium, Britain, and Germany.

Advertising

Beauchamp, Thomas L. and Bowie, Norman E. "Ethical Issues in Advertising." In *Ethical Theory and Business*. Englewood Cliffs, N.J.: Prentice-Hall, 1979. Ch. 7, pp. 445–522.
Case studies, legal opinions, and essays on such ethical issues as deception and creating consumer demand.

Capitman, William. "Morality in Advertising—A Public Imperative." *MSU Business Topics*, Spring 1971.
A reply to Theodore Levitt.

Cone, Fairfax. *With All Its Faults*. Boston: Little, Brown, 1969.
A sensitive practitioner looks at his business from the vantage point of 40 years experience.

Hopkins, Claude. *Scientific Advertising*. New York: Crown, 1966.
A classic (1923) view of the advertising process from one of the business's legendary copywriters.

Kottman, E. John. "The Parity Product—Advertising's Achilles Heel." *Journal of Advertising* 6 (4: 1977), pp. 34–39.
An examination of one of advertising's enduring ethical arenas.

Levitt, Theodore. "The Morality (?) of Advertising." *Harvard Business Review*, July-August, 1970.
A provocative positioning of advertising as a form of "alleviating imagery."

Mander, Jerry. "Four Arguments for the Elimination of Advertising." In *Advertising and the Public*, edited by Kim Rotzoll. Urbana: University of Illinois Department of Advertising, 1979.
A major attack on four presumably inherent dimensions of the advertising process.

Ogilvy, David. *Confessions of an Advertising Man*. New York: Atheneum, 1963.
A literate, insightful statement of how advertising should be practiced, by a most influential modern practitioner.

Palmer, Edward and Dorr, Aimee, eds. *Children and the Faces of Television*. New York: Academic Press, 1980, chs. 15–21.
Seven authors examine the behavioral, political, and ethical dimensions of advertising to children.

Rotzoll, Kim. "Gossage Revisited: Reflections of Advertising's Legendary Iconoclast." *Journal of Advertising* 9(4: 1980): 6–14.
A renowned practitioner and perceptive critic, Gossage examines the philosophies and practices of his business, and finds them wanting.

Rotzoll, Kim, and Christians, Clifford. "Advertising Agency Practitioners' Perceptions of Ethical Decisions." *Journalism Quarterly* 57 (Autumn 1980): 425–431.
Based on research reflected in this book, the authors examine key ethical dimensions of advertising agency practice, as seen by the practitioners.

Rotzoll, Kim; Haefner, James; and Sandage, Charles. *Advertising in Contemporary Society*. Columbus, Ohio: Grid, 1976, chs. 1–3.
Explanation of advertising's roots in the market and the world view of classical liberalism; four visions of advertising as an institution; the strains on advertising under the neo-liberal world view.

Terkel, Studs. *Working*. New York: Avon Books, 1975, pp. 112–147.
Terkel interviews six people involved in the advertising business.

Codes, Guidelines

The Advertising business involves a wide array of guidelines, codes, and standards dealing with the legal and ethical dimensions of the process. These are some of the more important sources:

Council of Better Business Bureaus, Inc.
845 Third Avenue
New York, NY 10022

National Association of Broadcasters
1771 N Street, NW
Washington, DC 20036

American Association of Advertising
Agencies
666 Third Avenue
New York, NY 10017

American Advertising Federation
1225 Connecticut Ave., NW
Washington, DC 20036

Association of National Advertisers
155 East 44th Street
New York, NY 10017

Television Bureau of Advertising
1345 Avenue of the Americas
New York, NY 10019

Radio Advertising Bureau, Inc.
485 Lexington Avenue
New York, NY 10017

Newspaper Advertising Bureau
485 Lexington Avenue
New York, NY 10017

Outdoor Advertising Association of
America, Inc.
1899 L Street NW
Washington, DC 20036

Direct Mail Marketing Association
6 E. 43rd Street
New York, NY 10017

Magazine Publishers Association
474 Lexington Avenue
New York, NY 10022

Business/Professional Advertising
Association
205 E. 42nd Street
New York, NY 10017

Entertainment

Alley, Robert S. *Television: Ethics for Hire?* Nashville: Abingdon, 1977.
Interviews of Norman Lear, Alan Alda, Earl Hamner, and others give insight into the aims and ethics of industry pacesetters.

Casebier, Allan, and Casebier, Janet, eds. *Social Responsibilities of the Mass Media.* Washington, D.C.: University Press of America, 1978.
Part Three of this collection of essays deals with entertainment programming: pro and antisocial images, controversial content, rights and obligations of producers. Included is a discussion of the issues by conference delegates.

Clor, Harry M. *Obscenity and Public Morality: Censorship in a Liberal Society.* Chicago: University of Chicago Press, 1969.
A reasoned moral argument for restricting certain kinds of communication in a liberal democracy. Legal and ethical issues are integrated in this critique of laissez faire freedom.

Ellul, Jacques. *Propaganda: The Formation of Men's Attitudes.* Translated by Konrad Keller and Jean Lerner. New York: Vintage Books, 1965.
An expansive critique of modern symbols and their threat to democratic freedom.

Mander, Jerry. *Four Arguments for the Elimination of Television.* New York: Morrow, 1978.
Some ideas are harmed by their treatment on television, says the author. Four provocative chapters and a radical conclusion.

Newcomb, Horace. *TV: The Most Popular Art.* New York: Anchor/Doubleday, 1974.
A critically humanistic approach to the art of television that raises ethical questions along the way.

Phelan, John M. *Disenchantment: Meaning and Morality in the Media.* New York: Hastings House, 1980.
Proposing that a public philosophy arises from the humanities, Phelan addresses the problems of new technology and cultural freedom.

Schwartz, Tony. *The Responsive Chord.* New York: Anchor/Doubleday, 1973.
A resonance theory of communication is the framework for exploring the ethics of television and radio. Advertising and news functions are also part of this discussion.

Two classic readers provide several articles of key importance:

Schramm, Wilbur, ed. *Mass Communication.* Urbana: University of Illinois Press, 1960.

Skornia, Harry J., and Kitson, Jack W., eds. *Problems and Controversies in Television and Radio*. Palo Alto, Calif.: Pacific Books, 1968.

TV Guide, often underrated as a mere timetable, is a goldmine collection of articles on television ethics.

Appendix A

Cases by Medium

Books

Magazines

Motion Pictures

Newspapers

Photography

Radio

Television

Appendix B

Cases by Issue

Censorship

Children

Confidentiality

Conflict of Interests

Deception

Economic Pressures

Explicit Sex

Fairness Doctrine

Health and Safety Information

Law-Bending for Information

Media as Accessory to Criminal Actions

Media Self-Criticism

Minorities and the Elderly

Privacy

Sensationalism

Stereotyping

Violence

Index

About the Authors

Clifford G. Christians is an associate professor of communications. He has a B.A. in classics, a B.D. and Th.M. in theology, an M.A. in sociolinguistics from Southern California, a Ph.D. in communications from Illinois, and has been a visiting scholar in ethics at Princeton University. He has published essays on various aspects of mass communication (including ethics) in *Journalism Monographs, Journal of Broadcasting, Journalism History, Journal of Communication,* and *International Journal of Mass Communications Research*. He has completed a third edition of Rivers and Schramm's *Responsibility in Mass Communication*, has co-authored *Jacques Ellul: Interpretive Essays* with Jay Van Hook, and has written *Teaching Ethics in Journalism Education* with Catherine Covert. He teaches courses in media ethics, mass media in a modern democracy, history of communications, qualitative research, and popular culture.

Kim B. Rotzoll is a professor of advertising. He holds a B.A. in advertising, an M.A. in journalism, and a Ph.D. in sociology from Pennsylvania State University. He is the senior author of *Advertising in Contemporary Society* and an author of *Advertising Theory and Practice*. He has published articles in *Journal of Advertising, Journal of Advertising Research, Journal of Consumer Affairs, Journalism Quarterly, Christian Century, Journalism Educator,* and several anthologies, and is the author of the article "Advertising" in *Colliers International Encyclopedia*. His teaching interests concern advertising as a social and economic institution as well as advertising and communication theory.

Mark Fackler is an assistant professor in the Department of Speech-Communication, University of Minnesota. He holds an A.B. in philosophy, an M.A. in communications, an M.A. in theology, and a Ph.D. in communications from the University of Illinois. His professional experience includes writing for magazines and radio, audiovisual production, graphics, and public relations. He has contributed to *Journalism Quarterly* and to a compendium entitled *Reader in Mass Communication Ethics* (Department of Communication, University of Utrecht, 1980).